LERO
TIGHTY '

BY PAUL SPENCER

Published by Starry Night Publishing.Com
Rochester, New York

Paul Spencer

Contents

Paul Spencer

Introduction to Tighty Whitey Edition

I was born in Montana, an only child, to a rancher. I enlisted in the military, the branch(s) I served under are outlined in my books, so no spoilers here. I retired after 23 years due to an injury and subsequently used my veteran benefit to obtain a college degree in Creative Writing. In the service, I was a Combat Engineer so the notion that I would pick up pen and paper might be perplexing. Yes, I do know about computers; what do you think, that I emerged from under a rock? I actually saw one in my biology class in college. I am certain my middle school English teacher, Mrs. Wells, would be rolling about in her grave, as I remember saying to her, "I can write good enough. I am going to be an engineer, so I won't be doing any writing anyway." How wrong I was! I wrote more in the military than I've ever written as an aspiring writer.

In college, the one form of writing I enjoyed most was "Flash Fiction" When I learned what the term meant I said, "Well, that is a short story." So, came to be Leroy's Shorts. IE: Short stories. What did you think it meant? The next concept I combined was writing from personal experience, followed by the rant. What is a rant you ask? It is what I do when something has me real worked up. My wife says I am the best at it because I do it all the damn time. I don't think she was singing me praises. So, what is a rant? This technique is pretty much as the name implies; a rapid-fire speech in an angry fashion about an issue, usually exaggerated, and quite frankly, comical to me. Maybe I have a sick sense of humor. Read the book and find out.

Since these stories are basically true, with perhaps some sprinkles of embellishment, I hope, that like me, you enjoy a movie a little more when the opening title says, "This is a true story.". Therein lies the formula. I hope you enjoy this book and that you will buy Leroy's Shorts Boxer Edition, the book that started it all, available on Amazon.com.

I have this current book, Tighty Whitey Edition and the first of the series titled Boxer Edition" and I am planning one more, Speedo Edition, that will be out next year some time. After this I am going to dive into some first person writing. Thank you for your interest in my books. I hope it gives a chuckle, a shout, and the ability to say, "I hate when that happens too! Halleluiah."

If you are reading my books, thank you. You will notice one change in this book. I am experimenting with giving Leroy an inner voice. This inner voice has eyes and a separate brain and can use reason for things where Leroy can't. You might think of it as an imaginary friend, a voice in the head, or a voice from above. However you envision the voice is great. This voice gives me the latitude to describe happenings as others besides Leroy may see them. Past readers know that Leroy often has a slightly skewed view of things, but the inner voice sets the stage as it really exists. I think the formula works; you be the judge.

What lies in store in this edition of Leroy's Shorts Tighty Whitey Edition?

This issue continues to explore consumer goods and services including LeafGuard, More of Lowes, Hulu, Angi and more. Some of these are quite the doozy of a tale so enjoy.

Last Edition we explored racism and hatred toward straight people among some in the gay community, specifically those bigoted homosexuals who hate cowboys for no other reason than they assume the cowboy hates them. I did try to inject some humor where possible, but sadly it is not a funny topic. This is an issue that continues to haunt America, so I will be hitting on it, but not to the extent I did in the last book. It remains a huge problem but one that, after writing to that issue in my first book, I feel the horse was declared dead.

This Edition seems to be metamorphosizing into a short story series on religion and family. I am a man of faith. I touched on my perceptions of faith in the first book. I am encountering this rift that has me disturbed. Read about it and learn more. And as always, family dynamics create a wealth of material,

This Edition will have several chapters beginning with the title "My Name Is" where I write about folks who have mentored me, inspired me, or any number of positive adjectives. Those folks include my Battle Buddy who was also my Best Man at my wedding.

This Edition also introduces the "and… Was His Name-O". If you see a short story titled like this, I promise at least a couple good laughs. These are the people who are polar opposites of the good folks' stories. Stories titled "Was his name-O" are where I write about folks who are the anti-mentor, the anti-inspiration, and any number of negative expletives. Curious who? Read the book.

It has been four years since my first book. As those who have read "Boxer Edition" know, I suffered a real breakdown after I was kicked out of MCC. Thankfully I went on to SUNY Brockport and ultimately met my goal of being a published author. It just goes to show that when bad people stand in your way, you simply walk around them and go find some good people. They are a lot harder to find, sadly, but I have come to learn, they do exist. Right alongside Big Foot, magic beans, and the like. You can order them on Amazon.com, said with a smile.

This book is a work of fiction, and although much of it is based on my personal experiences, all names, businesses, and circumstances are fictional. The one exception to this is the names of the two ships mentioned in the stories, and they are currently resting at the bottom of the sea providing a haven for the fishes and other creatures of the deep. If you believe there are any similarities to you in these stories, it is most likely because you truly see yourself as a complete unwiped asshole or maybe it's because you want to believe you are one of the figures in the story that proves that shit can be stacked six feet high. You are probably all that and more but you are not the one in this book. This is a book of fiction. It is not about you! Any similarities in these stories to persons alive or dead, any businesses, any circumstances, any occurrences within specific geographic locations and/or situations is completely coincidental.

Paul Spencer

Father Joe Was His Name-O

Leroy was an odd duck. He was born an only child of a rancher in Montana. He longed for adventure, including having dreams of tracking down elk and other critters. In pursuit of these dreams of adventure, Leroy strongly considered enlisting in the Forest Service. But ultimately Leroy settled for enlistment into the Armed Services. Just for a couple of years. A quarter of a century later, Leroy was nearing retirement.

Just prior to punching out, Leroy had gone to meet with Sister Deanna Carr. Leroy expressed interest in becoming part of what he hoped would be a place of solace from the haunting voices of guilt manifesting themselves within him. These voices came from Leroy's mistakes that had cost lives both in a literal sense and a real sense. These were not perceptions; Leroy had certainly made some mistakes in the heat of battle. Leroy wanted to be a tough guy and "suck it up" but he wasn't. He was a guy who would not wish to bring harm. He was a guy who longed for acceptance. Leroy would want it made clear that being accepted excluded people who believed their higher power was giving them a clairvoyancy that drove them to go kill people based on their religion. This is the enemy Leroy had fought his whole career. It was the mental battle scars he brought to Sister Deanna Carr, and it was Sister D that started Leroy down his faith path which began with RCIA, a rite which culminates in a person's full reception into the Catholic Church.

Sister Deanna Carr was nearing retirement during her encounters with Leroy. She would eventually go on to work in the church archives of a midwestern diocese and passed away recently. To detail the workings of Leroy and Sister D would bring an end to the concept "Short Story", so the bullet pointed version will have to suffice. Point number one: Leroy expressed fear that although he understood the mechanics of this faith he was exploring, he wasn't "feeling it." Sister D advised, "Just go through the motions and it will come to you."

Leroy stepped back thinking, "Go through the motions? That is hypocrisy! How dare she suggest such a…." Sister D had a gentle strength about her and she exuded confidence, as she should. She was running the church in its entirety and using surrogate priests to fill in where she could find them. She was doing this flawlessly. To observe the mass with all the talent working together like a Swiss clock was awe inspiring. Spiritual in its clarity. This was the only reason Leroy would agree to such a thought that he might just go through the motions. "Thank God", Leroy touted, "it was like dancing. I had no idea how good it would feel to move with the rhythm of the music until I 'went through the motions'."

And, as nuns were known to do, Sister D would also order Leroy about, "Leroy get those heavy boxes off the top shelf and put them in my office." Again, no one would get away with demanding anything from him ever. Ever. Except for Sister D. Leroy begrudgingly hauled the cross before the congregation every Sunday, he painted, fixed and scrubbed. Folks would ask Leroy "what gives?" and Leroy would explain," Sister D is competent, organized, genuine, and in need of folks around here to step up and give her a hand. The question needs to be directed at you, 'What Gives'? Don't wait to be ordered what to do and then get offended. Instead, ask "Hey, what can I do to help"

Now this is where the story takes a mad twist. Leroy had been married in a previous life to his childhood sweetheart Racheal Cook. Volumes can and will be told about this train wreck of a relationship but that's for another time. However, we do need to put in some highlights in order to complete the moral of this story. Leroy had certainly been in love with Racheal. He was young, dumb, and full of … ambition. But before any official ceremony, Racheal and Leroy had become pregnant. They then went off to the Justice of the Peace and formalized their love. Leroy understood the ownership and responsibilities he needed to take for his daughter and decided compromise was the best course of action. Three years passed, and Leroy grew ever more resentful of his loss of freedom. He wanted to go live his life of adventure. Racheal had become increasingly less desirable to Leroy, but again, Leroy took some responsibility for that.

Finally, when Leroy's attempted marital course correction failed to produce any positive outcome, due to no effort from the opposite court, Leroy made the toughest decision he has ever made; he chose to leave his daughters behind and go live out his dream of someday becoming a Combat Engineer. Leroy sent all of his paychecks home, out of devotion to his daughters and in amicable support of his wife Racheal, and shortly after leaving, Leroy's career was underway. Technology allowed Leroy to electronically deposit all his paychecks, which he did, and gave access to that account to Rachael. Leroy had literally spent his years in training and then more years deployed to the battle field, and as a result, he never had much need for money and was happy to provide it to support his wife and daughters.

As for Racheal, Leroy did not hate her but he had fallen out of love with her. The powerful feeling of love was long gone and had been replaced with resentment. Still, he did feel responsible for her and his daughters. An important aside here; Leroy still has a valued relationship with his eldest daughter, but sadly, Racheal has successfully alienated herself from everyone in the family, including her daughters. Simply put, for Leroy and Racheal the flame was gone and the marriage was purely obligation.

Fast forward to Leroy and Sister D. Sister D was desperate to get Leroy through the RCIA, the Rite of Christian Initiation. Normally, several adults would be part of this RCIA, preparing to receive their final confirmation into the church. The RCIA course, which is about 9 months long is the first step towards that confirmation. Upon graduation, the group of RCIA graduates become an integral part of the Easter service. This whole process is quite lengthy and involved, and the focus is on Jesus, of course. But in a much greater sense, the focus is on the folks getting baptized into the faith. Normally a 9-month process, it took far longer for Leroy because Leroy kept getting redeployed to another hot spot in Afghanistan which would put his RCIA journey on hold. But after finally completing the RCIA program, when the day for Leroy's formal acceptance into the church came, Leroy continued to be deployed and was therefore unavailable on the all-important day of Easter. So nearly three years into RCIA, a program designed to take 9 months, Leroy was at last ready to graduate. Leroy's course of

RCIA was complete and this Easter belonged to Leroy, not Uncle Sam. It looked like Leroy was finally going to become a full member of his faith.

But we know that things don't always go smoothly for Leroy and this was no exception. Much to Leroy's dismay, Sister D insisted Leroy get married in the church as part of his right of passage. Again, Leroy reared up, just as he had done with the notion of "going through the motions." Leroy had silently objected to lifting all Sister D's boxes, but the notion that he was supposed to get married? To whom? To Racheal? This was ridiculous. But once again, a well-meaning Sister D insisted Leroy get married. Leroy questioned this idea with, "We have not gone through marriage counseling, I do not love this woman any more, and this is a violation of church rules in so many ways." For Leroy, one of the major selling points of his faith was that it had rules to follow. Most of the rules made sense to Leroy, while acknowledging that no human operated organization was going to be without its flaws, but why were they not following their own rules? One of the rules regarding marriage was that both parties must attend 6 months' worth of pre-Cana, which is a discernment process, led by a priest or deacon and designed to help the couple discern whether this marriage will be something lasting and in line with God's will for them.

However, Sister D was adamant that Leroy and Racheal be married and as a result of that complete disregard for established procedure, in an instant the damage was done, and Leroy and Racheal were married in the Catholic church. Leroy was given complete membership in the church on Easter and was subsequently declared a full participating member of the Catholic Church.

After being home for a spell, Leroy's deployment to Afghanistan drew near. Racheal, who had always been overweight, pipes up again after 3 years of silence and announces that she is going to get gastric bypass surgery. She had spoken to Leroy for a couple of years about getting the procedure and Leroy had always been adamant, that if she insisted on doing such a thing, she needed to do it when Leroy would be home to help in her recovery and not to do it when he was about to be deployed. Now, on the eve of another deployment, was definitely not the time to be discussing it.

Leroy sternly stated, "If complications arise, the army will try and send me back to the states from Afghanistan to take care of you. Understand that I will tell them "No" and you will be on your own, unless your folks rescue you. Don't do it! If you do go ahead with this, I will consider it as a betrayal of my trust and we are done. No more nothing."

Later Leroy cornered the surgeon that was to perform the procedure. He unflinchingly stated that Rachel had not lost 10% of her body weight which is a critical prerequisite of the procedure to make sure the person can resist eating. Leroy further explained that he knew Racheal would not follow the post op procedures and complications would be inevitable. Leroy paused and gazed at the doctor, "If you do this procedure, you will likely kill her, and if you don't and she ends up a vegetable, rest assured I won't be coming back here to care for her. If you make the mess, then you are going to be the one to clean it up. Are we clear? Are we clear on all these points doctor?" The doctor's response was basically that he would default to Racheal's choices.

Leroy left in early December for his basic combat training at Fort Jackson. As a Combat Engineer he was focused on engineering but as a requirement of the deployments he was being assigned, he got combat training anyway. Leroy used to joke, "Putting a sailor through the army's basic combat training, is like teaching a sailor how to ride rodeo by putting him on a carousel."

On Christmas Eve, Leroy arrived in Northern Afghanistan and met Rob Lloyd. Please read "His Name Was Rob" about Leroy's battle buddy, a relationship which started right then and there.

I will tell you details of this evening which ends up bonding Leroy and Rob into "Battle Buddies", but for the purpose of this particular story, I will be relating how Leroy had arrived in Northern Afghanistan, gotten settled in and was making good headway both in securing the area and getting basic, as well as critical structures up and running. This is when it all changed.

Leroy was taking in the view, content with what he had done, and confident that he could see it through to completion. Suddenly he was jerked out of his daydream by an encroaching Command Sergeant Major. "Senior Chief, I need to talk to you,"

Leroy instinctively knew what it was about. He looked the smug Sergeant Major in the eye and began his famous rant, "My oldest daughter has a home of her own and will take in her sisters. I told the doctor that my wife did not lose the required 10% weight and if the doctor did the surgery, he would likely end up killing her because she would not follow the post op procedures." Leroy was sweating heavily at this point and a bit out of breath, but he continued, "I also made it clear to them, just as I am making it clear to you, I am not going home! Take a look around. Do you want to tell the General you sent me home over this stupidity? I didn't think so. Please excuse me, Sergeant Major. I have a base to build and an air strip to construct." Leroy walked away still muttering under his breath.

A few months passed and Leroy had word that his kids were doing better than ever under the care of their oldest sister. His youngest went to prom, which is completely amazing because, well, let's just say that she is mildly autistic and had never wanted to leave the house, let alone go to prom with her friend from church and yet off she went. Full credit for this transformation goes to Leroy's oldest daughter.

So, Leroy swore off Racheal for good and finally made a commitment to get a divorce, in spite of his new Christian beliefs that frowned on divorce.

It was around this time that Leroy met Lenora. Leroy had reached out to his Aunt Marcia for some Gold Bond Medicated Powder. His Aunt Marcia happened to work with Lenora at Johnson and Johnson. Leroy figured that since his aunt worked at J&J, she could get the Gold Bond powder for Leroy. She did get it… at a local grocery store, because it is a Proctor and Gamble product not a J&J product. As Leroy's aunt was preparing a package for him, Lenora passed by and asked, "What you doing Marcia?"

Marcia stopped preparing the package and went on to explain, "My nephew is in Afghanistan and he asked me to send him this powder."

Lenora asks, "Can I put something in there too, and oh, does he want a pen pal?" Later, Leroy found out that Lenora thought Leroy was 20 or 21 years old. In any case, Marcia gave Lenora's email address to her nephew Leroy, and so began the courtship of Leroy and Lenora.

Lenora was nearing retirement and Leroy was trying to decide when it would best for him to retire. On base in Afghanistan, Leroy had just gotten phones, internet, and other forms of communication up and running so the soldiers could reach out to their loved ones and Leroy was all too happy to provide daily lengthy operational testing of these systems. Thus, he was able to stay in frequent contact with Lenora. Their correspondence went on for nearly 8 months and near the end of this long-distance relationship, Leroy coaxed Lenora into letting him come and see her. On leave, Leroy would usually go to Thailand for a 2-week R&R where he would drink himself silly, venture into other risky behavior, like fighting, flirting, and f… but instead, this time he hopped a jet to Rochester, New York. This was the home of Lenora. Leroy knew he was going to get teased by the fellas. Here he was going to New York to meet this MILF he had only met via the internet. Leroy could only imagine the teasing he'd get. "What if she doesn't like you? Where are you going to stay until you catch your hop back here?" He didn't care. He was going to meet Lenora!

The two weeks Leroy spent together with Lenora were pure bliss. The two of them were like kids in lust. Truly a blissful experience. Leroy later told folks that going back to Afghanistan this time was the hardest it had ever been.

Shortly after returning to Afghanistan, Leroy was injured, as we learned in Boxer Edition. Just weeks before he was to rotate back to the states, he found himself being medevac'd to Balboa Naval Hospital for surgery. Thanks to a brilliant neurosurgeon, Leroy recovered well enough to walk and function at about 85%. This was much better than the doctors had expected.

After he was discharged from the hospital, Leroy made his way to Lenora's house. Lenora nursed Leroy back to health and due in large part to her kindness, Leroy decided 23 years in the service was enough. He dropped his papers and retired. On September 6th, Leroy took Lenora to the Canadian side of Niagara Falls and proposed marriage. This was the date Leroy and Lenora had first met in person the year before. Leroy and Lenora discussed whether or not they even needed to be married, but if they were married, she would be able to get Leroy's medical insurance. Lenora's medical insurance would expire upon her retirement so this was a major concern.

Because of this crucial benefit, they not only decided to get married, but because Lenora would be retiring in 2 years, they needed to get married before Lenora retired when she would be left without medical insurance.

Marriage is pretty easy these days, right? Nope. Not when you want to get married within your religious faith and that faith happens to be Roman Catholicism. Because Sister Deanna had insisted on the marriage of Leroy and Racheal before Leroy could be baptized and initiated into full membership in the Roman Catholic Church, that same marriage had to be annulled in order for Leroy and Lenora, who were also Roman Catholic, to be married in the church of their faith. It seemed particularly ironic that this previous marriage, which had not even been performed in accordance with the dictates of Leroy's faith, was now a gigantic obstacle standing in the way of Leroy and Lenora's desire to be married in the Roman Catholic Church.

Enter Father Joe. Father Joe was the priest at Saint Leo's Catholic Church in Western New York. The parish is so close to Leroy's house that he has included the parking lot in his running route. Now Leroy had mixed opinions of Father Joe. Leroy would go to confession and Father Joe would always assign Leroy to say the "Hail Mary" as his penance. It got to the point that when he would go to confession, Leroy would think, "So the sage advice that is going to guide me onto a path of right behavior should this sinful situation arise again is to recite "Hail Mary, full of grace..." That's fine for an add-on, but please tell me what to do to avoid that issue again, or if it is somehow unavoidable, give me the tools to deal with it."

The second thing that colored Leroy's opinion of Father Joe was that Leroy was invited to attend a weekend retreat called Cursillo. He signed up and went but the next thing Leroy comes to realize is that he has landed in some kind of sub culture within the church. Scary how we invite the devil in by deviating from long-standing traditions. Both me and Leroy belong to ONE holy and apostolic church, so, what is Cursillo? It is a cult, or a deviation from the rich heritage of the church. It has been around since the 1940's but it is my experience that most churches do not endorse it. If you want to look into it, that is great, but when Leroy was forced into it under the false pretenses that it was for the weekend and that it was affiliated with the Catholic church, he had no clue what he was walking into. It's a bit like the Knights of Columbus. God did not say to go out into the world to fight evil people looking like the grand marshal of the KKK, did he? Maybe it happened during the Spanish Inquisition. Not our proudest moment either. So, when Leroy arrived at the weekend retreat called Cursillo it was okay, but soon turned out to be something way beyond what Leroy had signed up for. Next thing he knew, the Cursillo leadership was hanging symbols and what not around his neck, while swearing him to a lifelong commitment to Cursillo. Leroy could take no more. He was not swearing allegiance to anyone!"

The third strike against Father Joe came shortly after the retreat when Leroy saw Father Joe's poor judgment of people in action. Allow me to explain. One evening Leroy and Lenora were in attendance at Father Joe's church meeting. The purpose of the meeting was to find ways to raise the money needed to construct a new entry to the church. Leroy was always generous with his finances, especially when it comes to the church, so Leroy showed up to write a check contributing to the fund for the new front entrance. A parishioner by the name of Dickless Dan Schwind, approached Leroy for a donation. He handed Leroy a donation card which required 3 sets of donations. Leroy explained to Dan that he was simply not, repeat not, giving any more than one donation. He was donating now tonight and was writing a onetime check for $1,200.00. Dan insisted Leroy fill out the donation card for documentation, so Leroy reluctantly filled out part one of three on the donation card. He marked $1,200.00, writing in bold letters "one time donation", drawing a line through the other two spots to make it perfectly clear this was not to be repeated, but Leroy knew what Dan was up to. Sure enough, about 6 months later Dan Schwind called Leroy and said," Leroy it's time to give your next $1,200.00 installment."

Leroy immediately saw red and began to rant in his anger, "See Dan? I told you this would happen. I came to the church, I spoke to you in person, I explicitly told you I was giving a one-time donation, yet here you are, just like I knew you would be, when you insisted, I fill out your card."

Dan responds, completely oblivious of what he has been told, and then asks the unthinkable: "Are you having financial trouble?"

Leroy loses it. "I am the opposite of financially troubled, you pompous ass!" Leroy winds up even tighter, "You are calling me a liar! You are telling me I agreed to payments I did not agree to and by the way, the reason my finances are so great is due to my dismissing dipshits like you and getting them out of my life. Do not call, write, email or in any way contact me any further. I am asking nicely this time and this time only. If there is a next time, I promise it will be the last time," Leroy takes a moment and then shouts over the phone, "ARE WE CLEAR?" Leroy never did hear from him further so Thank God he at least listened to that correctly. That Father Joe considered Dan an appropriate man for this kind of job spoke volumes about his continued poor judgment.

Strikes 4 through infinity against Father Joe took place when Leroy came to Father Joe to file for an annulment of his marriage to Racheal through the Seattle Archdiocese. Father Joe assisted in the initial filing and Leroy was most grateful. Leroy had explained to Father Joe that he knew the annulment would take a while. Leroy had good expectation management and Lenora still had well over a year with J&J, so as long as the annulment was done by then, Leroy and Lenora would be married in the church and Lenora would have the quality medical care she needed thanks to Leroy's retirement, because once married, Lenora qualifies to be on Leroy's medical insurance plan. Simple, right?

But Leroy never could sit still so he called the folks in Seattle to ask what the status of his annulment was. Lenora would be retired shortly and need Leroy's medical insurance, so there was good reason why they needed to get married soon. Leroy called Seattle and asked to talk to the "Head Honcho." Moments later some nun came on the phone and started berating Leroy about calling her a "Head Honcho." Leroy calmly asked her, "Are you Jesus?"

The sister shouted back, "Of Course Not."

Leroy sternly stated, "Then get over yourself!"

Well, needless to say, that Sunday after church, Father Joe grabbed Leroy and said, "Don't call Seattle any more about your annulment. I will take care of it." I am going to state that again.

Father Joe gave Leroy his word that he WOULD take care of it. Leroy assumed the sister who had come on the phone must have believed she was sainthood material and modest as well, ~ you know Sister Snooty Pants ~ and Sister Snooty Pants had obviously called Father Joe telling him to take care of Leroy.

Months went by and soon Lenora was 2 weeks from retirement and therefore 2 weeks from needing to be married in order to assure her continued health insurance. Leroy went into Father Joe's office and demanded "Where are we at with this annulment?" All of a sudden Leroy realizes Father Joe has absolutely no clue what he is talking about. He forgot, just like Dan Schwind forgot. The difference here is that Dan Schwind did not cause Lenora to be without medical insurance.

I later found out that Leroy went on such a loud tirade in Father Joe's office, that the kids in daycare were evacuated to the outside. Not one of Leroy's proudest moments. Leroy just couldn't imagine a priest could simply completely forget about something so critical to a parishioner's quality of life.

Leroy was aware that Father Joe was prone to bouts of forgetfulness. But unlike Leroy, as his voice of reason, I did not let Ol' Joe off the hook. I knew how good the Parish Staff was at keeping Humpty Joe Dumpty from forgetting things. If the staff was aware of it, it was taken care of, but in order for them to know about Leroy's annulment, Good Ol' Joe would have had to tell them. As Leroy's inner voice, I accept no excuse for Joe's demented buffoonery. And it only gets worse as we continue with the story.

After Leroy's tirade, Joe accused Leroy of not respecting the priesthood. Leroy snapped back, "I respect the priesthood with every fiber of my being. I do not respect you, Joe!" What enraged Leroy the most was Joe's glib attitude. It felt like Joe was metaphorically saying, "Gee, Leroy. We did not get you to the Olympics for which you have specifically trained during the last four years. I forgot to get the paperwork done. You would have won, too. Oh well. No big deal. We will try and get you there for the next competition in four more years. Okay?" It was this "I don't give a shit" attitude of Father Joe's that had sent Leroy into the tirade which caused the little kiddies to be evacuated. As Leroy's inner voice, I think all Catholics, large and small, should be aware of their priest's shortcomings.

Think what it would be like if such had been the case concerning pedophilia? What do they say in AA? Your secrets keep you sick. So Please! Assure me that we are not immediately and continually going to repeat the mistakes of the past. Unfortunately, it sure looks like it to me.

Another example of Father Joe's ineptitude and lack of sensitivity to people was his treatment of the deacon at the church. He had assigned the delivery of the homily to this deacon but the problem was that the deacon had suffered a massive stroke and could no longer speak coherently. Most of the parishioners grumbled about this but it went on for months. Not only was Father Joe's forcing the deacon to give homilies and participate in the mass cruel to the deacon, it made a mockery of the solemnity of the mass. But over all else, it was just plain wrong! If Joe had briefly experimented with allowing the deacon to give a homily, one could accept that as okay. But as months went by and the deacon was continually forced to give the homilies, no one thought it was okay. It was unbelievably insensitive of Joe to keep this up. Finally, someone complained to the bishop and the deacon was given his dignity back. Leroy would say with a smile, "I wonder who that was?"

Father Joe epitomized the adjective "turdish" as in "turd". He allowed inept people to interact with the parishioners on financial matters, he blew off his parishioners in their time of need, and he made a mockery of the mass by insisting a disabled deacon deliver the homily when the deacon's ability to speak was severely compromised due to a massive stroke. Leroy was also totally offended by Father Joe's trickery when he lied and told his parishioners that Cursillo was simply a weekend retreat instead of a life commitment. When your priest lies to you, nothing good follows.

When it comes to lifelong commitments, Leroy would only make two: one would be marriage, with no thanks to Father Joe, and the other, the most important lifelong commitment Leroy would make, would be to his Lord. Leroy might make lifelong goals such as catching the biggest fish during his favorite fishing derby or something like that, but he was not about to give a lifelong commitment to Cursillo when folks were using peer pressure to shove the doctrines espoused by Cursillo down his throat. However, when it comes to peers using pressure on Leroy, you have to be equal to him. As Leroy's inner voice, I can assure you there were no peers pressuring Leroy in that room, try as they might. Now, to avoid a scene and for the sake of the others who were with him who had not been lied to by their priests, Leroy went through the motions so that those who had chosen to make this lifelong commitment to the idolatry of Cursillo could do so without any unwanted drama.

Does all this sound like the actions of a well-oiled, competent, caring priest? It is no surprise that Leroy sought out a priest he could trust with the vitally important things like his immortal soul. Leroy whispered to me regarding Father Joe, "I wouldn't trust this douche bag to properly inspect and clean my backside

So given all the craziness associated with Father Joe and the necessary time constraints, Leroy took Lenora back to Montana and to the little church he attended as a younger man. The reverend at the little country church did a wonderful job and it was a lovely ceremony. Along with his oldest daughter. Leroy had a few of his buddies in attendance to celebrate with them. Lenora had a lifelong friend as her Matron of Honor and Leroy had his Battle Buddy Rob as his Best Man. Once married, Lenora and Leroy left on a 60-day honeymoon to include some of our country's greatest National Parks.

Some months later the Annulment was approved. It was all too little, too late. Upon returning home, Leroy sought out Saint Elizabeth Ann Seaton Catholic Church, Father Bill Spilly presiding, and the adventure continued until…

The End

Paul Spencer

Time Talent and Treasure

Leroy was an odd duck. He had grown up in Montana an only child of a rancher. He had enlisted in the military and after a few years of intensive training emerged a Combat Engineer. He had certainly engineered combat; a destructive end result. He had also engineered orphanages, hospitals, shelters and the like. They call it Combat Engineer because the most important aspect of this job is building all those wonderful shelters in a secure location. When none of those secure locations could be found, Leroy would make one. "Fire in the hole."

Leroy eventually retired and during his last tour to Afghanistan, he had met his wife over the internet. The complete story is told in Boxer Edition. Lenora was her name and she was reaching retirement from her career field with J&J. She lived in Rochester, New York. Since Leroy had moved to Rochester to be with Lenora, he had landed in the church of Father G.

Father G was new to Leroy's church. He was a good priest, true to his craft, his delivery of the mass was not scripted, monotone, or lacking any sincerity; quite the opposite. He was a joy to listen to, taking his knowledge of faith scripture and applying it to the lives of his parishioners. Father G also loved the history of the artifacts that represent his faith. Father G hit the ground running, stripping the proverbial banners from the walls and redecorating. Seems great, right? Well Leroy, though unconcerned about all that, did get concerned when his friends started leaving. Friends who seemed to hold the purse strings. "Wink-wink." Leroy was divided: should he go with his friends or remain loyal to his parish which had served him well thus far?

When Leroy questioned, "Why are you leaving?" the response was most often a version of "We all made our church and all that is within. Now it is suddenly not good enough! He said he came to FIX us. We don't need fixing!"

Leroy replayed the events in his head when Father G had said "This relic is 30 years old and should have been put on the roof 30 years ago. I smite ye for not having tended to this!" said with a smile. Leroy was finding the discourse affecting him because it was alienating folks, he looked forward to seeing. Folks whose kindness was almost as dear of a blessing as the Lord. Leroy began to ponder, "Maybe I need to find my friends and worship with them." As Leroy longed for a sign, new folks began to emerge that offered the brotherhood/sisterhood Leroy was beginning to crave. He was hopeful other thorns would be evaluated and removed.

Leroy had been a problem solver in the military and always considered himself equipped to do so with skill. Leroy failed miserably as soon as rank, discipline, respect, ethics, morals, and the like, were removed from the human interaction equation. He was now civilian scum like the rest of us. Leroy was afraid to say anything; he worried would people think he was hostile, would people be offended, would he think, "No good deed goes unpunished"??

Leroy wanted to respond to the church motto of "Time, Talent, and Treasure." The obstacles to Leroy satisfying these objectives were troubling. Leroy listened to the words, "I have gravely sinned in what I have done and what I have failed to do." Had he failed to speak up? "Well, no," Leroy thought, "I will address observations and additionally, reevaluate my discretionary money." Leroy said to himself that if he comes up with more money it belongs to the church as long as that church isn't sinking. Leroy does not throw good money after bad. God would be disappointed in Leroy for squandering God's gifts to Leroy.

Leroy was unwilling to give much of his time. He had attempted to help a parishioner once with moving. However, in the course of the move, far too many people arrived; all well-meaning, but organization fell apart, things were broken in the chaos for which Leroy felt responsible, so ultimately Leroy just grabbed his hippie van he was using for a moving van and left. Feelings were hurt on both sides and Leroy touted the words he uses all too often, "No good deed goes unpunished."

Leroy mulled over his talents, and his treasure and saw an opportunity to potentially provide both. He started out at the bottom of the parishioner food chain: The "Christ-Er"- those who only show up on Christmas and Easter. Leroy would sit in the cramped church during these glorious celebrations thinking, "If only you all came to church regularly and threw your change in the collection pot, we could afford a bigger church."

Leroy put it another way; you devotedly watch the regular season games in your spacious stadium, you grab an 8-dollar beer which is your contribution to the stadium, then on the commencement of the Super Bowl, all the "Christ-Er's" show up and you are now watching some guy's butt instead of the game you came to watch. The game means way more to you, a true diehard fan, who emulates the main characters, learns their playing styles and so on while the "Christ-Er" is just there because... Why are they there? In 90% of the cases, it is some stupid obligation they think they have. How sad to live in utter hypocrisy. Just stay home!

"Christ-Er's" are the last to fall when things go south in the parish though because they really don't care what is happening in the church. Juxtapose that with the folks who have put their every effort, including their sweat. Their talent, and a generous sharing of their treasure with the church and have faithfully attended and tithed "religiously." Leroy was asking, "Which of these fine folks are filling coffers, the Christ-Er's or the dedicated Christian?" Where are those dedicated Christians now?

Leroy heard the need for another $8K to satisfy the annual giving requirement for the church to meet the church CMA (Catholic Ministries Appeal). Leroy wanted to help meet the fund raiser goal. Before Leroy was willing to fork over the bucks, he began looking at the leadership with amazement because they were not seeing the cause of this shortage. Leroy knew from his experiences that the first step to solving a problem was recognizing the cause of the problem. This ensures success in fixing the problem. Instead of bailing water out of the proverbial sinking ship as the only solution to the problem, find out where the leak is. Part of the leak is the afore mentioned persons who perceived their efforts as having been dismissed and discarded. Leroy was quick to note this was only his perception. God had denied him the ability to see into the hearts of the involved characters. He gave that gift to His Son.

To remedy the shortfall in the CMA, Leroy would have to move funds set aside for other philanthropic ventures to come up with the $8K, but he did not want to plug a sinking ship and by golly that is exactly what would happen if he gave the funds. God again would not be happy with Leroy for wasting God's gifts. In this case, that would be the money in Leroy's deep pockets. Leroy wanted to see Father G making sure everyone understood what Father G was looking for. Father G said, "What am I looking for? For everyone to give as much money as you can!" Leroy thought of a showdown with Father G but when even the archdiocese would not rid him of his post, he knew that a showdown would be an exercise in futility. Thank God he is not a pedophile, not said with a smile. The Diocese turns a blind eye, where their church priests are concerned all the time. At this point, Leroy just put his head in his hands and said, "God grant me the ability to accept what is going to bite me in the ass anyway."

Leroy knew Father G's approach was destined to fail because he was watching it fail. Leroy grimaced and explained that these folks were civilian scum with limited mental capacity and pungent with greed. Said with a smile. Leroy explained that the parish needs a metric. Leroy knows, Jesus wants us to tithe according to our ability. He does not want us to deny our grandmother nursing home care so we can put a new gold moniker holder at the front door of the church. Said with a smile.

Metric, what did Leroy mean by that? He went on to explain it using a pizza analogy. You might feel that your weekly pizza outing is keeping the family together, and it is. You are having great family time and I just bet that you recognize that your faith in God is a big part of that successful family life. Now ask yourself what would you sacrifice for your family? A pizza, one week of the month, bought at the grocery store and heated up, consumed in front of your big screen TV that cost you more than your first house would be a good start. The pizza money saved is "free money." Giving "free money" to God to be used as He sees fit, which will not take away from any genuine need, IE: rent, food for survival, a vehicle to get to work, and such, is a gift you can share. However, you honestly need to ask yourself what is your true priorities are in life and give accordingly.

Give as you are able and really pray for discernment between being able and being unwilling to give up even a second of any of one's guilty pleasures. Leroy also suggested to Father G that he make a chart. IE: 10K a year should give $50, etc. Leroy wouldn't pretend to know what his faith guidance was because no one was telling him how to structure his charitable giving and he knew that was contributing to the failure. Bottom line: "People won't give what they don't know to give."

Leroy waited for a bit to see how Father G would address these facts. He had considered suggesting a bulletin memo or two, and maybe some direction from the pulpit but Leroy figured Father G to be much smarter, far more educated and even older and wiser than him (perhaps). Bottom line; Father G did not tell him how to kill Extremist Muslims for a living so Leroy figured he would not tell Father G how to fix his blunders. Leroy would shout, "Stay in your swim lane." The only reason Leroy had vectored from his swim lane was because his friends were no longer with him on Sunday, and he actually thought he might be heard. I know, Shit in one hand and provide logic to Father G. After the exchange is complete look what remains.

When Leroy still did not see any action or acknowledgment of the problem, he sought out a few of the fellas. Leroy explained to me that these were the guys that knew where the bodies were buried. I say that jokingly because I don't want to be one of the bodies, said with a smile. Leroy was not really friends with the fellas but he had been around awhile and figured he could ask, "What is up with Father G?" He was both saddened and relieved to find out that he definitely was not the only one concerned.

Leroy decided it was time to face off with Father G. He approached him one Sunday after worship and began to rant in front of all the remaining parishioners as they hurriedly filed past them on their way out of the church. Father G was tugging at Leroy to get him some place private but Leroy would not have it. He knew folks whose opinion of him mattered would agree with what he had to say. Leroy spouted off about all the facts he had brought to Father G's attention a few weeks back. Leroy knew his mental illness, a result of his military service, has made it difficult for him to confront people, and when his emotion button switched on, his thinking button switched off. Nevertheless, Leroy persevered and finally he finished his rant. He stared sheepishly at Father G. Leroy respected the priesthood better than most, equating it to a military rank structure. His sheepish look was a direct result of not wanting to face off with his priest. For Leroy, priests had always been an icon for love, peace, and understanding. Understanding what was going on here was lacking big time.

Leroy had hoped Father G. was aware of the facts now, that parishioners were leaving as a result of being offended, not only by father G's changes, but by the delivery of his sales pitch with verbiage like "This should have been done long before. This should never have been that way," and the ultimate salt in those devoted parishioners open wounds came when Father G was boasting and touting about how he "fixed" everything. A phrase that has always served Leroy well is "If it isn't broke don't fix it!" The devoted parishioners that built the church did not think it was broke, and with each change in décor, policy and lack of compassion and understanding from Father G, more and more of them took themselves and their thick wallets elsewhere. Father G continued to pump his chest and live in total denial. Leroy does have it on good authority that Father G is pumping his chest to a lot fewer parishioners. However, one thing about Western New York is that there is a Catholic church on every corner. Like Starbucks in Seattle. As a result, it is pretty easy to move on when a moron comes along. Ok fine, another moron comes along, I am already there.

Leroy hoped Father G would see that folks needed a measured goal of funds to donate and some direction about how to allocate that part of their income. Every organized Christian religion collects funds from their parishioners and many of the more successful ones like the Church of Latter-Day Saints (Mormons) ask for a percentage of income. Others ask for a weekly amount to give. Of course, there are exceptions, but people will give what they know they are supposed to give. Father G will never grasp this due to his moron status. In his world, folks will throw money at his pompous feet and he will save the world, with or without God or his parishioners, or the Diocese or even the Pope himself.

In frustration, Leroy then went to the Diocese to voice his concerns. Leroy's concerns not only fell on deaf ears from the bishop, the bishop also turned a blind eye to what is an extremely negative issue. Sound familiar? Leroy could not believe it. No wonder Father G was so arrogant. Apparently, for some reason unbeknownst to all but the bishop and Father G, Father G is the

Golden boy in Rochester. Once again, a blind eye is cast. It's a damn good thing that at least as far as we know, he is not a pedophile.

Leroy shared all the afore mentioned data with Father G. Leroy was not sure what to expect next but I can tell you with 100% certainty he did not expect what did come next.

Instead of offering any type of discussion, Father G responded, "Interesting." Leroy stopped in his tracks. Of all the words in Webster's Dictionary, in response to what Leroy had just stated, "Interesting" was not one of them. The nail in the coffin was when Father G said, "I will discuss this with you any time."

Leroy thought to himself, "Now where exactly did I say, 'Can I discuss, or can I talk about, or can I ask you something?' There was NO discussion to be had. There was just "fixing" to be done by Father G and he was fixing nothing but rather, he repeatedly behaved in a manner that weakened everything about the church he was supposed to be strengthening with his leadership.

Leroy spoke in a loud raspy voice as he choked back tears, "I was simply giving you facts. I would expect nothing less than for you to trust but verify." Leroy continued to stammer as he walked out the door for the last time, "But instead of listening to me, you just ignore me and offend me just like you did the folks I tried to tell you about in the first place."

Leroy sat in his car in the parking lot and as tears welled in his eyes, he asked himself how he had failed. Leroy had been trained to go on "observe and report" missions and he knew how to read people. He had fought in arenas where there was no clear enemy and no clear friend and where reading a crowd was often a matter of life and death. In the case of the church of Father G, Leroy thought any moron could observe that Leroy's friends were no longer attending and the annual financial goal was not being met for the first time in Leroy's 10 years at the church of Father G. It must not bother Father G because he continues to this day to try and determine the depth of his bowels with his head. 2 feet and counting. You go Father G. At least Leroy can cheer Father G on for success at that.

Was Leroy just "any moron?" Father G must have thought so, as if the bishop had whispered these same concerns in Father G's ear, would Father G have responded with, "Interesting. Let's discuss it?"

Before Leroy and the bishop had met, one would have thought at least some concern might have come from the bishop. You know; at least look into it. "Trust but Verify" is what Leroy did when his troops brought him problems. Leroy had discovered earlier that Father G was bullet proof, in fact the golden boy in the Diocese, the favored son of the local bishop. Father G was going nowhere. He would be staying on as the one and only priest of this church, and this awareness served only to strengthen his pompous attitude.

Leroy did not think himself the bishop. In fact, he knew he was the "any moron", which after all we know, is just one more reason for the reality that Father G must be worse than an "any moron" to continue being blind to all of this. Father G confidently carried out his own agenda, doing whatever it is he does, damn near breaking his arm while patting himself on the back, even to this day. Leroy runs into past fellow parishioners from time to time. Most have scattered to the wind, and Leroy has now become one of them. Leroy thought a priest was supposed to unite their church and embrace its parishioners. Guess that was wrong?

Leroy had learned the hard way and at a pretty young age that "pride goes before a fall." When would Father G. learn that? "Soon, and very soon." Leroy finally left the church of Father G with his tail between his legs. He also kept his ear to the ground as any good soldier would do. About six months after the CMA of which we spoke of earlier in this story; Leroy got word that Father G had missed the CMA fundraising goal by thousands of dollars. Leroy thought, "What if I would have dropped the 8K into the CMA?" What if in deed. Shortly after failing to reach the CMA goal, father G was removed for cause! YAAA! There is a God. A God that wants his 8K or else! Said with a smile. Leroy is back at his old church with old friends. It was like a reunion. As Leroy's inner voice, I am praying HARD that the new priest is great. Why was he not removed for cause for being a dick? That was the hole in the boat all along.

See the next book, Speedo Edition for the exciting update to this story. It is writing itself. Pride really does go before a fall. Stay tuned.

The End.

Hertric and the Heavy-Set Woman

After graduating boot camp and engineering school, Leroy reported to his barracks in Long Beach where he was to live for the time being. Leroy was told to report to base operations each morning until he was assigned to a department. If he had no assignment, then he could take off for the day and enjoy Long Beach. Leroy made himself at home in the barracks and noticed a fella a little younger than himself sitting at a bench with his feet propped up. Leroy was wearing civilian clothes and so was Hertric, the man sitting on the bench with his feet propped up. Leroy asks, "What's fun around here?"

Hertric responded, "I don't really know and I don't have a car to go exploring."

"What's your name?" Leroy asks.

Hertric responds, "Hertric."

Leroy pried a little deeper asking Hertric, "You got any money?"

Hertric responded, "I do have a little."

Leroy smiled and said happily, "Well Hertric, my man. We have here what they call a symbiotic relationship!"

Hertric looked a little puzzled, "A sim-bat-hot-chick? What did you say?"

Leroy volleys back, "My name is Leroy and someday I am going to be a Combat Engineer. The word symbiotic refers to two or more separate creatures needing the other creature or creatures to live while at the same time each creature gives and receives good from the other(s). Neither can live without the other; thus symbiotic." Hertric was still looking a bit like a stunned fish, so Leroy said, "Keep It Simple Sailor - I have a car and you have money for beer."

Within an hour Leroy and Hertric found themselves lying on blankets in the sands of a busy Los Angeles County Beach in Long Beach, California. A voluptuous woman came into view and laid down on her blanket just feet from Leroy and Hertric. Both Hertric and Leroy looked away from the phat voluptuous woman as if they were too self-conscious to look at her. In other words, Leroy and Hertric were posturing themselves as shy guys.

Moments later another woman lied down nearest to Hertric. She was wearing a pink bikini which left nothing to the imagination. To Leroy, her skinny body looks a bit emaciated. And herein lies the comedy of errors created by the situation. Leroy and Hertric both happen to like phat women; a fact that both Leroy and Hertric had been totally unaware of. The woman they both want to ogle is the woman closest to Leroy. She's the one who is voluptuous. She has large arms and legs and other wonderful large things that come in pairs. Most folks use the slang "phat" to describe this type of woman. It was Leroy's belief that he was the only one who admired phat women, so when Hertric turned toward the twig woman, Leroy assumed Hertric was ogling twig woman and therefore, Leroy was free to ogle the woman he nicknamed "Fun Bags" who just happened to be lying in a space that gave Leroy a clear view of her assets.

Hertric noticed Leroy had shifted his position away from twig woman and had his back to Hertric, presumably to look at some other hot skinny woman. So Hertric took advantage of the situation and unbeknownst to Leroy, Hertric began to ogle the same woman Leroy had locked onto. The two men would reach for a beer from the cooler they had carried in tandem to their beach spot, and with each new beer retrieved, they couldn't help but notice twig girl running her fingers inside her bikini and making many suggestive moves of a flirtatious and somewhat lascivious nature towards both Leroy and Hertric. These attention getting moves failed to interest either man, which made twig girl start to get annoyed. She felt she was God's gift to young horny men.

It did not take long before Leroy and Hertric both questioned why the other was ignoring twig girl and paying attention to different women, which we know is actually the same woman, but Leroy and Hertric still remain clueless to that fact. What finally gave it away was the childish grunts and cat calls each were making under their breath, "She makes me think of churning butter." These primeval noises were corresponding with this lovely phat creature's movements. For example; it did not take much movement from her for her voluptuous parts to start up and maintain a lovely jiggle.

These were the seductive movements that Leroy and Hertric were drooling over. So, it didn't take long before Leroy and Hertric figured out that they were ogling the same woman. Leroy and Hertric said at the same time, "You like phat women!" followed by, "Ya, so what?"

Leroy whispered in Hertric's ear, "That skinny girl in the pink bikini is getting openly pissed that we are not paying her any attention."

Hertric whispered back, "Now she knows how it feels to be on the other side of the blanket."

Leroy's and Hertric's friendship was supported by the fact that Hertric had beer while Leroy had wheels for travel, both of which was needed by each of them in order to further their common wish for adventure. This bond of common interest: beer, a ride, and phat women created a bond of brotherhood between Hertric and Leroy and served them well.

Hertric and Leroy knew they would both be working in some capacity for Naval Base Long Beach. At this point though, the only work they had was to check in each morning for an assignment, but because the assignments had not yet been handed out, after checking in, the two of them would simply spend the remainder of the day lying on the beach, drinking beer and ogling phat women. Leroy and Hertric joked with each other that they hoped they would never get an assignment, like maybe they'd get lucky and a glitch or something would happen, and they could keep spending their days on the beach.

As things go, the day did come when Leroy went in to check on an assignment and lo and behold it was there: Operations Department. Hertric was not with Leroy at the time and would not check in for his assignment for a couple hours yet. Leroy went over to his assignment at the Operations Department for Naval Base Long Beach. At the point this in the story, Leroy is about 23 years old and extremely wet behind the ears. However, he had obtained the rank of Second-Class Petty Officer, and as a result of his rank, he basically ran the daily activities and took care of some construction and repair. The Senior Chief in charge generally took oversight of most of that sort of issue, but he would always have plenty of helpers, like Leroy.

So, the following morning, Leroy nervously prepared himself to meet the sailors that would be working for him. Soon there were 19 sailors standing in formation in front of Leroy and the Senior Chief. Just in the nick of time, here came Hertric hurriedly walking into the formation where Leroy would have charge. As he spotted Hertric, Leroy got a sinking feeling in his gut. When he had first met Hertric at the barracks, he did not know Hertric was a Fireman's Apprentice. Leroy had been a Fireman's Apprentice almost 4 years before and had advanced to middle management. Leroy knew he was not supposed to be familiar with his subordinates, and knew being friends was about as familiar as one could get. Leroy also knew he had already become friends with Hertric before finding out that Hertric would work for Leroy. What were the odds of THAT? The odds were apparently 100%. With all that said, Leroy told himself that he could handle being both boss and friend.

A few days later, Leroy and Hertric decided there was a need to float check the white Ford pickup that had been issued to them for use in making the world a better place and in keeping the world safe for democracy. For example, using the white pickup, Leroy and Hertric would collect and dispose of 140 trash cans located throughout the base and then would go through the trash sorting out the materials suited for recycling before disposing of the trash for good. The final destination for this was above their pay grade. Knowing how critical this white Ford truck was to a better world, the notion NOT to float test the truck seemed insane. Leroy said he would drive, and Hertric gladly got into the passenger seat. Hertric figured if they got caught, he could always say he was a hostage.

Upon arrival at the beach, Leroy started to back the truck down the boat ramp that was generally used to launch small craft into the Long Beach Harbor. The rear wheels of the truck dipped into the salty ocean and slowly submerged further and further into the water. The game they were playing was one where you take the truck, back down as far as you can, but don't go so far that the truck wheels start to float and lose traction. Leroy had missed the "too far" mark and the truck sailed into the harbor. Sailed may be an overstatement, but the truck went in for a dunking of at least a few feet and then proceeded to sink even further into the harbor. Realizing the peril of their situation, Leroy and Hertric jumped out and began to push on the truck with all their might, trying to push it onto the dry part of the boat ramp. The whole time, having neglected to close the doors of the cab when they jumped out, water had been rushing in, filling the cab until the truck sunk again. Having finally gotten the rear wheels on semi solid ground, Leroy and Hertric, both covered in ocean slime from having slipped on the treacherous footing of the boat ramp, ran around to the cab which was drenched halfway up the seats, and jumped in. Leroy and Hertric were both engineers and knew the chances that the exhaust would be above the water were not good. If the exhaust was below the water, then the truck was now a raft. Since Ford did not supply paddles with their trucks it was pretty clear that using a pickup as a raft was not Ford's intent. To Leroy's and Hertric's astonishment, with one twist of the key, they heard that precious "VROOM" and the white Ford pickup roared to life. Leroy pushed down on the gas and drove the truck up the ramp, the truck now adorned with bits of kelp hanging off it and with a flood of water pouring out the back. Now you might think, "Hey, everyone has a right to be a kid once in their life." but Leroy and Hertric did not agree. "They were kids their entire life."

Some days later, Hertric had educated Leroy on how to use the cardboard compactor. This is basically a compactor that has a couple of wires that automatically secure the cardboard into a compacted cardboard bale. Now, Leroy and Hertric had been given use of the base walkie talkies. They each had one and frankly, anyone who was anyone had one. Heck, even the Base Commanding Officer had one in her office. Hertric and Leroy were given one so folks could call them into action, like when full trash cans attacked an unsuspecting population. The young duo had not been expected to communicate on them at all but Leroy decided there was an exception to the rule and grabbed his radio and shouted, "Fireman Hertric! I am here at the cardboard compactor and I cannot figure out how to use this bitch of a compactor! Get over here and help me, will ya?"

Leroy hears Hertric over the radio saying, "Leroy, you dumb son of a bitch. You can't say bitch over the radio."

Leroy shouts back at Hertric, "Son of a bitch! Now you tell me, you piece of shit!"

The next voice Leroy and Hertric heard over the radio was none other than the Base Commanding Officer and she was not happy, as evidenced by her tone in addressing the boys. "Fireman Hertric, Petty Officer Leroy, are you two listening?"

Leroy and Hertric, the two communications experts respond, "Yes Ma'am."

The Base Commanding Officer goes on to calmly state, "As fast as you can get here is not fast enough when it comes to getting yourselves to my office. Do you understand?" The Base Commanding Officer was a reasonable woman as example; she was skilled in telling someone to go to hell in such a way that they would ask her for directions and even look forward to the journey. Knowing that, hightailing it across base, in record time, Hertric and Leroy were soon standing at attention in front of the Base Commanding Officer. The Base Commanding Officer gave Hertric and Leroy her mother/son talk on respect and military bearing and in the end, they were better young men for it. Some kids never learn though.

Leroy and Hertric were assigned to paint a large set of bleachers which were next to one of the baseball fields on base. The purpose of this was to make the area all shiny so folks could have an awards ceremony. Leroy and Hertric were adept at painting and knew they could paint the whole set of bleachers in no time flat. It was this knowledge that caused Leroy and Hertric to go sit at a bar and continue pounding beers while flirting with the phat sexy bar keep.

At one point, Leroy said to Hertric, "Hey, it's getting dark out and pretty soon we won't be able to see to paint."

Hertric said, "Hey, no problem, Leroy. I will shine the lights of our white Ford pickup onto the outdoor seating area and then we can paint those bleachers in no time." Seeing the logic in that, Leroy and Hertric continued to pound beer and shovel chicken wings and flirt with the phat women who, in Leroy's and Hertric's estimation, had plenty more to offer than the twig girls running around. After challenging each other with many games of skill, the two tried to improve on their skills, which involved the continuous consumption of alcohol, which of course, improved their skills with each drink. Eventually, the two rebels without a clue got wind that the bar was closing. Closing, closing…. "Holy crap the bar is closing! We gotta go and get those bleachers painted quickly," Leroy said. In short order, the two sailors arrived with paint and brushes and the other tools required to scrape loose paint or sand areas before repainting. Hertric aligned the headlights of the white Ford pickup in the direction of the bleachers that were in need of preservation. Soon Leroy and Hertric were feverishly scraping, sanding, and painting.

Hertric stopped to ask, "Leroy, how long do you figure this paint takes to dry? It's an oil based white paint so I bet it takes a while."

Leroy looked on the bucket of paint for instructions which would include the drying time of the paint. Guess what the drying time of the paint was? All of 12 hours for light traffic. Were butts considered light traffic? As the Long Beach sun began to rise over the California mountains, Leroy turned off the lights to the white Ford pickup and soon the rows of seating were fully painted. Now as far as they could figure, the event for which they had cleaned and painted these bleachers was due to take place in 6 hours. Even if the first stroke of paint was laid down about 6 hours ago, it was not due to be fully dry for another six hours, which was about the time the ceremony would begin. As for the rest of the paint job, there was no way it would be dry in time for the party. What could Leroy and Hertric do at this point? All they could do is pray and hope that the paint miraculously dried before coming in contact with the butts that were sporting those thousand-dollar dress uniforms.

Hertric and Leroy went back to the captain's building and were rolled into a rotation of providing for the care and feeding of the officers during their celebration. Soon after the ceremony, folks began arriving and as the officers started to mingle with one another, Leroy and Hertric looked feverishly at their dress whites for any signs of paint. It was extremely difficult to see where the wet paint had found its way onto the officers' uniforms due to the astonishing coincidence that had the white of the paint being exactly the same color as the color of the pants. Hertric and Leroy looked at each other and said, "Gee, maybe we will actually get away with having procrastinated on that painting assignment." Weeks went by before the two men were finally able to relax and figure they were free and clear of trouble. One might be justified in feeling that these two men just kept falling, or to be more precise, jumping, into trouble.

Sometime after the wet paint scare, Seaman Fiddler showed up at the Base Operations Department. He was the same rank as Hertric and would be working for Leroy on the crucial activities around the base like trash removal and preservation of structures throughout the base. Fiddler was a man who quickly had all sorts of connections and hook ups in place and knew the lay of the land better than most. These skills would soon come in very handy for the dynamic duo.

Fiddler rapidly established himself as a valuable member of the team. One day, he convinced Leroy and Hertric to go down to the ocean with him to a spot where the waves smashed against the cliffs. The three men climbed down on the slippery cliffs in search of sea anemones. Fiddler found one and hucked it at Hertric, striking Hertric square in the chest with such force that some of the hard pointed spines penetrated and broke off in Hertric's skin. Hertric attempted to pull the anemones off but left several broken pieces of anemone spine embedded in his chest. Leroy felt bad for Hertric and wanted to chastise Fiddler for hurting his buddy, but Leroy's thoughts were, "If we make Fiddler mad by chastising him for the stunt with the anemone, he may not grace us with his hook ups." In hindsight, it must be said that Leroy has always felt bad that he did not defend his buddy Hertric and that he'd sold out his friendship for a hook up. On the other hand, there would be a silver lining to this decision as Leroy and Hertric continued to be trouble makers.

Leroy decided that he was going to take the white Ford truck up a mountain near Long Beach, California. Hertric and Fiddler jumped in and away they went. Leroy found the trail he was looking for that wound up and around through the small mountains, and as he approached the top there were several sharp jagged stones that created a sort of series of steps up the mountain. Leroy barreled and skidded and ultimately bounced his way to the top. All three men got out to enjoy the nice California view and feel the warm breeze when suddenly Hertric let out a gasp, "Look at the tires! The rubber is shredded on the sidewalls of all four tires. It's amazing they're not all flat."

Leroy said, "Get in fellas. We have to get back to base before we lose these tires."

Fiddler spoke up, "I can get us new tires, no problem. We just need to make it back to the base first." As they drove down the mountain and onto the California freeway, they all were wringing their hands, white-knuckled with fear, hoping they'd make it home. Finally, they crossed onto the base. The first obstacle was getting by the guard at the base entrance. To their amazement, the base guard did not ask why the tires where all chewed up. Fiddler then came through as promised and went in to talk to the vehicle maintenance person about getting 4 new tires. All three men feared that the vehicle maintenance guy would question how the old tires got all torn up, because one thing was certain: the tire damage did not occur on the base. Much to their relief, Fiddler convinced the vehicle maintenance man to install and balance four new tires, thus ending this adventure. All's well that ends well! And herein lies the reason why Fiddler got away with impaling Hertric with a sea anemone.

As you might suspect, the fun had not yet come to an end for these three. Fiddler had worked with explosives early in his career. Having already demonstrated in this story how he has a way of getting hook ups from anyone he asks, Fiddler's ability to access all the makings for explosives, would create another opportunity for adventure.

Fiddler gathered as much money from the other two peas in a pod as he could and went out and bought a couple gallons of potassium perchlorate and powdered magnesium. Then the three men took beer bottles and made them into bomb casings with about 4 inches of paper mâché formed around each bottle. This combination of chemicals does not explode in the way folks might think. The chemical mixture ignites very quickly and reaches extreme temperatures instantly, but this fast-burning material is kept contained within the beer bottle bomb casings. These bomb casings hold back the expansion of the fire until it ruptures the bomb casing and explodes with impressive force. To detonate the bomb, Fiddler took a brick of AA batteries and lined them all, up plus to minus, minus to plus, back and forth. Fiddler would then freeze the batteries for about 24 hours. He would take the batteries out one at a time as he soldered plus to negative and negative to positive, until the entire brick was soldered together. He then attached two wires running from the battery pack to the bomb bottles. The voltage from this device is powerful enough that one would not want to touch the wires. While the voltage itself may not kill you, it's high enough to give someone a painful shock.

Having attached the wires, Fiddler then hooked a rocket detonator from a hobby shop to the battery pack, minus the positive wire that will eventually be touched to the battery pack when Fiddler was ready to detonate the explosives. Leroy and Hertric began digging a large hole, piling the dirt directly in front of the hole to make a shelter from the explosives. Soon the fellas were digging holes and placing 55-gallon drums full of dirt into these holes. They hoisted an old console television out to the blast zone and then they took a bunch of 20-pound flour bags and stacked them over tubes that contained the bombs the fellas had made.

The first 55-gallon drum bomb was detonated. The drum shot straight up in the air about 300 feet. As the drum trailed to the ground, the dirt poured out the back of the drum until it plummeted to the ground. It looked pretty darn awesome to anyone, but to three pyromaniacs it was cause to shout and celebrate and brag on the success of the bomb.

The next drum was all positioned and ready to go. The three men stood to the left and right of the foxhole they had dug for safety, but as could have been predicted, no one was in the foxhole where they belonged. Fiddler detonated the second 55-gallon drum which did not go up in the air like the first one. Instead, it flew apart in many pieces, all of which rocketed in the direction of the Three Knuckleheaded Musketeers. It happened so fast that metal chunks whizzed by the men and landed in the desert sand nearly 50 feet behind the men, who at least for now, thankfully remained intact.

The detonation of the console TV was the most impressive. The fellas finally decided to use their grey matter and get down in the foxhole. When the TV detonated, a fireball shot out in all directions followed by hundreds of pieces of the console TV which also dispersed in all directions. It was magnificent!

Their final pyrotechnic challenge was to launch all the 20-pound bags of flour into the air where the bombs would presumably ignite the flour dust into a gigantic fireball. Leroy, Hertric, and Fiddler had climbed back out of the foxhole and counted down to launching the final explosive. Fiddler touched off the battery pack he had made and instantly the flour bags converted to a large circle of flour dust roughly 300 feet in diameter. In less than a second the dust ignited into a fire ball that would make Hollywood movie producers jealous. However, one thing folks don't learn watching Hollywood movies is that the fire ball is super-hot. The three men dove into the foxhole all shouting, "Hot … Hot … Hot."

The Good Lord looks out for folks like Hertric and Leroy and Fiddler. He must, or they would all surely be dead. Sadly, Hertric is dead, having met his demise in Iraq. Leroy only knows that Hertric had become a Combat Engineer, perhaps because of Leroy's influence. Fiddler did his four years in the service and then built up a pizza empire in Toledo Ohio.

But for this day in the California desert, they had exciting memories to share. Hertric spoke excitedly, "Wow! Did you see how high we launched that 55-gallon drum in the air?"

Leroy spoke with equal enthusiasm, "Heck yeah! And what about the metal drum that blew apart right in front of us?"

As the three congratulated each other and boasted about their parts in the weekend of manly fireworks, they all felt a warm fuzzy feeling. One might ask, what does a warm fuzzy feeling, feel like? It feels like friendship.

Given what is going on in the country today, picture what the perception of this might be. The three young men had legally acquired chemicals to construct some pretty mighty explosives. Fiddler, Leroy, and Hertric only looked at bomb-building as a hobby. The intention to do harm to anyone never even entered their minds. In fact, they took measures to ensure the safety of others. Aside from that, said jokingly, the forgotten use of the foxhole does not bode well for their futures. Also, one might ask how the chemicals and materials were acquired so easily.

Sadly, Leroy will never have these kinds of friends ever again. Cherished youth was the motivation of this story.

THE END

Paul Spencer

Toyota Survey

Leroy recently purchased a Toyota GR86. It should be called MLC86 or Mid Life Crisis 86. It is a great car and exactly what Leroy was looking for. Things were ok with his relationship with Toyota. Relationships with some were wonderful, mainly in the service department, and then other relationships were not so wonderful. Leroy had already picked out the GR86 before entering his familiar dealership, and in spite of the asinine behavior of certain folks in the dealership, Leroy was not deterred from buying the GR86 as he normally would be by such behavior.

Shortly after Leroy drove his car home, he started to get survey after survey from Toyota asking his opinion on the Toyota buying experience. Leroy filled one out and it was pathetic. Instead of determining Leroy's car buying experience, Leroy thought to himself that it was actually designed to exploit information pertinent to Leroy's potential future car needs. Keep up that kind of deception and Leroy's car buying needs won't include one make of vehicle. Care to guess which?

The portion that did pertain to the car buying experience was equally useless. One example is that you are given only two choices: My car buying experience was awesome like none other, or, my car buying experience was the worst ever like none other. The truth of Leroy's experience, is that it lay somewhere in the middle. Unfortunately, there was no option for any middle ground. Leroy and I both hope that the following very useful survey included below will be studied and that action will be taken to reward and discipline those involved in the creation of future surveys. Leroy tells me he is now in the market for a more practical SUV. With so many options available, his loyalty still lies with Toyota, unless key folks ignore him again. More on this to follow. With all this said, the main message to Toyota is "Stop sending the spam surveys today please, and furthermore, please provide some meaningful feedback to Leroy! And when someone promises to call Leroy about the survey then call Leroy about his survey. Promising and not doing is LYING!" So here is a useful and valuable Toyota survey that Leroy sent in. Here we go:

Toyota Buying Experience Survey

Leroy was an odd duck. He grew up a ranch boy from Montana and after high school he left for the military where he spent 23 years, retiring in 2011, as a Senior Chief, Surface and Air Warfare Specialist, Combat Engineer. Leroy shared with me that his 2005 Toyota Scion was starting to show some wear and the cost to repair her had exceeded her value. Leroy had his eye on a little sports car he had found on line. I said to Leroy, "Hey get whatever you want. You can afford it and God knows you earned it." Leroy had donated generously to his church, he had paid for everything to allow his step daughter to go on a family cruise, and he had paid his editor to edit yet another one of his "Leroy's Shorts" series that you are enjoying now. With all that generosity having come to fruition, I said to Leroy, "Buy yourself whatever you want."

Leroy responded, "I want a car that looks and rides like an Indy 500 Go Kart. I want a dark royal blue paint job, and I think this Toyota GR86 might be the match." (Please read the stand-alone review of the car. The term Go Kart is said with admiration, and I am not disparaging the car in any way.)

Having made his decision, Leroy made his way to the Toyota dealership. He went inside through the service entrance, a creature of habit, because for the last 10 years, Leroy had always gone into the Toyota dealership to get his Toyota Scion serviced. Allen worked in the service department and had always been such a joy to work with on service and the occasional repairs to Leroy's car. Sure, Leroy had been disgruntled on occasion. That's just the way the world works, but as one example, after buying ALL new brakes for the 6th time in 6 years, he questioned Allen about why new brakes were such a frequent necessity. Allen went on to explain that in New York State, the use of salt on the roads during the endless winter months was every vehicle's enemy. The brakes needed to be replaced so often because the corrosion causes them to end up seizing due to the corrosion caused by salt. Leroy could only hope the brakes on his GR86 are corrosion proof like the frame is. Allen had explained to Leroy that he could fix the Scion for about $7K but cautioned Leroy that the value of the car was considerably less than $7K, so it was probably time to look at a new sports car. That is exactly what Leroy did, on the advice of the Service Manager. Can we give HIM the commission?

As Leroy walked in, Allen the Service Manager spotted Leroy and in his typical fashion he said "Hello Leroy." Leroy excitedly told him he was coming in to purchase the GR86. Allen had always been brutally honest with Leroy, which is only one of his many great qualities and in fact, he ended up having more to do with the car sale than any of the numb nuts in sales.

When Leroy went to see Tony the Sales Manager, after telling Tony what he was looking for, Tony told Leroy, "Yeah, there's a red one sitting in the parking lot. You can go see it."

Leroy looked at Tony in disbelief. Wasn't he going to grab a sales rep that would help Leroy buy this car? Wasn't he going to stroke Leroy's ego just a little? Leroy just said out loud, "WOW! This is not the new car buying experience I am used to." Feeling dismissed and disappointed, Leroy left the showroom and went home, tail between his legs.

So, Question #1: Is it in the Sales Manager's job description that he is to play on his phone all day? Is it the norm that when a hungry customer with cash to spend comes along, Tony, in his role as Sales Manager basically shines them on and sends them home frustrated? If this is the measure of a good sales manager, then job well done. If not? Then DO something about it!

When Leroy got home, he went crying to his wife Lenora about his abysmal experience with the sales manager at Toyota. Lenora said, "Come with me Leroy. I will get you taken care of." She had leased RAV4's since Leroy and Lenora had first become a couple some 12 years ago, shortly after Leroy had been blown up in Afghanistan, honorably discharged from military service and subsequently began cohabitating with Lenora.

Lenora and Leroy went back into the sales department and Lenora walked right over to Eric, one of the salesmen on the floor. Leroy recognized Eric, as he had been the one to help Lenora with the lease of her 5 separate RAV4's during this 12-year span. In fact, the first RAV4 that Lenora and Eric tangled horns over went like this: Lenora wanted to trade in her Toyota Scion. She asked Eric what she would get for a trade in. Eric offered her $7K. Leroy's eyes went wide and he immediately said "SOLD" and wrote Lenora a check for $7K. It was at that moment that Lenora decided to lease, and has done so ever since. Leroy encouraged her lease idea as it gives her a new car every 3 years.

With all this history, Leroy thought for sure Eric would treat him right. He had demonstrated this courteousness with Leroy's wife, Lenora, during her many lease negotiations and transactions so feeling confident in Eric's abilities, Leroy explained to Eric that he wanted the GR86, and told Eric the specific features he wanted. In the end, Leroy decided to go with the basic model, including an automatic transmission, cloth seats and so on. After listening to Leroy, Eric responded with "The GR86 is hard to come by, and even harder to get the options you want including color, interior, transmission choice, etc. that you're asking for."

Leroy mulled all this over, decided it would be worth the wait and dropped $250.00 cash towards the car as a deposit. Leroy asked Eric, "Can you please text me every 2 weeks with an update on your progress in finding me this car?" Leroy then asked Eric if 2 weeks was too often for a text.

Eric said, "No. That's not too often. I will text you every two weeks."

Leroy left the dealership and a few days later Leroy sees an advertisement from Toyota.com on TV. It goes like this: "Pick out your colors, your options, and so on. Then pay for your car and when it comes into your area, you can pick it up at your local dealership." Now, Leroy and I are smart. We know that some of these criticisms are directed at corporate and some criticisms are directed at West Herr Toyota in Greece. Anyway, Leroy went online and spent close to 30 minutes filling out the information pertaining to the car he wanted. When he hit the final submit, within seconds, the phone rings. Leroy answers and hears, "West Herr Toyota. How may I help you?" Leroy threw his phone across the room!

Leroy's wife Lenora, just snickered and said, "They sent you full circle, didn't they?" Leroy began to visibly shake and his face turns a never before achieved red. This was a good indication of Leroy's anger.

Leroy yelled, "Take me full circle? Take me full circle? They absolutely LIED to me and you know how I hate being lied to. It is worse than any inept performance! It is worse than just about anything because the person did it on purpose, knowing full well that filling out that request for a specific car was a lie. The only purpose for that online form was to get my name and number to a dealer." Leroy was furious. He knew there was never any intention to build Leroy his specific car and get it to him. It was a full-on lie, designed purely to get Leroy's information to a dealer who would then sell him the car THEY wanted to sell him, rather than the car Leroy truly wanted. This is exactly what Toyota.com did and continues to do. If Leroy ever wins the lottery, he will take the whole lot of them to court for false advertising. Why don't we call it what it is? Lying to the consumer! Toyota knock it off now!

Leroy decided to take a break and try to employ some patience. He had looked at a Kia's sports cars and a couple other makes, including a line from Mitsubishi and all the domestic muscle cars. None of them measured up to what Leroy wanted. The Toyota GR86 had already sold itself and now all Leroy needed to do was figure out how to get one. He called back to Montana and his father said, "I will buy you one here and then you can come pick it up."

Leroy responded, "Dad, I appreciate your charity towards me. I know you say you are only giving me my inheritance early, but my silly human pride gets in the way of your generosity." Leroy continued, "Besides, you gave me the skill sets to make my own money." It was at this point that Leroy decided just to wait. He was 35th on the waiting list for the car and therefore did not expect to be getting his car until spring.

Sometime after all the afore mentioned drama had played out, Lenora went to Toyota. She was taking her RAV4 in for service. After she and Allen, the Service Manager, visited a bit, Lenora went to see Eric, Leroy's Toyota Sales Rep. As Lenora approached Eric's cubicle, she noticed Eric's entire desk was gone. She went to Tony the Sales Manager and asked, "Hey, where's Eric?" Lenora went on "He's not texting my husband Leroy as promised!" Then she tells Tony that Leroy wants the standard transmission for his GR86 that he's put a deposit on, and not the automatic he'd originally asked for.

Tony responds with, "Darn, because I have a blue one in Buffalo but it's custom and it has an automatic transmission."

Lenora went home and relayed the information to Leroy and then ran for cover because she knew Leroy was about to blow a gasket. Leroy immediately called Tony the Sales Manager and laid into him. "First off Tony, I want to know why you did not take Eric's customer list, and let ALL of us know that Eric was gone? I saw the data base. I was on the waiting list for the GR86, along with 34 others who were on the list before me, and the list was complete with all our contact data. As Sales Manager, when one of your sales reps is no longer with the dealership, you are supposed to call all 35 folks on the list, including myself, and bring us all up to speed. You are supposed to let us know who is taking over for Eric, along with the status of our orders. Did you do that? Did you not have time? How long has Eric been gone? How much time do you need?" These were all rhetorical questions. Tony certainly had long enough because all this should have been done on day one.

Leroy gave Tony a minute to gnaw on that rotten lamb shank, and then said, very sternly, "This car negotiation is now between you and me! I don't care who, besides me, comes in on my behalf. Just send them away! Yes, I wanted the standard transmission and I still do. Eric told me it was a pipe dream, and I believed him, which is ALL the more reason I don't want you holding out for one on my behalf." Tony shakes off the butt chewing. Leroy is always one to give credit where credit is due as well doing some ass chewings, and Tony deserves credit for going forward. Most folks that Leroy gives the raspberries to just quit. They choose vindictive behavior instead of professionalism. Leroy makes sure that such behavior becomes their loss!

However, much to Leroy's surprise, Tony called Leroy three days later and said, "Leroy come pick up your car. It is not exactly what you want, but please come see it for me."

When Leroy hung up the phone, he passed the information outlined above on to Lenora and Lenora just said, "You're welcome." Lenora is a dream and people love her, even the people Leroy deems incompetent, and worthless. Leroy on the other hand, keeps wondering why people hate him so much.

Leroy, hearing a potential car may be waiting for him, went to the West Herr Toyota dealership that day. Tony demonstrated his sales skills well by making Leroy feel good about his decisions. Leroy thought Tony, given the proper circumstance, could sell a ketchup popsicle to an Eskimo in white gloves, and Leroy means that as a compliment!

Tony took Leroy out to the car and began to ply his trade as a salesman. He said, "I know this color isn't Neptune Blue, but I think you will like it."

Leroy did not want to give credit to Tony after being ignored by Tony on several fronts, and what he would really have liked to say to Tony was "It sucks!" But damn if Leroy did not fall in love with the beautiful blue color that was before him. It was even better than the Neptune Blue. Of course, Leroy did wonder why this was his first time seeing this particular color. It never showed up as an option at the time Leroy handed over the deposit. But at this point, he didn't care. He loved it. The next mind blower was the interior. This was a deluxe model in front of Leroy and in the past, Leroy wanted to steer clear of the deluxe models due to the leather seats. Leroy was picturing the type of leather that looks like vinyl, is hard to maintain and cracks just like vinyl. Leroy scoffed, "This is the deluxe model!"

Tony calmly opened the door and ran his hand across the suede leather and said, "See Leroy, I'm a man of my word. These seats are not the leather you were complaining about. They are just like fabric in feel but they will last longer than fabric. Again, Leroy sheepishly admitted to Tony that he actually liked the seats. I could keep going with this interaction between Leroy and Tony but suffice it to say that Tony did a good job helping Leroy accept those things he couldn't change about the car and to be happy with what he could control.

Tony, the Toyota Sales Manager, then turned Leroy over to Savannah. Savannah is the West Herr Toyota Sales rep. I asked Leroy if he was over the kibosh between him and Tony. Leroy said, "I am not going to declare war on him. I am already at war with Leaf Guard for selling me a defective gutter system and with Lowes for selling me defective pressure treated lumber, so I can't afford too many more lawyer fees. In the end, Tony came through. Sadly, Leaf Guard and Lowes only understand lawyer talk." Leroy then said to me, "Surely you are going to put this in your latest book, are you not?"

To which I gladly responded, "Yes, of course. It is how I make my living."

Tony has presented himself as a person who, when brow beaten or worried what a customer might say about him, performs pretty well. But an ounce of prevention is worth a pound of cure. IE: Competent sales managing in the first place is far superior to always putting out fires! Putting out fires is a dirty set of words in Leroy's dictionary. Attention to detail is a must, not an option. Tony? Tony puts out fires, which is a horrible way to do business for both the customer and Toyota. Secondly, Leroy knew he was 35th on the list for the GR86. Leroy knew for a fact that Tony got Leroy a car, but Leroy also knew he cut in line in front of the other 34 folks on the list big time. If someone at Toyota wants to say Leroy is wrong, I hope they won't lie to him again!

Leroy called 2 of his buddies that he knew were before him on the waiting list. Earlier, he had shared Eric's info with said buddies. Although Leroy had procrastinated completing the purchase of his GR86, Leroy called his buddies to boast that he got his car before they did and he had cut in line on the playground, all thanks to Tony. How and why did this happen? It was solely because Tony only knows how to be a fire fighter. Tony needs to understand he is a sales manager, not a forest service fire fighter.

One last important note on Tony the Toyota Sales Manager. He almost lost this sale with Leroy, so when Leroy comes back in 3 years to trade up his GR86, if Tony the Toyota Sales Manager is still a member of the Toyota Team, Leroy is likely to walk out and go elsewhere. Leroy had purchased many Chevy vehicles before he retired and Bob Johnson Chevy did much the same as Toyota. Leroy's Sales rep at Bob Johnson left for good like Eric and Leroy never knew about it until near 6 months later. Leroy told me we won't be going there anymore. Leroy was telling me he wanted to get a new cargo van and trade in his old one with 50K miles. Given that West Herr now carries Chevys, he planned on buying a new van next. Eric, the old Toyota sales rep. was ready to pull the trigger. Wonder why that trigger was never pulled? Thank God there are a ton of dealerships and no one has the monopoly on vans. Leroy just looked at me kind of lost, kind of hurt and said, "I can just keep plugging away until I find professionalism. It has to be out there somewhere, right?"

To his credit, Tony tried, albeit with minimal effort, to apologize to Leroy. Leroy just blew past him because for one, Leroy and every other living human knows how one truly and sincerely apologizes. And secondly, with his new car, Leroy was having fun at long last. His shit eating grin most certainly gleamed as a beacon of his happiness. As he walked past Tony, he was following Savannah, who had listened to Leroy when he said he was in a hurry, and as a result, was moving past Tony quickly. Leroy was right behind her, hustling along, when all of a sudden and without warning, Tony sticks out his hand for a hand shake and says, "Hey Leroy. I am sorry for the mix up," It should come as no surprise that Leroy just brushed right by him. Again, it seems Leroy's 3rd grade education exceeds Tony's education. When you apologize with sincerity instead of just trying to put out another fire, you contact the person when they are hopefully not involved in something else. You do not try to shake their hand when they are running after their dedicated sales rep who truly is putting in a five-star effort. Instead, you take the person to a quiet place where everyone can sit and talk. One can argue that the recipient of the apology may not be cooperative, but Leroy is always more than willing to receive a well-deserved and WELL-EXECUTED apology. The reason Tony was throwing apologies at Leroy is that he was afraid Leroy would squeal to Toyota's upper management about Tony's attitudes, so as Leroy hurried by, Tony the Toyota Sales Manager had his fireman's suit on yet again. Spoiler alert! Leroy did indeed squeal, but the measure of a successful survey is that after receiving it, whether or not the company who requested the survey does anything that results in changes to procedure and policy, rather than simply file a collection of sales data.

Savannah the sales rep that Tony had assigned to Leroy was just great. She showed Leroy how to operate the custom gun turrets Leroy wanted installed, and then Leroy asked Savannah, "Which car is Tony's car? I want to test fire my gun turrets." Said with a smile.

Savannah showed Leroy all the features and though Leroy felt inundated by the sheer volume of information being rapid fire fed to him, he did his best to keep up. Furthermore, when Leroy did get home and was driving the car to church and back, it was during these trips that Leroy began to wonder how to operate all this cool stuff. A few weeks after getting the car, Leroy called Savannah who offered to show vs tell Leroy how everything in the car work, and not by having Leroy look on some website. No! She said she would show him anything on the car any time. Leroy told me that in his survey, Savannah is rated a perfect 5 stars. Leroy is hoping she can get him a new Chevy Express van from West Herr Chevy. Leroy is confident she can if she can get this survey to the right place. So far that is not happening, but hope springs eternal and Leroy figures anything is possible.

After orienting Leroy to his new car, Savannah handed Leroy off to Steve, the finance guy. Leroy was wondering why he was even going to Steve the finance guy? Leroy had always paid cash for every purchase he ever made, with the exception of a couple of houses and the purchase of this car was no different. There were no finances involved in this car transaction. As Leroy met with Steve the finance guy. Leroy walked into Steve's office a little confused, thinking to himself, "Why am I here?" Steve a more than adequately sized fellow, positioned himself behind Leroy in a posture that could only be interpreted as threatening.

Some time ago I had asked Leroy if he was intimidated by big guys. He smiled and said, "Honestly? The little guy scares me more. The little guy had to get tougher and more skilled than the big guys and always went into a fight as the underdog. The big guy is overconfident, often lacks agility, and in general, is easy to take down." But why are we talking about this in a car dealership? Because it's time for Steve to go find his calling. Customer service is not it. Maybe the circus is in town.

I asked Leroy if Steve standing behind Leroy and in effect blocking the doorway, instead of sitting in his desk chair next to Leroy, was making him anxious. Leroy really nailed his response. He told me he was not intimidated, but he recognized the effort to do so. It was pretty obvious that this yahoo was going to try and intimidate Leroy or hard sell him something? While Leroy does not know what Steve was up to, he sure was not up to making a good first impression on Leroy. I asked Leroy where he thought Steve should be and Leroy said, "Steve should be sitting at his desk, you know, like normal business people do when dealing with their customers, and he should try making some eye contact. The good cop/bad cop routine needs to go."

The next thing Steve did, really cheesed Leroy. Steve reaches over to the computer and turns on a propaganda video. The vocals pick up and say, "Welcome to the Toyota team."

Leroy looked at Steve and loudly exclaimed, "I am not a member of any more teams, especially this team!" Leroy invited Steve to sit at his desk and continued, "So, Steve, lesson learned: assume your customer is educated past the 3rd grade." Leroy told Steve to turn off the propaganda video. Leroy then asked, "Please get to the warranty packages." Leroy had spotted a single piece of paper on Steve's desk outlining the various warranty options. Now don't get me wrong; if Steve had some milk and peanut butter cookies, Leroy's personal favorites, then it's a pretty good bet that Leroy would stay and watch cartoons with Steve, but then and only then.

Leroy said loud and clear that he was very short on time and the sooner he could be driving the car, versus filling out forms about the car, the better. Watching a propaganda video is the polar opposite of HURRY UP! After all this with Steve the finance guy, remembering that Leroy had paid cash for his car, Steve finally handed Leroy the warranty paper which was the only thing he wanted to see. This paper outlined all the extended warranty options. Steve started hurriedly to explain the warranty packages and Leroy got thinking, "I just eliminated some 30 minutes of cartoons, so surely Steve has 30 minutes to explain these warranty packages." I wish I could say all went well but it was not to be. Leroy just asked Steve for the list and left. Steve had never explained diddly. Leroy ended up researching the options on his own. As far as Leroy is concerned, Steve served(s) no purpose. Again, reference Steve to a circus career. There you can switch from your head up your ass to being a horse's ass.

Once again on his own, seeing Savannah busy elsewhere, he grabbed his mini lap top, aka his phone, and started to weigh the options. While researching the various warranties, Leroy came up with what he wanted, and reported his decisions to Savannah.

I asked Leroy if he was sure he wanted an extended warranty. Leroy has only bought an extended warranty one other time. He had bought a washing machine from Sears and the extended warranty for the washer cost $800.00 for a 5-year period. A month after buying the warranty, Leroy's washing machine from Sears, fully covered under the $800.00 warranty, failed due to a manufacturing defect. The failure caused the machine to dance out from the wall, which then pulled the hoses loose, flooding the entire lower level of Leroy's house. Leroy promptly called Sears and as Leroy laid out details with the woman on the phone who was representing Sears, he explained to the woman that he was not angry about the damage as he felt that was an act of God. Continuing with Sears on the phone, Leroy said, "I am so glad we got the extended warranty. My homeowner's insurance is taking care of everything else, so I just need a new washer ASAP. I have 4 young kids so laundry mounts quickly and I am NOT wasting my evenings at the laundromat."

Sears' response was, "We can get you a new washer in 8 weeks!" Well, that's 2 months and predictably, Leroy exploded on the stupid woman who would consider 8 weeks as an acceptable time to wait for another washer. As always, Leroy could not let it go. Ultimately it was the legal staff at State Farm Insurance that went after Sears and Leroy was made whole from Sears for the cost of the new clothes washer. State Farm then sued Sears for the costs of repairing the water damage. State Farm took care of this quickly and in 3 days, from the time State Farm intervened, Leroy received the money and promptly went and bought a washer and dryer which Leroy has to this day from an appliance store called Orville's. Leroy's loyalty to State Farm goes without saying. Leroy's loyalty to Sears? Well, we all know what happened to Sears and after all Leroy had gone through, here was yet another proof that karma does exist. State Farm completely restored Leroy's house, doing a hassle free and professional job. No complaints.

.

So, Steve, you want Leroy to be, a member of the Toyota team? Then earn it. Leroy does not join a team until he sees what it is made of. The first time Leroy brings in a bent rim or some other problem covered in the extended warranty and Leroy gets the Sears treatment, Toyota will then discover the Leroy treatment. Leroy is much more action oriented than word oriented, which is a valuable thing to remember.

What ever happened to Sears? I am certainly not saying Leroy ran Sears out of business. Sears ran themselves out of business when they started screwing over their customers. Perhaps the decline of Sears started with one customer, and maybe that one customer was Leroy.

With all this talk of extended warranties, it is no wonder Leroy wanted to research his extended warranty options without pressure and intimidation. Instead, he would like to do this in a relaxed environment where those who possess higher than a third-grade education, like Leroy and who want to weigh their options are given the space and time to do so. How about it, Toyota? Put it all online and direct potential buyers to come in with an idea of what they want in a warranty. If they still want to sit down with Steve, watch cartoons and be intimidated by him, then that is their God given right to do so. At least have some milk and cookies available. Then by all means, they can proceed as they wish. I know some folks like to be dominated, but not Leroy. For the rest of us, give us a different option.

Again, Leroy is stating clearly, if in three years when he is ready to trade up to a new model of the GR86, Leroy sees Steve puffing his chest outside his office, Leroy will bounce. Screw me once, screw you, screw me twice, screw me. Leroy does not allow screw me twice to take place. Please don't test that conviction. It can only end badly for any idiot attempting the behavior.

Leroy did buy the extended warranty and the extended maintenance package and a couple other features, which added over $5K to the purchase price, but if the warranty comes through like it reads… I mean, come on folks. After the debacle with Sears, Leroy quit buying magic beans. I will keep you, my readers, informed in book three, Leroy's Shorts: Speedo Edition, updating you on Leroy's like or dislike of the warranty and maintenance options moving forward. Leroy is doing his best to remain positive, but he thinks this is going to be another George Santos, meaning just another New Yorker lying to him. How do you know if a New Yorker is lying? Their lips are moving. There are a few exceptions. If you find one of them, please let Leroy know.

When Leroy finally arrived home, he was exhausted. This car buying experience had been nothing like his car buying experiences in Montana. Instead of the friendly and professional service when Leroy walked in to buy a Chevy or a Toyota with his Montana Team, who would greet him as he walked in asking "Hey Leroy. How's the ranch? How's your dad? You want a scone and some fresh coffee?" Juxtapose this with the Toyota team in New York and voila! I have yet another short story to publish.

Home at last, Leroy settled into his arm chair, and as was his norm, routinely checked his email thinking he might be getting something from his editor or perhaps some news from any number of Leroy's other associates. Instead, Leroy starts to get emails from Toyota. Now one or two emails with specific info that needed to be imparted to Leroy, the customer, is fine. What is definitely NOT fine is being inundated with endless emails from Toyota. Leroy lost count at about twenty of them. And what are these emails? They are surveys. So, after struggling to find a solution, Leroy thought, "If I block all email from Toyota, then I won't get recall information, I won't get any rebate info, I won't get invited to a closed course experience with a professional driver, and in other words, I can't block all emails from Toyota."

When the annoying spam from Toyota persisted, Leroy thought that if he completed one of the surveys, perhaps it would stop. I know, I know. Little known fact is that Leroy was "Special" as a child. Said with a smile. The surveys did not stop and Toyota continues to inundate Leroy's email with endless inanities. The question Leroy is asking Toyota is, "Will the madness that is Toyota spam ever stop going to his email? Is there a way to decline emails? Can a person stop all spam or should Leroy go elsewhere for his vehicles and try to convince Lenora to start leasing Kia SUVs? Going elsewhere won't be hard. Leroy did not spend almost $50K just to have his email turned into a trash can for Toyota advertising. STOP NOW!

Here was the gist of the Toyota survey that Leroy managed to open. The survey was another folly of failure. The first question asked was, "Rate your car buying experience" but ONLY two choices are presented: choice 1: Worst car buying experience I have ever had. Choice 2: This is the best car buying experience ever had. Given only these two choices and with what you have read so far what would you mark? Exactly, Leroy marked "Worst experience ever". He certainly was not about to mark, "Best performance ever." Leroy was clear with Toyota: "Fix your stupid survey so it might actually have some benefit or stop spamming us with it."

One thing of note is that Leroy left the survey open on his "Fast" laptop. When he returned 30 minutes later, the survey had finally populated. It turned out there were choices 1 through 5 that finally materialized. Leroy was glad the ITs did not build his car, because this survey was an abysmal creation, obviously designed by ITs from the planet Gobbledygook. Leroy's GR86 would be in the scrap yard if the ITs built it. Fix it or get rid of it! When only two options appeared as outlined above, it actually let Leroy pick the option "Worst experience", even though the other options had not yet populated. I am no web designer, but even I can see what was wrong with that design. It's called Beta Test moron, look it up!

Leroy continued on the survey and quickly realized that all the questions were not geared to gauge his pleasure and to have Toyota be prepared to make improvements in the car buying experience. NOPE. The sole purpose of this survey became obvious when next it asked Leroy to get out of his chair, get out of his jammies, and go out and get the year, make, and model of all the cars he has. Note, it looks like Jay Leno lives at Leroy's but, nevertheless, Leroy painstakingly gathered the data, populated the Toyota survey with all the cars and then hit "next". Suddenly the survey was blank. Leroy tried multiple devices and the same thing kept happening.

Again, thank God Toyota's ITs didn't build Leroy's. Ask the ITs if they know what Beta Testing means? Leroy knows they must have a clue. When Leroy designed and built something like a weapon turret, for example, you'd better believe he tested it! That was his product and he would be the one to discover if it wouldn't work. How many projects of Leroy's failed? Take an educated guess. Right. You guessed it. None in 23 years! Leroy stood behind his product. Toyota IT's stand behind their product as well. Unfortunately, they stand really, really, far behind it and clearly, they don't have a clue what it means to have pride in their work or do the necessary beta testing of their work to make sure the final product will function properly. From the perspective of the customer, it absolutely does not, and is an epic fail!

As Leroy blindly carried out the task of gathering make, model, and year on a half dozen cars, Lenora asked, "What does any of this have to do with rating your car buying experience? Don't you know they are pressing you for your vehicle info so they can ascertain your future Toyota needs? It's that simple. Nothing more, nothing less." Just so you know Toyota, that is a really bad move! Not to mention sneaky and just plain wrong. And so, the lies continue.

After muddling through the most worthless survey Leroy had ever seen, Leroy thought, "I would be embarrassed as a CEO if I allowed this kind of tripe to take place on my watch. But I am not the CEO. If I was, I would want a layman like me to explain why business was down and what could be done to improve it." Thank God none of this is in Leroy's swim lane.

Shortly after Leroy hit "send" on a survey that should go up on the wall of fame as the worst survey ever, Leroy got a phone call from someone in regards to the Toyota survey that Leroy had just sent. As Leroy was unavailable, they left him a completely incoherent voice mail. What Leroy was able to make out was that someone was calling about the survey. The voicemail went like this: "My name is" Again, it was so garbled it couldn't be made out. The caller from Toyota continued to talk, "I see you sent a survey in and it looks like you're disgruntled." (Please note the above survey criticism. Leroy was not completely disgruntled, but then again, nor was he completely happy.) The mystery man from Toyota had just put his stupid survey to the test and showed clearly why it failed. "It looks like you are disgruntled." The Toyota man who called Leroy from his garbled phone to discuss Leroy's survey, rattled off a phone number should Leroy like to return the call. Again, like his name, the caller's phone number was so garbled that Leroy did not get either a name or a phone number. Toyota man from the survey then said with his final breath, "Don't worry if you did not get all this. You are super important to us at the Toyota Team, and I will keep calling you until we connect." Now THAT went through okay. But the promise to reach Leroy was yet another lie. Leroy has received no follow-up phone call from this mystery man from Toyota.

How about this mystery man? I know this requires a 3rd grade education so Leroy is anxious to help you out. Let's start with a text to include a name, phone number and when it would be a good time to chat. That will side track the fact that the moron was obviously calling from a location that disrupts everyone's cell service, including but not limited to inside a tunnel, inside a metal Toyota building, in the woods, on the beach, out in a gale force wind etc. You know what Leroy does in these types of situations when he needs to make a call and knows the call is going to be unclear? He goes outside, or goes next to an outside wall. More importantly, we can all tell when our cell phone is cutting out and that drives us to find a window, a parking lot, an exterior wall, or whatever it takes to sound like a professional instead of Yogi Bear talking to Booboo from a location that everyone knows is not connecting. Leroy wants to meet this person who left him that garbled message so he can ascertain the value this person brings to the Toyota team. He will start the conversation with this person by explaining this disaster that Toyota calls a survey and then ask them to figure out how to stop the spam emails from Toyota without stopping the recall data and such, which would be the result if Leroy blocked all emails from Toyota in some vain effort to stop the madness. That's the email equivalent of throwing the baby out with the bath water but seriously Toyota, that spam mail needs to STOP!!

Author's Note:

This survey has actually been a blessing because it gave me another short story to add to the collection of short stories in the Leroy's Shorts series available for sale on Amazon.com and B Dalton books. This book should reach those same shelves by midsummer 2023 and I am going to start on the third book in the series immediately after this edition gets published. I will follow up with what happens with this debacle going forward and build it into the next story. Pretty cool how these write themselves, huh?

Paul Spencer

The Toyota GR86 according to Leroy

Hello my name is Leroy. I grew up an only child in the wilds of Montana. My father bought me every toy a boy could want, so yes I am spoiled. I served as a Combat Engineer for 23 years. During that time, I lost my youth, as we all lose our youth, struggling through life. I had a Toyota Celica rear wheel drive as a young man before my 23-year military adventure. I had so many youthful memories behind the wheel of that car, that I wanted to recapture that youth. So, enter the Toyota GR86. The design takes me back to happiness, that is the best description I can give. It is the model for the midlife crisis man like me. It is more of a race car than a sports car. The suspension is like a buck board wagon but that is done on purpose because this tight suspension compliments the great handling the GR86 delivers. This car won't win at NASCAR, nor is it meant to. It will give you an exhilarating ride to the grocery store. It has an adequate trunk for all your groceries.

My only wish for my GR86 which has back seats. Can somebody tell me why? Even if your back seat passengers were paper cut outs, you are still not getting them into those seats. Toyota would be awesome to all us GR86 enthusiasts, if they dumped the back seats and put in a roll cage with a shiny diamond cut steel box for more storage. Toyota's ad shows us putting our child seats in the back. Yes, child seats will fit, but I seriously doubt that someone raising small children is going to buy a midlife crisis car. Or a car so tightly configured that putting a child into a child seat in back would require the flexibility of a Cirque de Solei contortionist.

The GR86 comes with a lot of bells and whistles that I know nothing about. Savannah, my sales rep, has offered to teach me about such bells and whistles. In addition, I have received a free invitation to drive the car on a closed course with a professional driver to assist and advise me as needed. Which is allot. My self-teaching has been pretty scary at times. Said with a smile.

It does not have a CD player that would allow me to listen to my CD collection, or even a port to plug a CD player into. I likely have about $10K of stuff I will never even learn to use, but there is no CD player! It took me 20 years to graduate from my 8-track to my CD, and I am too old to take another 20 years to learn "streaming" or whatever it's called. Even if I did figure it out, it wouldn't access my music. So, Toyota, going forward, at least supply an auxiliary plug one can plug a CD player into.

I bought the deluxe model, or whatever Toyota is calling it, only because it became available first. I did my research and both versions of this car will make you happy if upon reading why it made me happy makes you want to investigate acquiring one for yourself.

In conclusion, as I drove my GR86 to church the other day, part of my journey takes me down the Parkway. My wife and I have named our cars for years and I have named this beauty John Wayne. Going down the Parkway, I decided to put John Wayne, to the test. Heads turn as I pull into a parking lot. I admit this attention gets me off. I told my wife that John Wayne gave me a woody on my way to church and it felt great. If you want a laugh, make that same statement while waiting in line at Costco.

As I decided to put my GR86 to the test on the open stretches of the Parkway, I will leave the word "test" up to your imagination. If you are a State Trooper, test means up to and touching the limits of the law but never exceeding them. As I tested my GR86 on my way to church, I felt this weird sensation overtake me. What was it? It had escaped me for so long…. Oh yes. It was the feeling of sheer, unadulterated, Happiness.

As I walked into church, with a never before seen, shit eating grin on my face, folks thought I was possessed. They whispered, "Look at Leroy. What is wrong with his face?" Another whisper came from the pews, "I think he has a demon running through him." Next thing I know, I am in a sensory deprivation tank full of holy water.

But thinking about my GR86 made me feel as giddy as a school girl for the first time in thirty years, and at age 57 I sure can get on board with that experience. THAT is what the Toyota GR86 will give to you, do for you, be for you.

The End

Leroy Down the Parkway

Leroy had moved to New York in 2011, some twelve years earlier. He had met a woman by the name of Lenora when he was in Afghanistan and when he retired after 23 years of service, he wound up in Western New York. He had often wondered why it was that every time he would go down the Niagara Scenic Parkway, or any highway for that matter, people would drive slowly in the slow lane which was their prerogative, which is why it is called the slow lane. Because Leroy preferred the fast lane, the person Leroy did have the beef with was the person who, when Leroy was in the slow lane and getting to pass, they would zoom up next to him and then slow to the same speed as the old geezer in front of Leroy in the slow lane. Got it? This asinine behavior caused Leroy to have to slow down to "old geezer speed," and then be forced to hold that speed as there is no way around the old fella. I have heard Leroy ponder this over and over: "Maybe they are purposefully trying to box me in? At least that makes sense. There is no other reasonable explanation that makes any kind of sense." Leroy wondered, "Are these drivers totally oblivious to their surroundings at the exact moment they box me in? Are they completely unaware that their action of boxing me in as the most "turdish" (like a turd) thing a person could do?" It was another one of Leroy's pet peeves concerning common decency.

Regardless of all that, Leroy was going to the Toyota dealership where he had recently purchased his GR86. Lenora had insisted that the sales manager get her husband Leroy the Flip 8 manual transmission. Leroy had scolded Lenora for putting her nose in his business, explaining to Lenora that the original sales rep, Eric, that Lenora had originally introduced Leroy to, had told Leroy that if he held out for the manual transmission he would be waiting forever. Leroy chastised Lenora for her interference but Lenora only saw her meddling as being helpful, even though Leroy had driven a long hard road to break Lenora of her well-meaning intrusions. After deciding that an automatic transmission delivered now was better than a manual transmission delivered never, Leroy had picked up his automatic transmission GR86, and had driven away when he began to ask himself, "What are these flippers on the steering wheel?"

Leroy called his current Toyota sales rep. Savannah and asked her what the flippers were on the steering wheel.

Savannah said, "If you can come in, I will show you." Being a visual learner, Leroy preferred to be shown instead of told over the phone. Some days later, Leroy called Savannah to see if she had time to do some training. She responded with, "Sure Paul. Come by any time this morning I will give you all the time you need."

Leroy arrived at the Toyota dealership and found Savannah walking out of the boss's office. Savannah had her coat on in expectation of Leroy's arrival and was ready to go. Leroy said, "Thanks Savannah, I appreciate you teaching an old dog a new trick."

Savannah confidently said, "Leroy can I drive your car?" Before Leroy could even respond, Savannah continued saying, "Get in the passenger seat and I will show you how to do this." Savannah was about twenty-five years old; she was quite intelligent and she was good with people.

Now one might think, "Aren't all car salesman good with people?" Sadly, the pandemic destroyed that nice car buying experience when the microchips became impossible to obtain. Soon there were no cars to buy and when one did become avail for purchase, the salesmen just waited for us the customer to come begging on hands and knees. The whole thing was and is disgusting.

Savannah still remained quite skilled at making the car buying experience enjoyable again and the car teaching experience which she had offered to do without question was also much appreciated. Leroy marched to his race car, got in the passenger seat and buckled in. Savannah entered the driver's seat with ease. Leroy grumbled under his breath, "I can't get in like that. I have to lift my right leg into the floor then bend painfully like a clam shell as I grind into the seat." Savannah simply glides into the seat. Leroy could only shake his head in envy!

Savannah fires up the car, aggressively peels away and races out of the parking lot. Her aggressive driving continues down the busy road and out onto the interstate. Her driving is not reckless. It's just aggressive and very intimidating to an anxiety driven person like Leroy. She shot down the interstate, passing every car in sight. Leroy figured "She's driving, so it's going to be her speeding ticket." Within minutes she was turning off the expressway onto the Parkway which is normally devoid of any vehicles until about 3:30 PM when folks who live in the same village Leroy lives in start coming home from work. The Parkway was a shortcut from the city to the village. The time was 1:45 PM and there was no traffic.

As Savannah started to slow down to a stop, she said, "OK! Hold on and away we go!" She stomped on the gas and it was obvious to Leroy she had done this many times before. The front tires of the car came off the ground for a moment and then settled back down. She shifted a second time as the RPM's reached the optimum. The front end of the car lifted again as a chirp of rubber smoke emitted from the rear wheels. With each shift, the car responded the same, front-end lifting, though not as radically, as the speed increased and the rear tires chirped with a puff of smoke. When Savannah was in eighth gear the car was going 135 miles an hour. Leroy told me he figured it had a ways to go up from there, but Savannah down shifted with the same skill and returned the transmission to automatic. She said, "Any questions Leroy?"

Leroy was shaking a bit but also smiling. Leroy said, "I think you have demonstrated it well, When I get my drawers cleaned out, I will go practice it myself. But Savannah," Leroy continued, "I am confused. Did you just show me the flip 8 manual transmission that I wanted?"

Savannah was a bit confused by the question, since she rightly assumed Leroy had put the deposit down and subsequently paid for the precise features he wanted. Savannah did not know that Eric had talked him out of the manual transmission, and Leroy did not know that Lenora had gone and batted her big doe eyes at the Sales Manager, convincing him to get Leroy the toy he wanted.

Savannah showed Leroy where the automatic shifter said manual at the bottom and that the use of the manual transmission, as she had demonstrated, flawlessly meshes with the automatic. The flip 8 manual transmission gives this car a real racecar experience. Savannah roared back to the dealership and slid out of the car with ease. Leroy thanked her profusely and asked for some help finding him another "Hippie Van". Savannah smiled and said she would get to work on it.

Leroy went back to the Parkway and practiced the use of his eight-speed flip manual transmission. Every day he would get a little better until finally he could do what Savannah could do: chirp the rear tires with all eight gear shifts and allow the torque to lift the front tires off the ground all eight times, although you really do not want the tires lifting off the ground at high speeds, because for some reason the steering wheel and steering mechanism malfunctions and the car won't steer. Leroy keeps meaning to take it in for repair but when the wheels touch back down on the pavement the steering system resumes full operation. It is the darndest thing.

Leroy had chastised Lenora for her interference with the sales manager at Toyota. Now he had the flip 8 manual transmission. This was the ultimate toy for Leroy. It solidified his car as a true racecar. Leroy eagerly awaited the free class on a closed course track, complete with training from professional drivers. But what was he going to do about Lenora? He knew that as soon as she discovered that her nosy behavior is the reason Leroy had the toy of his dreams instead of having to settle, she was going to crow and then make Leroy eat that crow. Leroy asked me what I thought. I told Leroy that he had made his bed now he had to lie in it. Rip the band aid off and tell her you appreciate her butting in, just this once. Leroy followed my advice and Lenora took it better than expected. Leroy still has one testicle.

With all that drama behind them, Leroy was convinced he was ready to show off the full potential of his mighty race car to Lenora. He invited Lenora for an afternoon drive along the Parkway which follows the shoreline of Lake Ontario. There is lots of wild life and scenery to enjoy along this scenic byway. The Parkway has two lanes of traffic in each direction just like a small interstate has. Leroy entered the Parkway around 2:00 PM when he assumed the traffic would be minimal. Lenora was all strapped in and Leroy started to get up the nerve to make his demonstration of speed and torque, when just ahead there was a white Hyundai Elantra in the slow lane doing about 45 MPH. Leroy roared up on the Hyundai, though not to the extent of creating a danger if Hyundai Man has to slam on his brakes, but close enough to let him know Leroy is there. Just as Leroy was about to pass the Hyundai, a jet-black Jeep Grand Cherokee roared up in the fast lane. Does Jeep Dude just keep going at his same rate of speed? No. The idiot or asshole or both slows to the same speed as the Hyundai, and sits in the fast lane right next to Leroy who is now pinned in the slow lane. The medians on either side of the road are very narrow and Leroy really does not want to roll his $50K toy through the swamp. So, there is Leroy stuck and cursing, "These damn East Coast morons! Why on earth did he block me in?"

Leroy looks up at the Jeep and although he can make out the passenger, the driver is out of view. Leroy can see the passenger is a middle-aged woman and she is looking down at him.

The Hyundai suddenly takes an evasive move, God bless him, swerving into the fast lane in front of Jeep Turd. Leroy seizes the moment and rolls down his window and makes the sign of giving fellatio at the woman passenger and then points at her and then at himself with a shrug as if to ask the question…. Leroy focuses his attention and says, "Hang on Lenora. We are playing 'let's be chased by the turd.'" The turd is the Jeep driver.

Lenora asks, "Why did you do that to that woman?"

Leroy laughed, "She was just a prop! Collateral damage!" Leroy launched his new toy past the Hyundai and obviously past the boxed in Jeep. God bless the old codger in the white Hyundai. He continued to weave back and forth at around 45 MPH. Jeep Turd Man is honking his horn and eventually gets past the old codger and here he came toward Leroy. Leroy figured the Jeep Grand Cherokee had a 360 CU engine and was probably putting out 800 Horse Power. So, in theory, Jeep Turd Man should easily overtake Leroy in his little toy that only puts out around 280 HP. As Jeep Turd Man got closer to Leroy, Leroy said to Lenora, "Brace for Shock" as he stomped on the gas, shifted through the 8 gears and left Jeep Turd Man, whose mother has no living children, wallowing in the dust. Leroy had figured it out: his GR86 weighed a third of what the Jeep weighed, so it was like strapping a rocket to the space shuttle or strapping the same power rocket to a tin can. Leroy's GR86 was the tin can, or as Leroy affectionately called it, his Go Kart. Leroy eventually grew tired of toying with Jeep Turd Man but the experience had definitely given Lenora the full affect. Leroy went back to automatic transmission as Lenora and Leroy enjoyed the view. Leroy said, "So what do you think of my flip 8 manual transmission you got me?"

The Old Geezer in the White Hyundai Elantra

Willie Privette was born in Long Island New York. He graduated from high school as one in a class of 35 and went on to be a small-town sports announcer before landing a job as a civilian working for the Department of Defense, specifically the Department of the Navy. After many years of working in the Washington, DC area he decided to go to work for Catholic Charities and had since retired from that career some 20 years ago. Willie was kind to all as evidenced by his mantra of "Peace and Love." Willie was a practicing Catholic and a practicing Buddhist at the same time. Willie put it best: "When I say Buddha, I am saying Jesus." Leroy would concur with Willie. As long as a religion teaches love and acceptance of all others, then Leroy could get on board with that. The religion he worked to eradicate was one that believes in killing all those who don't believe as they do, including killing those within their own faith. Like if Leroy walked into a church of Baptists and started killing them because they were not Catholic, there would be plenty of consequences! I have it on good authority Leroy was about to find a different Christian religion himself, but he sure wasn't going to go kill anyone… in or out of the church. Willie met with several individuals each week just to be a friend to those who definitely needed a friend and that included Leroy. Willie was just shy of Sainthood.

Willie loved to drive the Parkway in his White Hyundai Elantra. He would drive slowly, maybe 40 MPH, and even though Willie was a vegan, he would look for meat eating birds along the Parkway. The Parkway hugs the coast of Lake Ontario and for many stretches of road one can see massive expanses of the lake. Willie also looked for humpback whales in the lake. I can't say if he ever saw any.

It was that fateful day when Willie was driving along slowly in his Hyundai, that Leroy came racing up behind him. Willie recognized that Leroy was just being a kid and he always was kind about passing him, like not blowing his windows in when Leroy drove by and not riding his rear bumper. Knowing Willie was being a looky-loo, Leroy would get beyond Willie's wildlife viewing area before lighting up the loud exhaust as Leroy would continue to play. Since Willie had no beef with Leroy, he just assumed Leroy would continue around him. Willie looked back when he did not see Leroy passing and saw the Black Jeep Grand Cherokee blocking Leroy. Willie was all about Peace and Love but he could also see that Jeep Turd Man was demonstrating the opposite of Willie's mantra of peaceful coexistence by being a turd and totally oblivious. Worse, it may be possible that he was being a turd and vindictive.

Whatever Willie's motivation, he swerved onto the fast lane and blocked Jeep Turd Man while Leroy sped past. Then Willie went back into the slow lane just as Jeep Turd Man went into the slow lane. Then Willie went back to the fast lane as Jeep man continued to try and get past him. Willie was feeling rather alive. This purposeful stirring up of trouble was definitely not in Willie's nature, but he was enjoying the change of pace. Finally, Jeep Turd Man got around Willie, and Willie settled back into the slow lane to resume his whale watching.

Turd Master in Black Jeep Grand Cherokee

Dan Schwind and his wife Judy had done OK for themselves. They had been married for nearly 40 years and had six adult children with too many grandchildren to list. They lived in the same village as Leroy. Leroy had gone to the same parish as Dan and we all know what Dan did to Leroy at that time. (Father O was his name O) Dan and his wife were not aware it was Leroy and Lenora in that beautiful blue Go Kart that they had decided to screw with. Maybe karma does exist? Dan elbowed his wife Judy and said, "Hon, watch this! I am going to block this old fart in just so I can be a warm festering fresh turd, and that way I'll keep him from getting around that old geezer in the Hyundai. I mean what other possible reason would I have to block him in?" Dan remained quite proud of his asinine behavior until he shouted, "Hey Mr. Hyundai! Get the hell out of my way!"

Judy let out a gasp and turned suddenly in her seat. She yelled at her husband Dan, "That son of a bitchin old fart in that little sports car just told me to give him a blow job."

Dan responded as he tried to get past the old codger in the Hyundai, "How do you know he told you to give him a blow job?"

Judy started to demonstrate with her cupped hand up to her mouth as she responded, "Because he did this!" Finally, Dan slipped by the white Hyundai Elantra and with an increasingly red forehead beading with sweat, and his wife pretending to give a blow job, Dan pushed the gas pedal to the floor and began to quickly gain ground.

Dan was enraged now as he shouted, "I am going to teach you a lesson old man! No one asks my wife for a blow job! She won't even give me a blow job!" Dan caught up to Leroy and as we know, Leroy immediately left Dan in the dust again and again until Leroy had had enough fun and just left Jeep Turd Man in the dust far, far away.

In conclusion: Isn't it interesting how one man's old codger, is another man's young whipper snapper? Isn't it interesting how everyone perceives the intentions of others? And finally, if you be a turd, please flush!

The End

For Home Repairs Don't Call Angi

Leroy found himself in need of heat tape. If you read *LeafGuard* you learned that the LeafGuard gutters Leroy had purchased were a complete failure. In about 30 minutes time, the melting water running off the snow from the roof subsequently freezes the opening slot where the water is supposed to flow into. The waterway opening is then completely frozen over and all the remaining roof melt water pours on all the walkways, freezing and rendering them unsafe for use. LeafGuard, recognizing their system was defective, agreed to have heat tape installed on their worthless gutters in an attempt to appease Leroy, hoping he would back off with the attorney General and the Better Business Bureau and the other consumer agencies Leroy had engaged. Leroy had no plans of backing down but if LeafGuard wanted to pay for three outside outlets which Leroy had wanted for many years in order to supply power to the heat tape, then Leroy would happily let LeafGuard foot the bill for the exterior outlets which he would then be able to use for Christmas lights and other electrical outdoor decorations.

Leroy was not familiar with electricians in the area so he decided he would try Angi. This was the worst thing Leroy could have done. If you need a service like Angi, do yourself a favor and call elsewhere, anywhere else. Angi is the worst call you can make. Unaware of this reality, Leroy called Angi and got ahold of a woman whose English-speaking skills were maybe 10% effective. Why do we hear about all this unemployment while at the same time we hire all of these foreigners who cannot speak a lick of English to take the call center jobs? There are plenty of Americans on welfare who are perfectly capable of doing those jobs instead. Can somebody tell me why?

Leroy dialed Angi and the call center answers, "How I help Mr. Leroy?" Leroy responded in great detail as to what he needed. The full explanation took nearly 30 minutes to convey the following information: Leroy stated "I need three electricians to call me and give me an estimate on my heat tape installation which will include installing 3 outside outlets." Leroy attempted to communicate with the half-wit from Angi, explaining that he did not need an all-purpose type handyman, because they aren't qualified to wire in the electricity for the outlets. Leroy then tried to overcome the language barrier and explained that he needed three electricians who would also put up the heat tape. The Asian woman responded," Do you have air conditioner?"

This was going to come back to bite Leroy and he knew it as he said it, "I have a little wall unit A/C which is worth about $300.00, so if it breaks, I will throw it in the garbage and buy another one." Looking back Leroy should have just answered, "NO"

What this foreigner who can't speak English heard was, "Blah blah blah yes I have an A/C blah blah blah" and heard nothing about the fact the A/C is disposable and that, if need be, Leroy won't work on it, he will throw it away and go buy another window unit. Leroy was blissfully ignorant as to what was about to come.

The English challenged woman next asked Leroy what his energy costs run. Leroy fires back at the Angi lady, "Look, I do not want air conditioner repairs or a new air conditioner. My energy costs are completely irrelevant to my request for an electrician so there is no need to ask me about it."

Angi lady responds, "We can install solar panels on house and lower energy for you. You interested in getting solar panels, Mr. Leroy?"

By now, Leroy was extremely agitated because he could tell that Angi Lady is obviously using a flow chart and therefore oblivious to what Leroy is actually saying. She is listening only for key words that will prompt her to continue following her flow chart regardless of the real needs of Leroy, the Angi customer.

Then the presumably Asian Princess of Stupid transfers Leroy to another person. The second person, equally challenged in speaking the English language, asks Leroy, "What you need help with?"

Leroy was rightfully pissed and loudly exclaimed, "Why on earth did I spend all that time with a woman who could not speak English, being forced to give her all the grueling data concerning the project for about 30 minutes, only to have you tell me that she passed none of that information along? Why did I waste 30 minutes giving her the project details to pass onto the potential contractors so they know if they can bid on the job or not, but now I have to do the exact same thing with you? Put another way, you're telling me that you know nothing of my needs that I just spent the last 30 minutes explaining. WHY?"

The woman Leroy was talking to looks through her flow chart but nothing exists that states all morons must go to the next text bubble. So, with a sigh of resignation, Leroy explained the whole thing again for a second time. Can you believe it? And yet this is a thriving company. How can that possibly be? After hopefully getting through to the fine folks at Angi, Leroy said his goodbyes and waited for the phone calls from electricians who wanted to work on Leroy's project to come rolling in. Leroy would then get the estimates he needed and forward them to LeafGuard to chew on before Leroy and Lenora would be taking them to court.

The first call came not from an electrician about installing the three outlets and the heat tape, but from a 3rd Angi representative. Leroy had now been in contact with three Angis without even a single contact from an electrician. The Angi representative started to ask Leroy every single question he had clearly answered twice before and had repeatedly explained in great detail as to what he needed. Now this third Angi person was asking all the same questions for a third time. It was another completely worthless phone call, insofar as Leroy was concerned, and Leroy realized he had spent a total of 1.5 hours of his time on the phone with Angi, answering and explaining his needs three different times, when one time should have been enough. Anything more is a clear sign of complete inefficiency and Angi demonstrated inefficiency to such a point that their company logo appears in Webster's Dictionary next to the word inefficiency. The liar from Angi said, "We get you take care from here" which could only be another catch phrase imprinted on all Angi employees, poor English and all.

Later that afternoon, Leroy got one phone call. The person on the phone was calling because Leroy expressed an interest in solar panels, or did he! Leroy answered the phone only to hear the person on the other end of the line say, "Leroy I see here you have requested information on our solar panels."

Leroy asked the man, "Who told you that I was interested in solar panels?" Leroy continued his questioning asking, "Who told you to call me?" The man responded that he did not know who recommended Leroy. Lie! Leroy said, "Look, I do not want any more calls from anyone associated with solar panels, are we clear? Solar panels are horrible for the environment and are not an effective source of energy for the home, unless you want to cover your whole yard and house with them with the intention of going off the grid. If you can't go off the grid then why bother with solar panels, because you still need all the power sources you have now. Don't even think of getting me started on the maintenance costs. Does this sound like I would request anything concerning solar panels? No!" and hung up on the man. Leroy had to assume that according to an Angi representative, Leroy was super interested in solar panels because spam phone calls from solar panel installers continued for months.

The next morning while Leroy was enjoying play time with his four-legged friends, the phone rang. Leroy thought, "OK! My first electrician calling me, thanks to Angi."

Leroy answered the phone and the man on the other line says, "I am calling you about your air conditioning unit." Leroy was cautious but perhaps the air conditioner service company was unaware about Angi's complete lack of a brain. Leroy asked the air conditioning representative how he got his name? The A/C rep lied and said he did not know.

Leroy shouted back, "You are a liar! You got my number from Angi and I was adamant with three separate Angi employees that I DID NOT NEED an air conditioning repair/installation person, and yet here you are! Worse, I still have not gotten calls from the folks who are capable of installing my heat tape." Leroy hung up and shouted, "CAN somebody tell me why?"

Finally, Leroy got one phone call from a handyman who stated the obvious, "I cannot wire up the electrical outlets but I can put the heat tape up once I have a manufacturer's instruction sheet detailing the installation of the heat tape."

Then Leroy got a phone call from an electrician who, of course said, "I don't install heat tape. You'll need a handyman for that." These requirements were all VERY clearly explained to Angi three times, and therein lies the problem. If you can deal with one competent person, you avoid confusion. In the case of Angi, constant confusion is absolutely unavoidable. After 1.5 hours of explanation, one would think Leroy would be getting his choice of the cream of the crop in electricians, but instead they were all brain dead on arrival. It was glaringly clear that Angi had not given any of the information Leroy had painstakingly detailed over to the contractors because if Angi had, the contractors would have been able to quickly ascertain if the job was within the scope of their expertise, thus avoiding wasting both Leroy's and the electrician's time.

Now Leroy tells all his chums around the neighborhood that not only is Angi a swing and a miss, but any contractor who would put their customers through that kind of wasted time and energy cannot be the least bit concerned about their customers who have to suffer through Angi's incompetence. Instead, contractors should make a simple website which clearly states their qualifications. Leroy subsequently used such websites, and with very little culling of morons, was able to find folks to provide the three estimates he needed to forward to LeafGuard.

Leroy finally gave up on Angi. Not one usable referral from Angi panned out and there were a ton of stupid calls leading up to this final failure point. Leroy got the estimates on his own and each of the installers asked for the instructions from the manufacturers detailing the installation of the heat tape from LeafGuard. Everyone quickly found out there were no instructions for heat tape applied to LeafGuard gutters because heat tape or no, the system will still be defective. Soon LeafGuard will answer to Leroy's lawyer and the judge overseeing the case. (Read about it in *LeafGuard*)

Starting the following week after Leroy fired Angi, his phone started ringing, his text messaging app blew up and he was inundated with calls and texts from every worthless contractor who uses Angi. Leroy made it clear to all Angi contractors by responding to them with, "If you thought Angi was a good choice to meet your customers' needs then your judgment absolutely sucks and I would never do business with anyone whose judgment sucks. Imagine what foolishness they might impose!"

The calls from worthless handymen and contractors with poor judgment due to their use of Angi, eventually began to subside. What still has not subsided is the texts and phone calls from the business that calls itself "Angi". Leroy deleted all the Angi contacts in one day almost a year ago, and still the nuisance messages and calls keep coming, sometimes as many as 3 or more a day. If Leroy blocks the call, they just call from another line. What does all this say about the integrity of the American public? The above debacle is getting worse by the day. What is the solution that will allow us to hire a reliable and competent person to care for us when we need it? Or in 20 years, will we all be forced to move to Zimbabwe just to escape the corruption, laziness and induced starvation faced by all Americans?

THE END

Leroy Two Time Land Speed Winner

To best understand this story, one needs a few logistical points first. Before Leroy was a Combat Engineer, he was a Machinist Mate. If you are a reader of this series, you may recall that Chief Guardado, Leroy's boot camp company commander, had used a yard stick to convince Leroy of his career path. At the time, Boiler Technicians were getting $2K more as a sign-up bonus than what Machinists Mates were getting and Leroy would have sold his soul to the devil for $2K. But by becoming a Boiler Technician he would not have been eligible for Combat Engineer. It was the convincing yard stick of Chief Guardado's that saved Leroy from himself. Now Leroy was not only a Machinists Mate, he was a Propulsion Machinist Mate which means his job was to operate, maintain and repair the plethora of equipment that made up the WWII technology engine room including steam generators, distilling units for water, and the ships engines themselves. The Boiler Technicians, who had gotten their signing bonus which, incidentally was $2K more than Leroy's signing bonus, were tasked with operating the boilers. If you know anything about boilers you know there are no moving parts in a boiler. Leroy used to jokingly say, "The reason they made you a Boiler Technician is because it has no moving parts for you to screw up." Leroy meant it as a joke. He relied on these men and women to all do their jobs.

To operate these old steam ships required a team of many more skilled people than were required to operate the modern diesel electric or gas turbine engines. Nearly 100 Propulsion Engineers worked in the engine room, and during the evenings, the engine room required a minimum of 30 engineers on hand to operate the equipment. The engineers are required to work grueling shift work, which sometimes meant 6 hours on and 6 hours off, continuous around the clock. Unless a repair is needed, which happens far too often. Then all bets were off on how much time one would be spending in the engine room. Consider this comparison: Take a 30-year-old car and drive it down the interstate as fast as you can for 6 months. As you barrel down the interstate, you have to fix the car while it is being driven, fuel the car without stopping, and the constant wear and tear on the vehicle never stops for at least six months. Amazingly, these ships persevere. We all know a car of that age would not.

The second bit of information you need to have is that in the Navy, there is a contest every year for which ships can set the fastest land speed record. In the Navy, a land speed record is called that because GPS is used to measure the speed of the ship and it does not take into account side to side drift. All the same class ships in the fleet participate in the race, but each ship may be in a different region of the world, so each ship conducts the race as they are able. So, to conclude, it is the "highest" speed reached that wins the race. Once you began the race, you had 30 minutes to reach the highest speed possible.

When race day arrived, Leroy anticipated he would be needed by the Chief Engineer, Bruce Becker, so he ran to his office early that fateful day and popped his head into Commander Becker's office. He asked, "You looking for me sir?"

Commander Becker, always of calm demeanor, responded, "Why would I be looking for you? You should be looking for me."

Leroy smiled. "Yes sir, you are correct." Leroy idolized Commander Becker. He even kind of got a kick out of his calm and elegant sarcasm. To this day, Leroy uses many of those gems of sarcasm that he learned from his boss. Read *His Name was Bruce Becker* for the whole story.

Commander Becker told Leroy to grab some breakfast and meet him and the skipper in the skipper's stateroom. Commander Becker, always the prankster, asked Leroy, "You gonna wear those coveralls up to the Captain's stateroom?"

Leroy hadn't even thought about it and replied, "Sir, of course not. I'll put my khakis on."

Commander Becker laughingly said, "Well, okay, but your khakis are gonna get awful dirty while you show us around your engine room. Just wear what you have on. We need to win this land speed record, and of course we are including you in our plan."

The Commanding Officer of the USS Sacramento AOE2 was a Captain in the Navy. When Leroy became a Combat Engineer for the Army, he learned that a Captain in the Army is like being a bus boy at a restaurant. No judgment here ~ Leroy knows what it's like. He started at the bottom of the well also and he is still drowning. Leroy knew the power of the Commanding Officer and would never make light of any situation surrounding him. The Skipper said, "CHENG and Chief come on in and sit down." CHENG was slang for Chief Engineer and of course Chief was in reference to Chief Leroy. The Skipper then said, "Okay Chief. So how do we make this ship faster than all other AOE's in the fleet?"

As the skipper was talking, Leroy was thinking about a great many things. He knew that the skipper was going to be up for admiral and that these AOE's were deep draft ships, just like an Air Craft Carrier, and Admiral is exactly where this Commanding Officer was headed. Would Leroy's Commanding Officer want to take any risks at all? If so to what extent? Would the skipper want to risk that fancy career for stupid bragging rights? With all that running through his mind, Leroy asked the skipper, "Sir, I need to ask what part of risk versus reward are you willing to take?"

The skipper exclaimed, "No one hurt, no one killed. Show us what you have in mind and we will decide."

Leroy felt a little relief and replied, "Thank You, sir. May I get a big sheet of paper and a pencil?" The Skipper grabs some chart paper and a fat tipped pencil and hands it to Leroy. Leroy lays it out on the skipper's table. Commander Becker and the Commanding Officer pull in closer to see what Leroy is drawing. Leroy draws a square then dissects it once from the top and once from the side until four equally sized rectangles exist. Leroy then labeled the four boxes as follows: Feed Phase, Generation Phase, Condensation Phase, and Expansion Phase. Leroy then explained the crude drawing he had created and how this would give them the tools to figure this out.

First was the Feed Phase. That consisted of steam driven pumps that forced the water from the deaereating feed tank into the boiler. There was no steam that could be diverted to the ship's engines. There were only steam driven pumps in use.

Next was the Generation Phase. This involved the boiler generating steam for the ship's engines. Leroy suggesting using JP5 AKA jet fuel and not using the standard DFM, the Navy's incomprehensible way of shortening Marine Diesel Fuel into a three-letter acronym. To Leroy's amazement the skipper agreed to the use of jet fuel. In fact, the skipper continued to prod Leroy for details on what limits they could reach. As Leroy remembered what Becker had said, "We will win this race", Leroy started to see that the skipper was serious when he said, "Don't kill anyone and don't hurt anyone and otherwise do what you do."

Leroy then went onto the Condensation Phase. This is where the steam from the ship's engine gets condensed back to water. Leroy knew the bigger drop in pressure at the end of the final phase of the ship's engine would actually pull the steam through the engine, creating greater velocity and would make far more efficient use of the steam, thus, making the engine go faster. Leroy put into operation all four of the air ejectors knowing this could only be maintained for a short time. Normally, only 2 ejectors are supposed to be used. Leroy explained to his watch stander on the ejectors to activate all 4 on his command and that the command would be given just before the race started.

Continuing to think outside the box, Leroy asked permission to put as much of ship's power onto the emergency diesel generator as he could. When the skipper asked why, Leroy explained, "If I can get enough ship's power onto the diesel generator, then I can shut down one or even more of the steam generators and put all that steam towards the main engine.

Without missing a beat, the skipper said, "Do it. Carefully!"

Leroy responded with confidence on the outside while being scared shitless on the inside, "Yes sir." Leroy sheepishly asked if he could take the steam stops off of the ship's engine ahead valve. The stop was a sleeve that screwed onto the valve shaft. The sleeve was held stationary by a couple of Allen screws. If the stop was removed, an inexperienced operator might screw the valve stem out too far and uncouple it from the valve, thus controlling the ability to slow the ship is gone until it can be reassembled.

The skipper looked at the CHENG and the CHENG gave the skipper a nod. The Skipper looked at Leroy and stated," Don't hurt or kill anyone. With that said, do it!"

The Expansion Phase was the final thing Leroy could think to manipulate. The ship's evaporators would be shut down for the 30-minute duration of the race and then turned right back on. It is important to know that these evaporators which were made in the

1960's provided all the ship's freshwater for cooking, cleaning, showering, and drinking. Most importantly, they provided pure water to the boilers so the boilers could operate. Leroy had taken a calculated risk that the reserve fresh water would last until the evaporator could be put on line again. This process can take up to an hour before it starts to generate water with a quality good enough to feed the boiler. So, what did the skipper say? "Make it happen Chief."

Commander Becker did not say one word during the entire time Leroy was explaining his thoughts. He simply sat there and every now and then gave the skipper a nod. It was no surprise to Leroy that the skipper trusted Commander Becker with his very ship, but Leroy was sure struggling to understand why Commander Becker seemed to trust Leroy.

Soon the moment of reckoning was at hand. Leroy was the restricted maneuvering Engineering Officer of the Watch. They had managed to shut down one of the steam generators after starting the Emergency Diesel Generator (EDG) and put as much ship's power on the EDG as they could. The boiler fuel tank was full of jet fuel. Leroy ordered the sailor to start the second set of air ejectors. Moments later the order came from the bridge, "All ahead Full." Leroy had placed his most senior throttle operator on watch and she began to turn the ahead valve. The ship started to shudder as the speed picked up. Leroy gripped the edge of the table. He knew folks were counting on him to pull this off and he would take it very personally if he and his shipmates lost the fastest land speed record to another ship.

Soon the ship was at a speed rarely achieved. All pressures and temperatures were higher than Leroy had ever seen them. It gave "red line" a new meaning. Soon Leroy called up to the bridge saying, "For better or for worse, this is as fast as we are going to get with this old beauty. Permission to come down to a 2/3 bell and resume normal operations."

Leroy could hear the familiar voice of the Commanding Officer, "All ahead 2/3." The Throttle Operator began to turn her ahead valve in the direction of shut.

The skipper continues on the radio, "Great job everyone. Win or lose, we worked together like a well-oiled machine. Chief Leroy, get yourself a relief then meet me up at the CHENG's office."

Leroy called for another Engineering Officer of the Watch and once he was relieved, he hightailed it up to Commander Becker's office where the skipper also sat in wait. Commander Becker said to Leroy, "Close the door and make yourself comfortable."

The skipper said, "We made 32.4 MPH." If you are wondering why they are talking MPH and not the nautical speed measured in knots, it is because this was a land speed measured in MPH. What the skipper, Commander Becker, and Leroy all knew is that the AOE class ships were rated for 20 knots which is approximately 30 MPH. They had exceeded the maximum; one could not do much better than that.

The AOE was built with battleship style engines and were designed to keep up with an aircraft carrier when refueling the carrier. In case you were wondering where Leroy got jet fuel for the boilers from, it was not a problem, because the AOE holds millions of gallons of both Marine Diesel Fuel for the aircraft carrier and jet fuel for the jets on the aircraft carrier. Leroy was able to siphon off some jet fuel from the ship's storage tanks and use it to fuel the boilers.

The AOE also carried a huge bomb payload for delivery to the battlegroups. She had large freeze boxes which were always full of frozen food to deliver to the fleet. There was a rumor going about that some of the frozen food, like crab legs, were suspected to contain salmonella so just as a test, these were immediately boiled and eaten. When, after many, many tests, there were no ill effects, what packages were left got marked as safe for consumption and delivered to coalition ships.

A few weeks later when all the AOE class ships had completed their attempt at the fastest land speed record, the skipper came on the main speaker called the 1MC, which can be heard throughout the ship. "Good morning, all. This is your Captain speaking. The results are in for the fastest land speed record. All the engineers and even a few other ringers deserve tremendous praise because due to their efforts, we are this year's winner of the fastest land speed record! Congratulations to all involved."

Shortly after this record was set, Leroy would be among those critical to the process involved in the decommissioning of the USS Sacramento AOE2. What does decommission mean you ask? It means the USS Sacramento AOE2 is now an artificial reef off the coast of Florida. Soon after the Sacramento was readied for the decommissioning process, Leroy would take his next tour of duty on board the USS Camden AOE1. As Leroy and Commander Becker said their farewells, Leroy had no idea that this would not be the last time he'd see Commander Becker, as you will learn in the story titled *His name was Bruce*.

Leroy reported to the USS Camden AOE1 in the midst of a major overhaul period in the shipyard. Leroy hit the ground running and familiarized himself with the engine rooms where he would spend the next couple of years of his life. The ship had a different feel to it than the USS Sacramento. The USS Camden, being the first of the AOE class built, was obviously the oldest ship of that class. The poor condition and run down feel on the ship were primarily a result of neglect and a don't give a shit attitude. Leroy struggled to figure out what was causing the bad attitudes that lead to the copious amount of neglect and filth he saw on board. Then he found the source. Remember Commander Becker, also known as the CHENG? Well, on this ship the new CHENG was proof that donkeys do give birth to humans, from time to time. He was a feminine hygiene product incarnate.

Now, during the course of his day, Leroy had given a sailor all the tools, training and tricks needed to replace the burst disk on the evaporator. Meanwhile, Leroy was in his office doing these things called "8 O'clocks." These are reports that tell the Commanding Officer what is wrong with his ship. It is important to be truthful on this form and never sugar coat anything, but this new CHENG was of the opinion that one should not put any sort of "bad stuff" on the 8 O'clocks because he thought it made him look bad. Leroy wanted to say, "That ship has already sailed!" but Leroy kept silent as he didn't see any value in making an enemy of the CHENG unless he absolutely needed to.

Almost as soon as Leroy thought it, the CHENG gave Leroy everything he needed to justify making an enemy of him. The CHENG said, "Why are you not down there supervising the evaporator repair?" There was another chief in Leroy's office who was filling out his 8 Oclock reports with Leroy's help. The CHENG said to that chief, "Chief go down there and supervise that evaporator repair."

Leroy stood up and looked the CHENG right square in his beady little eyes and said, "You send another chief down to interfere with my repair and you might as well keep him down there because I will not work for you ever again, mark my words. Furthermore, I'm gonna bury your ass, if need be, so keep that in what passes for a brain under your shiny little pointed head." Leroy was not sure what was to come next. Would this pea brain take heed or would he bust Leroy? The pea brain took heed. That should tell you what a turd he was. The Skipper and Commander Becker on the USS Sacramento would never have tolerated that tone of voice from Leroy or anyone else because they damn sure would never do anything stupid to deserve it. I guess it is only insubordination to call an officer a used tampon if it is not true. If it is true as outlined so far then I guess you must get a mulligan.

The Commanding Officer of the USS Camden called Leroy up to his office. Leroy took note of this because in the past, when Leroy was the Engineering Chief for the Sacramento, Commander Becker was the one who told Leroy to meet him in the skipper's stateroom. Commander Becker was welcomed by the skipper. Now in this scenario, the Commanding Officer was calling for Leroy directly. Normally, cutting someone out of their chain of command is bad etiquette, but Leroy knew on some level that the skipper did not want the CHENG in his presence.

So here we are. Leroy and the skipper were sitting across from each other talking. The skipper looks at Leroy and says, "Explain submergence control."

Leroy was completely puzzled; this was a question for the first day of school. Nonetheless, Leroy answered, "Submergence control is a phenomenon whereas the depth of the condenser water begins to get low, empty air will flood the main condenser if allowed to drain. The pump that removes the water is built so that it cavitates on purpose. Cavitate means that bubbles start to form in the fluke of the pump and the pump loses suction, preventing the condenser from running dry."

The skipper said, "That's the best answer to that question I've ever heard." Leroy suspected the skipper might be teasing him but nothing prepared Leroy for what the skipper said next, "Congratulations Chief. You are now the USS Camden's Restricted Maneuvering Engineering Officer of the Watch." EOOW. The restricted maneuvering portion of the title meant Leroy would always be the only EOOW during ship's maneuvers that are in tight spaces, like moving next to a pier or working in close proximity with other ships. Leroy had qualified as an EOOW a couple times before and unlike this time, each line of questioning took nearly 6 hours. This time, Leroy had qualified in less than 5 minutes. The skipper explained that the reason he had qualified Leroy so quickly is that he knew Leroy was the chief who had won the fastest land speed record just last year. The race was coming up and the skipper looked Leroy in the eye and said, "I want that trophy this year. Do you understand me? And that I am your Commanding Officer?"

Leroy beamed with confidence as he said, "Yes Sir!" Leroy shuddered on the inside as he thought, "What if I let the skipper down?" The next competition for the year's fastest land speed record was upon them in no time.

Leroy anticipated he would be needed by the Chief Engineer, Dilbert Jobbernowl during the competition. However, he had no use for this champion of stupidity. He was Leroy's boss and as much as Leroy was not thrilled with that situation, he had to make sure he kept the high road while he rode out his time with this particular turd bird. Leroy knocked on the CHENG's office door, having been chastised by Dilbert for coming into his office unannounced. The CHENG called Leroy into his office but left him standing while he talked, "I don't want you breaking anything today over this silly land speed record," he stated.

Those words had barely left Mr. Jobbernowl's mouth when the skipper got on the 1MC. All hands on the ship could hear, "Chief Leroy report to my stateroom ASAP!" Dilbert tells Leroy to stay put and that Dilbert is going up to the Commanding Officer's stateroom by himself. Approximately 10 minutes from the time the CHENG took off for the skipper's stateroom, the skipper comes back on the 1MC telling the entire ship, "Chief Leroy, what part of get to my stateroom are you not hearing?"

As Leroy scrambled to the skipper's stateroom, he ran into Dilbert, whose face was bright red. Dilbert yells at Leroy, "What are you up to chief?" Leroy just kept walking by. Dilbert's ferocity grew exponentially as he yelled at Leroy, "Chief! I said stop right now."

As Leroy kept hustling towards the skipper's stateroom, he yelled back down the hall towards the CHENG saying, "Maybe you would like to come back up to the skipper's stateroom and tell him you're the reason I did not follow orders the first time and come see him right when I was ordered to. Sound good to you Mr. Jobbernowl? Let's go." It goes without saying that at least this guy was smart enough to know he was stupid. Most idiots do not possess that skill. He shut his trap as Leroy pushed on, continuing on his way to the skipper's stateroom.

When Leroy arrived at the skipper's stateroom, the skipper said, "Chief, I'm sorry about the situation you're in." Leroy knew what the skipper was talking about in broad strokes, but Leroy wanted all the dirt.

Leroy not so innocently asked, "What situation would that be?"

The skipper said, "I see you're going to make me say it. Well fine. I am talking about the stupidest Chief Engineer I have ever commanded. He won't work with me on any modifications to the ship's engines that would give us even a shot at winning this thing. His behavior is just short of me being able to fire him, so where does that leave you Leroy? It leaves you in charge of winning this thing and for the duration you answer to me. This is not an option."

Would the skipper want to risk that fancy career for stupid bragging rights? Leroy was thinking that would be a definite yes. Leroy asked the skipper if he has some paper and a pencil. The Skipper grabbed a large sheet of paper from an easel board, tossed Leroy a black marker, and Leroy began to draw. The Commanding Officer slid his chair closer to the table to see what Leroy was scribbling. Much like his previous plans from the Sacramento, Leroy began by drawing the four squares, labeling the four boxes as before: Feed Phase, Generation Phase, Condensation Phase, and Expansion Phase.

Leroy began to explain his plan to the Commanding Officer, "Sir, this game is all about preserving the use of steam however, wherever and whenever possible as I will explain. Then we channel as much of the steam we have as is safely possible, into the main engines. A final trick is to put another set of air ejectors on line strictly for the duration of the race. This creates a tremendous pressure drop as the steam gains velocity across the turbines of the ship's engines.

Leroy started by explaining all of the pumps in the Feed Phase are steam driven so there is no way to siphon steam from there. Next came the Generation Phase which was the boiler generating steam for all steam driven equipment and the ship's engines. Leroy gave his current skipper the same suggestion about using JP5, also known as jet fuel.

The skipper listened carefully and then said, "Done and done. What next?" The skipper continued to pick Leroy's brain for what limits they could safely exceed. Leroy explained the Condensate Phase where the steam from the ship's engine were condensed back to water. Leroy knew the bigger drop in pressure at the end of the final phase of the ship's engine would actually pull the steam through the engine, creating more velocity and a much more efficient use of the steam thus making the engine go faster. Leroy would put into operation all four of the air ejectors knowing this could only be maintained for a short time. As stated earlier, only two ejectors are supposed to be used. Leroy explained to his watch stander of the air ejectors that he was to activate all four upon Leroy's command and that this command would come just before the race started.

Leroy had learned from his success on the USS Sacramento that he could place into operation the ships Emergency Diesel Generationer (EDG) and if he fully loaded the EDG he could shut down one Ship's Service Turbine Generators (SSTG) and divert all that steam to the Ship's Engine. The skipper did not blink an eye at Leroy's plan. Leroy asked with great hesitancy if he could take the steam stop off the ahead throttle valve. The steam stop was a sleeve that screwed on the valve shaft. The sleeve itself was held stationary by a couple of Allen screws. Leroy explained to the skipper the risk involved in doing that was if the stop is removed, an inexperienced operator might screw the valve stem too far and uncouple it from the valve, thus controlling the ability to slow the ship is gone until it can be reassembled.

The skipper looked at Leroy and asked, "Did you do this on Sacramento?"

Leroy answered proudly, "I pulled out EVERY stop, sir."

The skipper was not impressed and sternly said, "Then pull out all the stops and then pull out some more for me!"

The last thing Leroy could think of doing was to shut down the ship's evaporators for the 30-minute race and then turn them right back on. We learned earlier that these evaporators made in the 1960's provided all ship's freshwater for cooking, cleaning, showering, and drinking, and that of upmost importance is that the evaporators provided pure water to the boilers so they could operate. Leroy had taken a calculated risk on the Sacramento and had won the odds. Would he be so lucky this time? Would the reserve fresh water last until the evaporator could be put on line again? Going back on line can take up to an hour before water with of a quality good enough to feed the boiler begins to generate. What did the skipper say? "Yes. Do it. Now what else?"

Leroy was tight with most of his fellow Chiefs and was generally in good standing with the Officers that he was assigned to. With that said, there is also the CHENG who as we will soon learn is even a bigger turd than first envisioned.

Another power turd ranger was the Navigation Chief who was one of these self-centered folks who will make sure they can take credit for things even when they were completely uninvolved. For example, this guy would show up to a painting party to help out the Boatswain Mates and would make a big show as he dipped a brush one time, and then he'd go shoot the shit and drink beer for the duration of the project while watching everyone else work. But when it came time for the credit, he'd have everyone believe he was the one who single handedly painted the ship. We all know these people and, sad to say. They run rampant among the civilians and are becoming increasingly more and more common.

Leroy went to the Navigation Chief and said, "Hey, the skipper wants us to win this thing. All I can do is tie my old record but if you put us downstream from a gulf stream, in theory we should then gain what, 1 or 2 knots? I am sure you will brief the skipper." The Navigation Chief would do the research, present the plan, and get the deserved credit. Okay, so do you think Leroy did what he would normally do with a typical Navigation Chief or did he choose to make this a learning opportunity for the self-centered asshole disguised as a Navigation Chief?

Leroy said, "Well sir, there's one more thing. What I have requested your permission to perform will give us a tie at best and I do mean at best. This is the oldest ship in its class. I am certain things were improved with each new ship so we need an edge and quite frankly this edge should not be coming from your Engineering Chief."

The skipper, still aggravated that he did not have the guaranteed win, said to Leroy, "Okay, fine. Spit it out. What is your ace in the hole?"

Leroy smiled as he said, "Have your Navigation Chief find the gulf steam about 200 miles out from Peru and aim the ship to go directly down current of the stream. No one has to know we are doing that and it will give us the win… I hope?"

Leroy was not even done talking when the skipper was on the 1MC saying, "Chief Navigator! This is your Commanding Officer speaking. Report to the bridge NOW!" Leroy sat there a bit nervously as the skipper engaged him in small talk. Understand that Leroy worshiped this man. The skipper had helped him with several messes, both personal and professional, and Leroy knew the skipper's gruff harsh attitude was merely an act required to achieve absolute perfection and loyalty to the ship from the entire crew. The skipper certainly had that loyalty from Leroy.

Finally, the Navigation Chief arrived on the bridge and before he could even get through the door the skipper said, "Stay right there! Chief Leroy is telling me we can gain 2 knots if we put the ship in the gulf stream. What say you?"

The Navigation Chief nervously put his left toe onto the floor and twists it back and forth, and finally speaks saying, "But sir, that's cheating." If Leroy could have gotten on his knees and kissed the skipper's golden ring he would have. The skipper was a God. Leroy could barely contain his laughter.

The Commanding Officer loudly said, "If you ain't cheating, you ain't trying! Now go figure this out now. I want us in that gulf stream by the start of today's race. Chief Leroy, it's all up to you now. Don't fail me, and keep it safe as I know you will. Oh, and Leroy, make sure folks are having fun. At the end of the day, this is supposed to be a great morale builder." It's no wonder the skipper went on to be an Admiral shortly thereafter.

Soon the moment of reckoning was at hand, Leroy was the restricted maneuvering Engineering Officer of the Watch. Leroy learned from his experience on the Sacramento that they were able to shut down one of the steam generators after starting the Emergency Diesel Generator (EDG) and putting as much ship's power on the EDG as they could. The boiler was full of jet fuel. Leroy ordered the dedicated sailor to start the second set of air ejectors. Moments later the order came from the bridge, "All ahead Full."

Leroy had once again placed his most senior throttle operator on watch. The ship started to shudder. This shudder is literally the metal of the hull of the ship being twisted by the torque of the ship's engines as they pick up momentum. As always, folks were counting on Leroy to pull this off and he would take it very personally if he and his shipmates lost the land speed record. However, on the other hand, the engineers on the USS Sacramento are about to lose the trophy and Leroy felt he might have just a tiny bit of responsibility for that.

Soon the Camden was racing along at a speed rarely achieved. All pressures and temperatures were maxed out just, as Leroy had experienced on the USS Sacramento. After the 30-minute duration of the race was complete, the skipper called down to the engine room, "All ahead 2/3 bell and resume all normal operations. Chief Leroy get yourself a relief then meet me up on the bridge."

Leroy called another Engineering Officer of the Watch and once he was relieved, he scurried up to the bridge. When Leroy stepped onto the bridge the place lit up with clapping and pats on the back for Leroy.

The skipper asked Leroy what the speed he had obtained on the USS Sacramento was. Leroy proudly answered, "We made 32.4 MPH." As we learned, 30 MPH is the max speed of the AOE class.

Leroy quickly realized that his current skipper wanted the record and he had promised he would deliver. The skipper grinned as he put a strong hand on Leroy's shoulder, "We made 33.7 MPH. Assuming the Sacramento only does a piddly 32.4 MPH again this year I think we did it Chief!"

A few weeks later when all the AOE class ships had completed their attempt at the fastest land speed record, the skipper came on the 1MC, and throughout the ship everyone heard him say, "Good morning shipmates. This is your Captain speaking; the record is in on the fastest land speed record. Everybody who participated deserves a Bravo Zulu. Because of them, we are this year's winner of the fastest land speed record. All hands congratulations! I want to give a shout out to Chief Leroy, who all of you know, was the Engineering Chief for the USS Sacramento. Chief, how does it feel to beat your own record with the oldest AOE in the fleet?"

Leroy did feel proud at that moment. He was given a placard for both wins and has told this story many ways, but this is the way it really happened. Google USS Sacramento and USS Camden. Being older ships, they both are now artificial reefs at the bottom of the ocean, swimming with the fishes as they say.

So, what became of the Chief Engineer with the turdish qualities? Leroy found some badly failing fuel piping and told the CHENG it needed to go on the 8 O'clock report and that it needed to get fixed before he killed more people. The CHENG whirled around on Leroy, "What do you mean MORE people?"

Leroy looked him in the eye. Without blinking he said, "I know what you did early in your career. You ordered sailors to use a wizbang to pump out fuel." Wiz-bang was a slang term for a pneumatic pump. It very clearly stated not to pump flammable liquid with it. Leroy continued, "While it was pumping it started to leak and began to squirt fuel across the engine room which then ignited on a hot surface and cooked three men to death."

The CHENG looked like a ghost, but sadly he felt no remorse for the dead sailors. His only concern was saving face and keeping that incident hush-hush. Leroy reiterated, "So you are going to get this fuel piping repaired by the shipyard ASAP, right?"

The clueless Engineering Officer told Leroy to just leave it alone and that the fuel piping was just rusty. What do you think Leroy did next? He grabbed a needle gun, which is an air powered device that drives metal rods up and down, thus giving it the name needle gun. It is used to chip paint and rust off surfaces. It is NOT for use on fuel piping. The most junior person is taught that, so where do you think Leroy was headed with his needle gun? You guessed it, he went right to the old fuel piping. Leroy figured the CHENG said there was just rust on the piping so a little needle gun action should clean that right up, right? Within a minute the needles of the gun punched right through the deteriorated fuel pipe. Leroy went to town on the fuel pipe and by the time he was done, that fuel pipe would no more transfer fuel than a flying monkey would depart Leroy's ass. Leroy figured he better get up to the CHENG's office lickety-split and report the damage. Leroy entered the CHENG's door to his office after knocking briefly on the door frame, of course. The CHENG boldly spoke, "Engineering Chief Leroy. Come in and sit down and tell me what you need."

Leroy had this arrogant poor excuse for a man right where he wanted him as he spoke, "Sir, I went down to ensure that you were right about the fuel pipe just being rusty. I needle gunned the entire area of rusty fuel pipe and well sir, the needle gun punctured the fuel piping into Swiss cheese which only got worse with each passing minute." Furious, the CHENG pushed from his desk to stand. He was such a fat bastard that the desk slid forward with his weight and the CHENG, with his hands flat on his desk, slid forward and ended up on his knees with his fat belly spilling out from the bottom of his shirt. This is not the kind of man who demands respect and wins confidence in his subordinates.

The CHENG had finally floundered enough to get to his feet and began to dress down Leroy, "You are going to be court martialed for this Leroy. How dare you ignore my orders." The

CHENG picked up the J-dial. (Telephone) and called the Commanding Officer, "Sir," he asked, "Do you have time to see me and Chief Leroy? I have some bad news to share with you." The Commanding Officer's dislike for the CHENG had him worried as he wondered what his Engineering Officer had done now.

The CHENG arrived at the skipper's stateroom with Leroy in tow. He knocked at the door and from inside they heard the skipper's voice say, "Come in!" The CHENG told Leroy to remain standing at attention. The skipper stepped in and said, "Whoa, whoa, whoa! Hold on. What is the issue here?"

The CHENG said, "Engineering Chief Leroy tell the skipper what you did with the fuel piping in Main One."

Leroy grinned like a mischievous toddler, "I went down to test the CHENG's theory that the fuel pipe was only rusty and would not rupture and kill a bunch more sailors like it did when he used a wiz-bang to pump out fuel. Sir, I know not to use a needle gun on fuel pipe but the CHENG knew not to use a wiz-bang to pump fuel, so which of these order violations saved lives and which of these order violations cost lives, sir?"

The Commanding Officer immediately dismissed Leroy who knew right away that his dismissal meant that the Commanding Officer was a consummate professional and would never chastise Leroy's supervisor in front of Leroy. It sure seemed to Leroy like the skipper wanted to do that though. Leroy was subsequently able to get the fuel piping fixed as well as taking care of the other dangers in the engine room that had been neglected due to politics.

The deployment came to an end and the USS Camden came back to rest in the city of Bremerton in Washington State. Leroy left the ship for a few days and tried to salvage his family life. One afternoon while Leroy was working in his wood shop, his oldest daughter brought him the phone. The man on the phone spoke, "Is this Chief Leroy?" Leroy recognized the person's voice on the phone. It was the skipper and Leroy knew it was unheard of that the skipper would call any of his Chiefs at home. If there was a death in the family or some other catastrophe there was no way in hell the skipper would not give the news in person. So, what on earth was the skipper calling for? Leroy lurched into gear and answered the skipper, "Yes sir, this is Chief Leroy."

The skipper, with a smile in his voice says, "No, I beg your pardon but this is not Chief Leroy. You are a LIAR! Now who is this?"

Leroy was totally clueless to the fact that he was the subject of the skipper's good humor and sheepishly said, "Sir, if I am not Chief Leroy, then who am I?"

The skipper sternly said, "You are not Chief Leroy because you are Senior Chief Leroy. Do you understand me?" Leroy was grinning from ear to ear. He had made Chief as a young sailor in only nine years. He had now achieved the rank of Senior Chief, the second highest rank in the US military. Leroy could have no way of knowing at the time how much his life was to change and in such a radical way. It was shortly after this story that steam propulsion became obsolete and along with it, the job of Machinist Mate.

Upon return to the ship all the engineers were gathered up and introduced to the new CHENG Commander Abbott. Commander Abbott was extremely competent and much to Leroy's pleasure he took Leroy under his wing. The two had discovered, over small talk, that they both had longed to work for the Forest Service, but neither had any regrets about having chosen a life in the military. Commander Abbott was always asking Leroy for intel on the state of Montana, and particularly the area where Leroy had grown up.

During their time serving together, Commander Abbott took Chief Leroy out for some rest and relaxation in the Spanish city of Valencia where the Nina, Pinta and Santa Maria had hailed from. Commander Abbott took Leroy around and introduced him to Limoncello wine and many delicious local dishes. Leroy would soon be moving on to his next duty assignment but Commander Abbott and his many kindnesses would never be forgotten.

So, knowing that the job of Machinist Mate was phased out, as Leroy moved on, we have to wonder what Leroy would do in order to keep himself at the tip of the spear in the battlefield. Many stories are told of how Leroy would go from being a sailor to being a soldier, working for the Army as a Combat engineer and you may read some of them in the many short stories about Leroy.

The End

Author's Note: This is as close to the truth as I can recall. It's noteworthy to point out that some of the names in the story I remember because of the outstanding nature of the person. The skippers are the exception as I just did not interface with them much more than what is described in this story. The people's names that escape me are due to the person's turdish nature. Folks like that do not deserve a lasting place in our minds, right? If you'd like to read more about the USS Sacramento and USS Camden, Google them for an in depth look at these two ships.

Paul Spencer

Leroy Learns the Meaning of Sibling Rivalry

Leroy was an odd duck. He was born in Montana; the son of a rancher. As soon as Leroy graduated, he left home, having decided that ranch life was not for him, he had decided to embark on a career in the military. Many stories have been told about Leroy's experiences in bootcamp and how he had become a Combat Engineer, but this story takes place in Olongapo Philippines when Leroy was just a young lad. He was assigned to an Amphibious assault ship which was designed to carry a large detachment of Marines who would be deployed wherever they were needed to answer the call of duty. Leroy was an only child so he had never experienced sibling rivalry but he was about to encounter something pretty darn close to this and so this story goes.

"Fireman Leroy, welcome to the Engineering Department," Chief Rucker barked out. Chief Rucker was a large black man with tattoos and scarification on his arms. The scars made images that Leroy assumed meant he had been in a gang or something. Leroy was immediately intimidated by the size of this man and would come to both fear and respect him in the coming months that they worked together. Leroy was called a Fireman as this was the lowest rank name for an engineer. There was some firefighting training because Leroy would be working with explosives, flammable fuels and such. Most of Leroy's focus was on engineering. Perhaps it had historical ramification from when the new men would shovel coal into the boiler to produce the fire that would boil the water into steam that would then propel the ship.

As low man on the totem pole, Leroy soon found himself assigned to the most disgusting work on board. He would have to open up condensers which were large chambers that salt water from the ocean would flow through at a high capacity in order to return the steam that had been exhausted from driving the turbines of the propulsion engines back into fresh water which would then be pumped back into the boiler to repeat the whole cycle over and over again. The problem with this is that fish and other sea life also got scooped up in the condensers and then needed to be cleaned out of the system. Imagine a bunch of rotten fish and other sea life heated by the condensing steam; rotting away, and you can only surmise the smell. "Stinks enough to gag a maggot," Leroy would say.

One of Leroy's best chums was called Hodgie. Well, that is what Leroy and the rest of the gang called him. In reflecting back on this time, the War on Terror, was about to become a reality, and Leroy wondered if they would have given this nickname to him. Hodgie was a Hispanic man and at the time Leroy never really gave it much thought that everyone called him Hodgie. Seems like it might even be racist. But that is what he was called and nobody even remembers what his real name was, so that is how the story goes.

Hodgie was short and a bit over weight. He had been born and raised in Compton, California. He and Leroy never spoke about their childhood or young adult lives much but it was safe to say he had grown up tough. He was quick to throw down on someone if they were to insult him and this would prove to be problematic.

After several days of cleaning condensers, scrubbing the deck plates in the engine room of the ship and other bottom-feeder jobs, Hodgie, Leroy and the rest of the engineering gang were finally granted some time off to go out on the town and blow off some steam. Hodgie suggested they go and check out the California Club, whose name was the only thing Americanized about the club.

The back wall of the California Club was little more than corrugated tin roofing material lashed together with hemp rope. The roof looked to be made of the same type of material and barely kept the outside elements at bay. There was a makeshift bar made of roughhewn timber and a bunch of tables and chairs laid out, none of which matched. It was pretty evident they had been scavenged from many different sources, because some were folding chairs, some were roughhewn wooden chairs, there were stools of varying heights and the like. At the far end across from the bar was a cement slab with a disco ball dangling from an extension cord. This area was fashioned into a dance floor. There was no air conditioning and the hot, humid, tropical evening was only slightly relieved by some strategically placed hurricane fans that were plugged in with extension cords hanging loosely from the ceiling. It would probably be safe to say that in the United States, the entire establishment would have been shut down instantly due to a million code violations, but this was the Philippines and things were allowed here that certainly would not be tolerated in the United States.

Hodgie and Leroy bellied up to the makeshift bar and commenced to drinking Sam Miguel beer, which was not regulated in any fashion. Rumor had it, the beer even contained formaldehyde to keep it fresh. The alcohol content had no consistency either. Sometimes a six pack would not even generate a buzz while other times the alcohol content would be such that a skinny fella like Leroy would become quickly inebriated.

Having grown up in the wilds of Montana, Leroy had never experienced anything even remotely like this and he was fascinated by it all. As he sat at the bar, a young Philippine woman came up to him and asked him if he wanted some company. Leroy was certainly happy to oblige. She was quite petite and was wearing a rather provocative pink blouse with a dark blue pencil skirt, some white tights and a pair of simple, but elegant short heeled shoes.

Leroy noted that the bar had very few Philippine men other than those who were operating the club, which included some behind the bar and a few at the door. Conversely, the place had nearly an equal number of Philippine women as there were American sailors, Merchant Marines, and American Marines and it soon became evident to Leroy that these women were available for the evening, if you know what I mean. This included the young lady named Ronella Punogbyon who had come to show her attentions to Leroy.

As he sat there enjoying Ronella caressing his neck and flirting with him, a stout Marine approached. "What are you?" he jeered as he ruffled Leroy's hair. "You some kind of hippie?" The Marine's hair was high and tight while Leroy's hair was just about as long as military standards allowed, and by wearing it that way he knew he was pushing the envelope as some kind of means of protest.

This Marine was clearly feeling no pain due to the quantity of beer he had consumed and Leroy quickly ascertained that this move was a means to start a fight. Leroy thought quickly as he spotted an instamatic camera tucked in the belt pouch on the Marine's waist, having already noted the Marine's comrades in the background watching intently.

Leroy calculated his plan carefully and grabbed the instamatic camera from the Marine's belt pouch with his left hand and waved his right hand so as to gesture to the on looking Marines in the back ground to approach their buddy for a photo opportunity.

Within moments a barrage of marines rushed over, and hoisted Leroy's would-be assailant into the air. Leroy snapped off a few photos of his would-be aggressor and handed him back his camera. The aggressive marine's buddies carried him back into the crowd. Leroy breathed a sigh of relief and returned to his courtship of Ronella and his beer drinking.

Moments later the Marine returned with a full can of San Miguel and handed it to Leroy in what Leroy could only surmise was some sort of peace offering. Leroy thanked the Marine and beamed with satisfaction believing he had thwarted a fight using brains over brawn.

One could only hope any fighting would be averted that night, but just as the dust settled from this potential outbreak of testosterone, Leroy looked over to witness Hodgie, who was sitting a few paces down the bar from him, haul off and sucker punch the same Marine right across his jaw. In an instant, there was a flurry of frenzied fists flying. Men were running at each other, chairs were being picked up as weapons, men went crashing onto the flimsy tables, crushing them to the ground, women went running for cover, and it was as if the whole place had gone mad. Thinking back to those John Wayne cowboy westerns, this event was a spitting image of those films where over the slightest provocation, a bar fight would inevitably break out.

Leroy had learned how to fight while growing up in Montana, He had encountered his share of playground adversaries but here in the California Club, he knew two things. First, he was significantly outnumbered by Marines, and second, they were all going to be in a heap of trouble for tearing up the bar and fighting. Suddenly in the midst of all the chaos, the edge of a chair leg caught Leroy on the right side of his lip, splitting the skin. The buzz of alcohol and adrenaline of the fight allowed Leroy to remain physically unaffected, but psychologically, it immediately sparked his need for retaliation. Luckily, just as Leroy turned with raised fists to look for a target, his attention was drawn to the front door of the establishment.

Without warning the Shore Patrol had shown up. This is the police force of the military, by the military and for the military. These Shore Patrol officers were made up of Sailors and Marines whose job it was to deal with these types of outbursts. Shore Patrol burst through the front door of the establishment. At the sight of this, sailor and marine alike dropped their broken chair weapons, lowered their fists and looked at each other no longer as enemies, but as folks who were about to get into a world of trouble. Leroy, always the planner, yelled out, "Shore Patrol is coming! Let's get out of here!" Leroy kept shouting as he ran to the back of the bar, which as previously noted was nothing more than corrugated tin sheets held together with hemp rope. Yelling ever louder, Leroy said "We can break the wall down if we shove on it! Come on guys! Help me out! We really gotta get out of here." Sailor and Marine suddenly united as they all rammed into the back wall, knocking a portion of the wall loose enough to allow for their escape. They all ran down the steep decline behind the bar, through the swampy jungle and scattered like rats deserting a sinking ship as the Shore Patrol rushed into the establishment right on their heels.

Leroy and Hodgie headed back to the ship, cleaned up their cuts and scrapes as best they could and climbed into their bunks to sleep off the hangover, but as it turned out, there was to be no rest for the wicked. As the tropical sun rose into the sky, Chief Rucker rousted everyone out of their bunks and ordered them to report to the helicopter platform located at the back end of the ship.

When Leroy, Hodgie and the rest of the engineering sailors arrived to form up, they witnessed the Marine detachment also forming up opposite them.

This was the location they always were called to formation when they needed to be debriefed and when head counts needed to be conducted, but today they all knew the reason for their formation. It was to answer for the fight that had broken out.

It seemed like hours that they stood there at attention. Leroy's head pounded from the hangover of far too many San Miguel beers. He was dehydrated. His mouth dry and pasty. His upper left lip was throbbing from the blow of the chair leg. It was clear that many of the other men had scrapes and bruises as well, and were undoubtedly as hungover and wasted as Leroy was. It seemed an eternity that the men stayed standing there out in that heat and years later, Leroy would speculate that the men were left standing there on purpose as they baked in the heat and humidity of this tropical paradise, as a punishing reminder of what they had done.

Finally, out of the corner of his eye, Leroy saw Chief Rucker and the Marine Colonel approaching their formation from the right. Leroy had only encountered the Colonel on one other occasion when he had flown with him on an operation a few weeks back, and if you think Chief Rucker scared Leroy, Leroy's fear of the Marine Colonel was exponential to that.

"I want to know who was involved in this fight at the California Club," The Colonel said in a firm calm voice that sent shivers down Leroy's spine.

The Colonel approached closer and began to dress down the sailors and marines; many of whom had obvious scrapes and bruises. He stopped in front of Leroy and with a stern look that would intimidate the toughest of men asked, "How did you get that cut on your lip Fireman?"

Leroy looked down at the ground sheepishly and said, "I fell down the stairs last night as I was going to my berthing compartment."

"That's a bold-faced lie and you know it! Who hit you?" The colonel's fiery blue eyes bored into Leroy. "Every one of you can stand here all day long until one of you wants to talk!"

The Colonel walked over to the Marine's side of the formation and continued his interrogation. He got no answers from them either.

Leroy had never had a brother or a sister, but it was at that moment when he recognized that these fighting men were his brothers. No one was going to rat out Hodgie or the Marine who ruffled Leroy's hair, or anyone else who inflicted even one of the ensuing blows.

After what seemed like an eternity, the Colonel stepped back from the men and said, "You can all rot in this sun today until I get some answers!" and with that he turned and walked away with Chief Rucker.

It's hard to say how long those men stood there in that hot tropical sun, the effects of which were completely exacerbated by the dehydration and hangovers, not to mention the throbbing of teeth, noses and other battered extremities. Some guessed that they stood there for approximately four hours.

Leroy began to recognize that although they had been enemies while the brawl had ensued last night, today they were brothers. He was certain they recognized, as he did, that it wasn't going to be long before they would be in Iraq facing a real enemy and that they would all need to have each other's backs. Leroy now knew he had brothers he could count on to have his six in Iraq, just as they all had each other's backs when nobody ratted out the two who had started the brawl. It gave Leroy a real sense of fraternity and security. These were people he could count on with his life.

After an excruciating amount of time baking in the tropical sun the Marine Colonel walked briskly back to the men and in a loud voice called them to attention, then shouted, "Get out of my sight all of you! I better never hear of another incident like this again. Soon you'll all be in a real battle and you better have learned that all you will have out there to survive the real dangers you will be facing will be each other." The colonel snapped tall, "You're all dismissed! Get the hell off my ship and stay out of trouble. That is an order!" Leroy and his chums scurried off the ship and went in search of their next adventure. Hodgie said, "I hear tell Rosie's Tavern is a good place."

The End

Paul Spencer

Leroy has a Showdown in Sturgis, South Dakota

Leroy sat in the driver's seat of his car, the engine still at idle, having just pulled into a convenience store in Sturgis, South Dakota. He was ultimately enroute to his daughter's house in Seattle, Washington, but on his way to Seattle, he planned to stop in on his parents who lived in Montana. He had never been to his daughter's house but had made the trip to his parents' home in Montana numerous times. Given that Montana was Leroy's home state, he knew the roadways like the back of his hand. Leroy remembered there was a shortcut he could take from Sturgis that would get him to Montana faster, but he could not remember the exit number. Leroy pulled out his GPS device which gives verbal directions as you drive. Leroy remembered that when he was a kid, before the GPS, driving places was navigated with the help of a map or by using written directions from a passerby. Leroy doubted he was even capable of using those old modes of navigation any more.

Wondering exactly what exit he needed, Leroy plugged in his GPS and a sweet female voice responded, "Low Battery." Of course, with the vehicle still running, the Garmin should have been getting power from the car. Leroy investigated and found the problem: the tip of the plug had broken off. Leroy had looked at his toolbox before departing and concluded that he would call AAA if he experienced any vehicular troubles, figuring he did not know how to fix these electronics on wheels anyway. But it sure would have come in handy now that he needed to fix the GPS. So here is Leroy with no tool box, but he does have a pen, a glasses handle, and some prayers, which he used while trying to fix the end of the GPS. Lo and behold, after about 40 minutes, Leroy got the end on and breathed a sigh of relief, until he plugged it in. This time, a tauntingly nasty female voice growled, "Low Battery."

Leroy snapped and became furious. He yanked on the plug of the GPS, and with it came the cigarette lighter plug, right out of the socket, rendering the power source inoperable. Leroy's meltdown grew worse. His mind began to race with thoughts of despair. Leroy remembered the time several years earlier, when he and Lenora had fallen away and Leroy had driven to Spokane from New York. He could not find a GPS at any of the truck stops and even when arriving in Spokane, there was no GPS to be had. All this was a moot point with the cigarette lighter apparatus now ripped out of the console. The thought of the Spokane trip now resonating in Leroy's mind, he went from furious to fearful as he thought to himself, "If I lose control, like I did in Spokane, I am going to get placed in a mental ward. And unlike Spokane, this time I won't get out, EVER!"

Full of fear and anxieties, Leroy got back on Interstate 90 heading East and began to make his way back home as quickly as he could. Leroy's fear was so palpable, it was causing him to flee for home, not just drive home. To reiterate, it was the fear that sent Leroy running for home. This fear stemmed from feeling out of control, and desperately wanting to avoid being institutionalized. Leroy was so afraid that if it happened, this time it would likely be permanent. Whether the fear was actually valid or not, for Leroy at that time, it was REAL!

But before Leroy fled that gas station parking lot in Sturgis, he texted his daughter, updating her about his current mental state, explaining he needed to go home and wouldn't make it to Seattle as planned. She responded with compassion and understanding.

Leroy then took a deep breath and texted his folks in Montana saying, "I am sorry but I am not going to be able to make it. My anxiety has flared up and I fear I will end up in the nut house again, and this time it will be for good, so I am getting home as quick as I can." Leroy felt bad that he could not even muster enough strength to have lunch with his folks. Before he began the trip, he had texted his father and locked down a date for lunch. In the text, Leroy explained that after lunch he would have to get going on the next leg of his adventure. Telling his parents that his anxiety had flared was Leroy's way of simplifying a much greater mental health issue, but getting his folks to understand even the simplest of issues was impossible, unless it was something that interested them. Unfortunately, Leroy's interests rarely aligned with his folks' interests.

Sometime later Leroy's step mom texted back, "I am sorry you decided not to come. Your grandson wants to beat you at basketball. I also have a bunch of yard work that your dad cannot do so I need you to do that also." Leroy just clenched his fists in despair. Sadly, this sort of response from his step mom was not unusual. Leroy knew from experience that they would take a mile when only an inch was offered. Leroy could hardly walk and his grandson beating him at the game of basketball was like shooting fish in a barrel. Yard work? Leroy's Step Mom regularly boasted to Leroy about her financial dominion. Leroy agreed she was a successful woman. His feeling was that if she was so financially successful, she should go hire a grounds keeper and not her 100% disabled combat veteran son.

If we step back here a moment, we can learn what led to this sudden bout of mental illness in Leroy and the complexity of it. During the week that Lenora had been on a cruise with her kids, Leroy had stayed home with their newborn Yorkshire Terrier puppies and in the quiet hours alone, Leroy began to think about the last time he had seen his daughter. It had been over 13 years and Leroy had never even seen some of his grandkids. So, Leroy worked out the details with his daughter and the trip was on.

Leroy's first mistake was trying to cram too much into the trip, including a stop to have lunch with his folks in Montana. One might think that having lunch with one's folks is a pleasant thing to experience, but for Leroy, that's not the case. As the drive westward continued, Leroy's anxiety about interfacing with his parents mounted and was certainly among the catalysts that led to Leroy racing home in fear.

The trip had started out well. After Lenora had returned home, Leroy told her he was planning a trip to see his daughter in Seattle and Lenora thought that would be great for Leroy. When he was ready to start packing, Leroy asked Lenora "Where is my luggage? It is gone from the spare bedroom."

Lenora said nonchalantly "The wheel on it was broken so I threw it away."

Leroy spouted back, "I did not even use the stupid wheels!" He substituted a black plastic trash bag for the now absent suitcase and Leroy headed for Seattle, Washington.

Leroy had chosen to drive his little red car that he had bought from Lenora some years earlier. As he drove, Leroy's mind began to race with thoughts of his folks and thoughts of his daughter and thoughts of his own life when suddenly he noticed the blue and red flashing lights of a State Highway Patrolman. At the same moment Leroy looked down at his speedometer. The speed limit was 55 and the speedometer read 86. Leroy quickly found himself over reacting. He was visibly shaking. His eyes reflected the anxiety so much so that as the trooper approached Leroy's window, his first words were, "Are you okay?"

Leroy tried to remain calm, to appear normal answering, "I am just heading to Seattle, to see my daughter."

The trooper collected Leroy's vehicle data and asked Leroy, "Am I going to find problems when I run this license?"

Leroy looked a bit puzzled but said to the trooper, "No sir. There is nothing on my record."

The trooper returned sometime later and said, "I am reducing this to 10 MPH over the speed limit. Consider it due to your military service." Leroy was very glad he had slipped his military retirement ID to the Trooper with all his other documents.

Then the trooper said, "When you get the citation in the mail, make sure you plead not guilty. It will lower the cost of the fine even more." Leroy did just what the trooper directed and as the trooper promised, the court reduced a misdemeanor 10 MPH over the speed limit, to a penalty equivalent to a parking ticket.

As the trooper finished up, he again asked Leroy, "Are you sure you're okay? You look really frazzled." Leroy confided in the trooper that he was feeling distraught but he would pay closer attention and most importantly that he would use his cruise control. The trooper went back to his car and Leroy gingerly pulled out onto the interstate.

As he resumed driving, Leroy began to weep, gasping for air, tears welling heavily. Leroy stammered out loud, "How can so many people who know me, who have a vested interest in treating me nicely, choose to just shit on me, while meanwhile, this state trooper who does not know me from Adam and certainly had every right to shit on me, treats me with compassion? I was the one speeding, not the state trooper. Lord, will you please explain this logic to me?" Leroy noted his overreaction for the first time on the trip, and his concern about these mental health issues started to mount.

The rest of the day's trip remained uneventful until evening came. Leroy's plan, much like his plan when he went to Spokane some years earlier, was to get a motel each night to sleep. The Spokane trip had worked out well in that regard, but as usual, it fell apart on this trip. Leroy's visit to a half dozen motels revealed NO vacancy signs. On the 7th try Leroy got good news. "Yes Leroy, we have a vacancy. It will be $289.00." Leroy just walked out in disgust. He had the $289.00, but the reason Leroy had a little money was that he would not piss away that amount of money for the paltry 4 hours of sleep he expected he'd get.

Leroy drove another 100 miles before nestling into a dark corner of a rest area. He tried to find comfort in the little 2 door sports car he had opted to drive, thinking he would be able to sleep in motels, but there was no comfort to be found. Leroy certainly had slept in worse places and despite his racing thoughts and hypersensitive emotions, he finally drifted off. I imagine the actual amount of sleep Leroy got was likely about 5 minutes because all of a sudden, Leroy was startled by someone pounding on his car. The would-be aggressor says in a badly inebriated voice, "Dude you got a light?" Leroy looks out the window and the haggard fella pounding on Leroy's car has a lit cigarette dangling out of his mouth.

Leroy told me once that the only thing that saves us from most thieves, this fella included, is that they are just plain stupid. As a result, they are pretty easy to outwit. If you are going to rob someone by asking for a light, then do not leave a lit cigarette in your mouth.

Leroy yelled through the closed glass, "I have a 44-caliber revolver in my door here. If I take it out, I am going to use it. I am going to take it out in about 30 seconds which gives you enough time to leave right now while you're still standing or leave in a body bag about 29 seconds from now. Make your choice quick!" Leroy started to count and when he got to 20 the fella lit off.

Now it's important to note that Leroy has not had any firearms in his possession since his retirement as a Combat Engineer. I am not sure that a confrontation like that would work with just anyone, but if you ever saw Leroy or encountered his demeanor when he's angry, you would know it would work for him. Leroy felt bad that he was not able to get a license plate off the "got a light" guy's car because the man was so obviously impaired that he was a danger to himself and everyone else on the road with him.

Leroy tried to settle back down but his overactive paranoia and with it, his intense feelings of anxiety, were growing worse. He was convinced that the robber asking for a light would return with his buddies and try to seek some kind of revenge.

So carefully, Leroy began to drive again, knowing that now there was no chance of sleep. Soon the sun came up and Leroy was feeling okay despite having had no sleep in 30 hours due to the absence of vacant motels along his route with a reasonable price point.

Leroy continued on and next he went to the Mitchell Corn Palace in South Dakota. He had always wanted to see how they engineered a building out of corn. As Leroy approached the Corn Palace, he laughed out loud. It was a concrete building, like any other, but it had corn husks attached to the walls.

Leroy then went to the Wall Drug Store near the Corn Palace in South Dakota. He searched through different souvenirs. A woman approached Leroy and asked him if he needed any help. Leroy said, "Why yes ma'am. I would like to know why these souvenirs are all stamped Made in China. When I go to China, I don't buy souvenirs made in South Dakota, so why would I buy a souvenir from Wall Drug that are Made in China? I'll bet there are a ton of local Native Americans who would love to sell you souvenirs, and more importantly, I would love to buy them. I have a ton of Made in China stuff in my house already." The woman just looked at Leroy in disgust and disappeared into another part of the store.

Leroy left Wall Drug and made his way to Sturgis, South Dakota as his next stop. He was trying to remember the exit number that led to a shortcut he had learned many years ago, but he could not remember the exit number. He figured that when he stopped to get gas, he would pull out his GPS and find the short cut. For now, Leroy just drove on, happy that his tourist visits went well, and that he'd even managed to find a few souvenirs made in South Dakota.

This takes us back to the beginning of our story and what happens next as Leroy races home, panic stricken and beyond frightened that his behaviors will land him in a second mental facility, from which there will likely be no return.

After driving for some time Leroy thought, "I need to eat and if I cannot sleep, I can at least get cleaned up and maybe rest a little. Leroy found success at just the right time, finding a motel with a reasonable rate that had a vacancy.

I don't want to say the motel name because Leroy was pretty whipped and could not remember for sure, and I would not ever wish to wrongly disparage any company, but I sure do disparage them rightfully, said with a smile.

With all that said, Leroy walked into the room and immediately felt a vibration in the floor like there was a huge steam pipe passing through just under the surface. Leroy cursed under his breath, "Well, crap! That will make sleeping a breeze!" He then thought, "Well, maybe I will watch some TV." Leroy reached for the remote, and after some exhaustive minutes realized the TV did not work! Leroy then thought, "I will get the coffee maker ready so I can have coffee in the morning," only to find that the coffee maker was missing a piece, thus rendering it useless! He then thought, "Man, a shower would sure feel good." Leroy turned the light on in the shower room to discover the shower floor littered with black pubic hair.

Now I agree with Leroy on this. He says "I do not mind the hair; the hair will not give me any sort of foot disease." He would pause, "But how the hell are they cleaning the foot eating bacteria from my shower while leaving me the hair! Answer me that!" After cleaning the shower floor and taking a shower, Leroy turned into bed and laid there as the bed vibrated in a bad way and the floor rumbled loudly.

After a fitful night with little to no sleep, Leroy sluggishly arose, got back into his little red car and powered along Interstate 90 East. As he drove, Leroy began to calm down a bit. He felt as though he could now control his fear and anxiety to a small degree, enough so that he slowly began to feel a little safe. Suddenly Leroy noted a sign and looked up in a panic, "Interstate 80? How the hell did I get onto I80?" Note the GPS is gone!

Leroy saw a gas station and service area just ahead and pulled into it. His plan was to take a picture of the highway map that was displayed on the wall of the food court. Leroy noted his ability to function without melting down and he began to relax a bit. When Leroy centered himself in front of the map on the wall, he looked at his phone and mumbled, "I wonder if this cell phone has a GPS on it?" He embarrassingly found a GPS and punched in Interstate 90 and just like that, he was in business. Note the GPS is back!

When he returned back to his car, he realized he could not safely use the cell phone while holding it in one hand as that would be no different than texting and driving. Leroy pondered, "What to do, what to do." Then he remembered that he had used a roll of masking tape to tape the "EZPASS" onto his dashboard and instead of putting the tape away like his usual OCD behavior would dictate, he had thrown it on the floor of the car. So, with cell phone taped to the dash, belching out orders that would put Leroy back onto Interstate 90, Leroy was on his way. His spirits began to lift and he knew he was on the way home where he would find safety and comfort, a clean shower and both a working coffee maker and working television.

Upon returning home, Leroy was racing in both body and mind. Having gone more than 2 days without sleep still did not make the lights of Leroy's brain dim. Leroy's psychiatrist would later scold him for being impulsive in his pursuit of this trip. Leroy would argue, "This trip was in the works for years and only needed me to have the courage to go, which I have failed at. Next year I will not go anywhere but my daughter's home. This should avoid any unanticipated problems." Leroy's session ended all to soon as usual, and the issues and the trip were put to rest.

Leroy was eventually able to sleep. When he laid down in his bed, he laughed out loud. The vibrating and rumbling bed had followed him from the motel of many wonders, all the way to his house. Leroy realized he was experiencing the feelings of vibration and rumbling as a result of driving so many hours straight. As we know, Leroy was a sailor first before becoming a Combat Engineer, so Leroy described it to me in this way: "It is a little like getting your land-legs after being on a ship for a long period of time." The mental illness was improving and Leroy felt certain he would not be ending up in any mental facilities today.

THE END

The Story of Hulu

Leroy was an odd duck and it was not hard to prove that. He would watch situation comedies over and over again. He would learn about the actors and kind of make himself a little family out of the characters in the sitcom. Leroy found comfort in this; his routine was to watch a couple episodes early in the morning while he played "Boogieman" with his Yorkshire Terriers, otherwise known as the kids. What is "Boogieman" you ask? It is where Leroy would hide the kids' favorite treats around the family room. Leroy then gets the kids all riled up with the word "Boogieman," which they clearly recognize as meaning, "There are treats hidden all over." Leroy remained amazed at the intelligence of the kids. They were capable of understanding well over a hundred words. Leroy continued to find more diabolical ways to hide the treats but the kids amazing sense of smell thwarts all efforts to trick them.

As Leroy observed his morning make-shift family on the sitcom he was watching, he sure wished he did not have to watch commercials. Leroy was of the opinion that if he was paying for the product that gave him the sitcoms, there should be no need for the commercials. After watching his sitcom, Leroy would then go off to work. He would work on his gardens or in his wood shop or at whatever chores Lenora had set out for him. As the day came to an end, Leroy would wind down with a few more episodes of whatever series he had latched onto. Again, Leroy would grouse about the damn commercials.

Some months later, Leroy caught wind of a program that was being offered to the public by appointment only. The program was offered by the state of New York and the objective of said program was to give a person coping skills which would help them deal with anxiety and the onset of panic attacks. For those who have read other Leroy's Shorts sagas, we know that Leroy suffered from anxiety and panic attacks, to name a few, so this outpatient program was a welcome occurrence and Leroy signed up to attend the two-week intensive treatment program. The first day proved to be very kindergartenish. The curriculum was so basic that Leroy was learning nothing new. He was hearing just more of the same blah, blah, blah, and to make matters worse, he had a doozy of a panic attack one morning. In desperation, Leroy went to the front window to ask for help. He explained, "I am having a panic attack as we speak and it is all I can do to stay in here. I need to see the psychiatrist on scene that I was told would be here to help me."

The woman who had checked Leroy in and who had greeted him each morning with pleasantries, responds to Leroy's urgent demand with, "Fill out this form and the psychiatrist will see you in the next seventy-two hours."

Leroy took a deep breath and bit his tongue clean off, metaphorically, as he restated, "Look! I am having a panic attack NOW! Not in seventy-two hours!" Nothing Leroy could say or do could overcome the complete block in the woman's brain. This was the same woman who had been singing Leroy's praises each day while apparently feigning concern. Feigning concern at least until concern is actually required. Leroy managed to eventually talk himself down from his panic attack so maybe that was all done on purpose by the staff of the facility: "How to talk yourself down from the brink of total panic?" Nah, just more example of Flow Chart stupidity. That term means that the person can only follow a flow chart. They have no mind of their own, no ability to think or act independently. A problem occurs when a crisis falls outside of the flow chart. The defeatist attitude that ensues because of this is beyond disgusting. I am certain I am preaching to the choir on this. Folks - it is only getting worse.

Here Leroy had found himself in the cloud of despair at this two-week seminar which consisted of propaganda videos otherwise known as commercials, for a bunch of different facilities, and a complete lack of the promised psychiatric care, coupled with daily board games that seemed to serve no real purpose other than to occupy a space of time. The silver lining in all of this occurred when Leroy met Journalist Senior Chief, Surface and Air Warfare Specialist, Ben Tiller.

Leroy's title was; Machinist Mate Senior Chief, Surface and Air Warfare Specialist, Leroy. Ben and Leroy immediately hit it off. Each morning they would face each other at attention and rattle off the other's title and then make some militaristic statement like, "Senior Chief Ben reporting as ordered." It was clear to these two men that the only ones finding any amusement in this ritual were the two men, but they enjoyed their morning routine and cared little for what anyone else thought about them.

Ben was a master at Scrabble and basically unbeatable. He would win the tournament every afternoon, but it was through these games that Ben and Leroy cemented their friendship within the program.

Ben and Leroy determined that they both suffered from the same affliction. Ben shared with Leroy how, as a journalist, he had documented the horrific wars of Iraq and Afghanistan. He had captured on photo, far too many gruesome examples of humanity's cruelty to herself. In the course of their many conversations, Leroy and Ben placed each other in close proximity during the overthrow of Saddam Hussein. They were both in Baghdad; one causing the damage and one documenting it for the propaganda value. It was no wonder these two men were suffering from mental illness. It was also no wonder that these two men in their fifties bonded, especially in a room full of teeny-boppers. These young whippersnappers were not old enough to have anxiety and panic attacks. What the hell do they have to be uptight about? I say this jokingly of course.

One day as Ben and Leroy began discussing world problems, Leroy brought up his issue with commercials on Hulu. He told Ben, "I hate having to watch commercials when I am watching Modern Family or any of the sitcoms on Hulu. I am already paying for their service, so why do I need to watch commercials on top of my payment?"

Ben responded, "Leroy, you simply need to bundle your Disney, Hulu, and ESPN. Pay for the Ad Free package and you will no longer have to watch any commercials. The whole thing will cost you an extra $8.00 a month."

Leroy was really excited. He thanked Ben several times that day and as soon as Leroy got home, he said to Lenora, "I met this fella at that treatment program I have been going to and he told me how to watch my programs on Hulu, free of all those obnoxious commercials."

Now, to fully understand the comings and goings of the next part of the story, we must recognize that Leroy and Lenora had made many promises and stipulations in their marriage vows. One of them was a 50/50 shared responsibility of all things. However, to divide and conquer, Leroy and Lenora agreed that Leroy would do all the grunt work and heavy lifting including things like mowing the lawn, shoveling the snow, digging the hundreds of holes for all the plants and bulbs planted around the house, cleaning out the gutters, cleaning out the Koi Pond, taking out the trash and doing any other duty Lenora came up with. For her part, Lenora agreed to take care of all administrative duties, including things like getting Hulu upgraded to be commercial free. Leroy started the clock to completion by telling Lenora, "Please get the upgrade on Hulu so it is commercial free. I will give you my credit card so you can charge it to me."

One month goes by and Leroy asks Lenora, "So. Can you get us signed up for Ad Free Hulu today?"

Lenora responded in her stubborn voice, "Not today, but I will get it done soon."

Two months go by and Leroy again asked, "How are you coming on the Ad Free package for Hulu?"

Lenora responded, "I just have not gotten to it yet. I will get it done soon."

Leroy tried to remain patient, especially when ten minutes of stupid ads take up what would otherwise be a twenty-minute sitcom. Three months go by and Leroy inquired again, "How are you coming with Hulu?" Lenora sheepishly admited that she gave up because the Hulu customer service rep said payment was being made by a third party, and they whispered "Apple". I am not sure why that was a secret.

Leroy asked, "So what does that mean for getting rid of my commercials?" Lenora explained that she must have used PayPal through Apple to make the payment and for reasons unknown to all sentient beings in the universe, this mode of payment somehow precludes upgrading to the ad free package. Can somebody tell me why? Leroy asked Lenora again, "So what are you doing to fix the problem?"

Lenora stated, "I need to drive to the Apple store and, and, and …"

Leroy asks in a rather perturbed voice, "Why are you driving to the Apple store? Don't they have access to a phone?" Leroy is in a depressed state and going forward he just does not have the energy to continue to chastise Lenora for her horribly executed plan as it had played out so far and resigned himself to watching commercials for the time being.

Four months pass and Leroy again asks Lenora for an update and the update is that there is no update. Leroy sternly orders Lenora to just cancel the whole thing. Once the television package is canceled then she can take Leroy's credit card and get a whole new package to include Ad Free. Leroy waited uneasily as he became more and more hurt by Lenora's blatant neglect of her duties. If Leroy did not mow the lawn for four months, what would Lenora be saying?

Five months comes and five months goes. Leroy tries to mention the Hulu issue to Lenora but he is met with a retort that was sharp enough to separate his head from his body. Lenora, in response to Leroy's inquiry, said, "Nobody at Hulu seems to know how to close the account and I don't understand what I need to do with Apple. I closed the PayPal account so Hulu won't get paid any more." Leroy is happy with that but that does not get him any closer to commercial free!

Six months had passed from the time Leroy first requested that Lenora get the Hulu package commercial free. Six months gone and Leroy was no closer to getting his commercial free programing. At this point, Leroy was starting to feel better and his mental illness was starting to give way to some happiness. His imagination returned and his motivation came back as the depression lifted.

Now, over time, Leroy has often wondered why some of his friends had committed suicide when they went on antidepressants. The VA, in their ultimate wisdom, oops wait – sorry - the VA is definitely not synonymous with wisdom. Quite the opposite. Let's try that again: the VA tried to convince Leroy that he could safely take antidepressants without adverse side effects. BULLSHIT! This is one example of how the VA seriously tried to kill Leroy, and sadly it is not the only time. If Leroy where a little less savvy, he would be dead! The VA said, "Here. Take this mind-altering drug that will only take effect really slowly, so you won't realize that you are now on the path to suicide until it is too late."

Leroy was/is so fearful about taking these medications because along with some of his fellow service members, he has done some horrific things that haunt his days and nights, and some of his friends have not survived. Leroy knew the antidepressants were responsible for the suicide of many veterans. So, although Leroy was following the orders of the higher ups and believed that the cause for which they were fighting was just, he remains to this day tormented by what he had to do in the name of his country and self-preservation. Leroy felt blessed that he was not suicidal. It would be easy enough for Leroy to say, "I do not deserve to live!"

And so, you go on antidepressants. As someone who feels the horrors of war, some carried out by your own hand in the name of your country, you believe these actions warrant your suicide. You are depressed and you have no energy. Believe me, I have seen depression take even Leroy down and leave him with no motivation, including any motivation to take care of Hulu, even though it was obvious Lenora had reached the limits of her capabilities. Anyway, back to our suicidal fella. He has no motivation to make a ham sandwich for lunch let alone pull off, what I suspect, has to be an elaborate plan to successfully do himself in.

Now, the way antidepressants work is that they start to slowly alter your brain chemistry and before you know it, you feel better, you have some energy, and you are ready to uphold your commitments. The commitment that many take on first is the commitment they made to kill themselves. Of course, thanks to the substandard care of the VA, which neglects to follow up with people after prescribing these brain altering drugs, the task is completed with flying colors. Way to go Veterans Administration led by John Fiero. Okay ... supposed to be led by John Fiero.

I give you this parallel because as Leroy started to emerge from his depression that came as a result of his bipolar cycle, the upturn in his mood had finally begun working to his advantage, giving him energy instead of depression, Leroy also began to get back his imagination. As you might guess, this is very important for a fiction writer and a artistic wood worker. But most importantly, Leroy got back his sense of motivation. Thank God it was not a motivation to kill himself! However, among the things that Leroy was motivated to take care of was the issue with Hulu. He was determined to resolve that issue once and for all!

Lenora was still asleep when Leroy laid out his strategy and made preps to pick up his cell phone and commence "Operation Hulu." With Lenora still dozing, Leroy was hopeful he could get the whole thing done before she woke up and then Leroy could really lay into Lenora about her taking more than six months and still not getting it done. Leroy's second thought was that there must be at least 100 or more customer service reps, so the odds were that at least ten percent of those 100 customer service reps would be decent people like Leroy and would not immediately start the conversation with a defeatist attitude. Leroy figured he would give the customer service rep enough time to demonstrate concern and competence but figured the more likely scenario would end up being a demonstration by the customer service rep that epitomizes an attitude of complacency and disregard for all other human life except their own. If Leroy encountered the latter, then he would make a game of how long the dipshit customer service rep would tolerate the humiliation and sarcasm that Leroy would deliver. There would be no yelling. Lenora did not like yelling. There would be no shaking with anger or getting upset. Instead, Leroy would just humiliate the service reps to death when they deserved it.

So, Leroy had his credit card ready and pen in hand. Of note, it was nearly impossible to find a customer service number for Hulu to begin with. I wonder why? But having finally located it, Leroy laid back in his easy chair and began to dial.

The phone for Hulu rang several times and finally Taylor answered the phone and introduced herself and asked how she could help Leroy. Leroy said calmly, "Yes, my buddy told me about his commercial free Hulu and I want that. I just need to upgrade my package." Taylor seemed to give a refreshing response, "No problem Mr. Leroy. I just need some information from you." Leroy provided the standard data to Taylor and Taylor put Leroy on hold for a bit and returned saying, "Mr. Leroy I can't help you. This is on a third-party payment. I can tell you it is one of three companies…" Taylor lists Apple and two other companies.

Leroy responds, "Apple. Is it Apple?"

Taylor responds, "I can't say,"

Leroy tried to figure out why the HIPPA law applied to his Apple TV application, but whatever! Leroy then asked Taylor, "So what are we going to do? I still want the commercial free package, so how do we proceed?"

Taylor then drops a whopper of a lie. "Mr. Leroy, you do know that only Hulu originals will be commercial free. All your other shows from Fox, CBS, and the like will still have commercials." Thus, Leroy realized he had found the first of what will soon to be many, total piece of shit customer service reps.

Leroy said to Taylor, "You are a filthy liar, Taylor. I know full well that CBS, Fox and other network channels are all commercial free with the package. If you would stop wasting time making up lies and excuses and instead start applying that effort to your job of getting me commercial free Hulu then you would complete the requested task as a hero instead of not completing it because you're a zero!" Leroy was amazed Taylor had not hung up on him yet.

Leroy decided it was best to fight fire with fire or, in this case, lies with lies. Leroy gets his head straight so he does not start laughing. He said to Taylor, "Taylor what is your mamma's name?" As predicted Taylor does not answer. Leroy sounds off again, "Oh never mind. I have it right here." Of course, Leroy has nothing.

At this point Taylor becomes agitated and asked, "How do you have my mamma's name?"

Leroy recognizes that he had Taylor right where he wanted her. Leroy asked, "What is your mamma's phone number?" Taylor begins to protest and Leroy interrupts with, "Never mind. I found it. I have it right here. When we get off the phone, I am going to call your mamma and tell her what a lying little hussy you are!" Finally, Taylor slammed the phone and hung up just as Leroy had planned. Leroy mumbled to himself, "Only 99 customer service reps left to go."

Leroy picked up the phone and next he found himself talking to Neil. Neil was as worthless as Taylor, but at least he did not try to lie and cost his company money while at the same time completely alienating the customer. No, his level of incompetence was enough to alienate any customer all by itself. Leroy did not take long to put

Neil in his place when he asked, "Neil does your mother have any living children who are not brain dead?" Click. Neil hung up. Leroy just smiled. His heart rate was fine and he was not seething mad at all.

Leroy picked up the phone a third time. This time he reached Claire. It took about 2 minutes before Claire was at a standstill and of course quickly began to demonstrate her defeatist attitude before giving up completely. Leroy asked, "Claire, if you were me, in other words a customer who called Hulu customer service to spend more money on a Hulu product to get the ad free bundle Hulu offers, and the response you get from the customer service rep is a simple "no", what would you do if you were in my shoes today?" Click. Claire hung up.

Leroy went through three more customer service reps. Each proved to be more incompetent than the last. None of them seem to have access to a supervisor to help with the apparent brain teaser issues. Leroy belittled each of them with no mercy.

I always laugh to myself when Leroy's sarcasm gets so thick that his stupid and unwary adversary is unaware that Leroy is telling him to go to hell. In fact, some even ask Leroy for directions. I know who his mentors are and where he gets it from. He has learned from the best.

Along came the 7th customer service rep and Leroy decided to try a different tactic. The 7th customer service victim answered the phone with, "Hello, this is Tim. How can I help you?"

Leroy responds, "Hello Tim. I am calling to cancel my Hulu bundle so please take care of that as soon as you can."

Tim asks, "Sir, do you mind if I ask why you want to cancel?"

Leroy responds in a slightly sarcastic tone, "Yes, I do mind if you ask. I'm telling you cancel it. That's all you need to know!"

Tim puts Leroy on hold for a bit and comes back with this sad news: "Leroy, I am sorry, but I can't cancel it. It is on a third-party payment and I cannot tell you what that is."

Realizing he could not keep going through all that again, Leroy shouts back, "I am sick of hearing "NO" today. I have heard it quite enough. You go get your supervisor if you can't figure this out. I am not going to put up with one more shit head from Hulu today. Click. Tim hung up.

Lenora emerged from the bedroom, well rested, and sat next to Leroy, enjoying her coffee and listening intently to Leroy and his efforts to get Hulu commercial free. Leroy was reminded of his commitment not to yell and lose his temper during this evolution of idiocy. Leroy started to razz Lenora saying, "I am going to have this Hulu thing, a project that has taken you over six months, taken care of today."

Leroy was committed now. If he failed to accomplish this task, Lenora would make him eat crow, and his foot would be stuck in his mouth for decades to come. Failure was no longer an option! Leroy called the 8th customer service rep and brow beat him into finally canceling the membership completely. No more third-party Apple bullshit. It was finally canceled completely. Now, did the 8th customer service drone empty the account of Leroy's email, phone, address and such? Of course not. Leroy's personal information was not deleted as required, which unfortunately Leroy didn't know until he was talking with the 9th customer service rep.

The 9th customer service rep went by Matt. Leroy said to Matt, "Hello Matt. I want to sign up for the commercial free Hulu application and the bundle that goes with it." Matt tells Leroy he can get him signed up and just needs his personal info including Leroy's email. Leroy provided all of that to Matt and Matt said he is going to put Leroy on hold for a minute. Matt then comes back on the phone and informs Leroy that his email is already in use because it was on his old membership. Matt then tries to convince Leroy to create a new email. Leroy methodically explains to Matt how stupid his request is, "Matt, if I change my email, how are all my battle buddies going to know how to reach me? If I just make an email just for Hulu, I will never check on it and Hulu will try to notify me and guess what? I won't ever see it. So, NO! You figure out how to make my email work!" Click. Matt hung up on Leroy.

At this juncture I am certain Lenora was grinning on the inside as she saw Leroy about to fail at something she too could not do. After hearing Leroy repeatedly make it sound so simple, and now Leroy was going to have to admit defeat. Leroy decided he needed to press on. There were still at least ninety customer service representatives left that Leroy could vet for signs of intelligent life.

Leroy picked up the phone and dialed for the 10th time. The phone rang a few times and Dana answered the phone with, "Dana here. How can I make your day?" Leroy explained the dilemma he had faced on the phone with all these previous customer service turds and how he desperately was trying to just get the commercial free programing on Hulu. Dana immediately went to work. Her professionalism was 100%. She explained to Leroy several times that she needed to put him on hold so she could get this done. Clearly Leroy had found one of the 10% of quality customer service reps. Thank God!

At one point during this whole process, Leroy said to her, "Dana, I am so grateful for all your time. Do you have all this time to care for me?"

Dana responded, "Leroy, I need to pick up my kids this afternoon and get them home but until then you are my only customer. I promise you Leroy, we are going to fix this before I leave."

Dana did all she promised and more. Lenora, realizing Leroy was going to pull this task off in just under four hours, stepped in to fill out the data to pay for it with Leroy's credit card. No more 3rd party payment hoopla or needing a new email address or any of the other nonsense Leroy had suffered through during the 4-hour exchange of turd filled munitions with Hulu.

Today Leroy sits happily in his home theatre room watching his commercial free Hulu programs, which, incidentally are all commercial free, not just the programs produced by Hulu. It was great that as Leroy's depression lifted and his energy returned, he did not carry out any plans of suicide but instead tackled nine morons to get to one angel named Dana.

The End

Paul Spencer

Leroy and The Step Kids

Leroy and Lenora met nearly 13 years ago now as this is being written. Lenora had grown up in Rochester, New York and as her kids left home, they literally moved within single digit miles of their mom, Lenora. They are both mamma's boys and girls respectively. Leroy shared with me that he was disgusted by the mama's boys and girls, but at the same time, Leroy was jealous due to the fact that he would never have those kinds of close-knit relationships for himself. Leroy did cherish the relationship he shared with his oldest daughter who lives in Seattle, and has a house, kids, a job, and a life of her own. Leroy has not even seen his oldest since she and her husband moved from Fort Drum, New York over ten years ago. Leroy has shared with me that this jealousy slightly mars the relationship with Lenora and her children. I believe it may be the catalyst that makes Leroy less tolerant of the circumstances about to unfold in this story. You be the judge going forward.

Cindy is Lenora's daughter. When Leroy first arrived on scene, Cindy was working at a respectable, yet underappreciated, job as a nursing aid at the "Sky View Nursing Home." You know, the one in Pittsford where your meds come in the form of raspberry Jell-O shots. She had been given accolades over and over by patient and staff. She doted on the folks that were in her care. Sadly, she would later self-destruct and implode at this job like she had done at all the other jobs she'd held. In the meantime, and shortly into Leroy's and Lenora's cohabitation, Cindy showed up at the house asking her mother for money to pay her rent. Leroy listened as Lenora said "No, I cannot afford it." What she was really saying is, "Look, go get your own money. We are not going to continue doing this." Leroy told me once that the word "gullible" was not in the dictionary. I thought he was joshing me but no, he really believed that. It is with that naivety about the pattern of normal family dynamics that Leroy blurted out, "Hey! I do not give money. I believe you give a woman a fish you only feed her for a day. If I give you a job so you can earn the rent money then I will be feeding you for life. Do you want to earn the rent money?" Leroy noted Cindy's eyes were swimming in her head and she had completely lost the pearl of wisdom Leroy hoped to impart. So, he resorted to a military term. KISS- Keep it Simple

Stupid Soldier, Stupid Sailor. Leroy had been called them all. He had also used that tactic when teaching others so he said "Cindy, shovel my dog-gone snow and in return I will pay your rent." Leroy's back injury from Afghanistan still throbs, especially when he shovels the snow, so Leroy welcomed the help. He gave the rent money to Lenora's daughter Cindy and Cindy lit out like her butt was on fire to go pay the rent.

Cindy then returned to shovel Leroy's walkways, driveways and such. Leroy did not pay her much mind as she began. Within moments Cindy came in the house crying, "I twisted my ankle, it hurts so bad, I am sorry I can't shovel your snow anymore!" Now, Leroy had been trained as a Combat Medic and while the training was only a few weeks long and Leroy was never going to perform heart bypass surgery, you know where you bypass the heart. Leroy could, however, brace a strained ankle and determine if a doctor was needed or if he could DIY the ankle repair. It was during Leroy's treatment that he found the problem. Cindy was wearing high heeled stiletto boots that were in no way designed to walk on, let alone to be worn while shoveling snow on Leroy's icy walkways. Leroy was beside himself but then he started to recognize that Cindy was truly just a little girl on the inside. On the outside, Cindy was an attractive woman, very voluptuous, like Marilyn Monroe, and at first glance seemed like any other attractive young woman. All these factors, along with Cindy's chronological age, combined to fool Leroy and were the reasons Leroy did not see her as a child.

Leroy and I have talked, and we figure her mental and emotional age are somewhere in the neighborhood of twelve years. Later that day, when it finally dawned on Leroy that Cindy was not the capable adult she seemed to be, Leroy barked at Lenora, "How could you let me give her that task of shoveling snow for rent? She is twelve years old in her brain. Had I known that I would have never made that learning moment a reality. Maybe I would have just given her the rent money."

Lenora looked down, ashamed, and said, "We were trying to keep it from you because we did not know how you would react. Maybe you would stop liking her."

Feeling mad and betrayed, Leroy fired back, "What if I had sent her up to clean the leaves out of the gutter and she showed up with her Hello Kitty ladder designed to hold a real twelve-year-old and Cindy then used it to ascend to the roof and then when it collapsed under her adult weight, she fell and broke her neck instead of twisting her ankle? How horrible would I feel then? I'll tell you! I'd feel about as horrible as I feel now."

Lenora did seem to recognize what happened and took ownership for keeping her daughter's affliction from Leroy. Leroy never shared this with anyone but me. He shared that what really concerned him was that Lenora was keeping her daughter's childlike behavior from him for any number of possible reasons, but that anyone of intelligence would know a person like Leroy, a profiler, a man who worked with young people daily, would make Leroy skilled at spotting what was going on with a person. Leroy would notice this behavior soon enough, so why keep it from him unless the relationship initially was supposed to last just a few weeks? Put another way, the judgmental neighbor comes over and Mom keeps Cindy's disorder a secret because the judgmental neighbor is a jerk and she does not want the neighbor in her business. Juxtapose that with a lifelong live-in partner to whom that mom does the same thing. Why? Does she doubt the commitment of her partner, his understanding of mental illness, his kindness and generosity? If Lenora did not hide Cindy from Leroy for one of these reasons, then what reason is there?

After this debacle, things with Leroy and Cindy went along pretty well. Leroy would go string her Christmas lights for her because she does not feel steady on her ladder. Leroy mowed the lawn of her new house while it was still in limbo and Cindy had not yet moved in because his thought was that she would have a nice lawn upon moving in, instead of a jungle she'd have to try and mow. On other occasions, Leroy made cookies with Cindy and Lenora, and always enjoyed their various get togethers. Still, Leroy had a tad of negative thoughts. His own children were scattered to the wind and Lenora had made it very clear she wanted to maintain the close relationship that she had with her kids both physically and emotionaly. Meanwhile, Leroy was homesick for Montana and all his powers of persuasion had failed to convince Lenora to move there. The kids were the real issue as Leroy had discovered, much like he had discovered that Cindy was mentally still a child. Yes, that's right. These issues were revealed to Leroy as if he had been slapped in the face by them without warning.

The real magic applesauce occurred just recently. The family was planning a cruise and was inviting Leroy along. Trouble was, Cindy could not afford the cruise. It seemed to Leroy that Cindy was exactly who should be coming on the cruise along with her brother, her mother, and other close relatives. So, Leroy did not hesitate. He told Lenora, "I will pay for Cindy's cruise with no strings attached. Cindy does not need to shovel snow, mow the lawn, or do anything other than enjoy this once in a lifetime experience." However, true to form, the odds are always against Leroy and this time was no exception.

Lenora and Leroy were in the beginning stages of birthing yet another litter of Yorkshire Terriers. Many might recall from other Leroy stories that Leroy and Lenora, unable to birth kids on their own, had created a hobby of breeding Yorkies. Leroy and Lenora had even kept 5 for themselves over the years. This current litter of puppies came just before the cruise and on the day before the cruise, it was obvious that the puppies still needed close care. Frankly, I am not sure how they and their litter mates survive in the wilds of Sherwood Forest. Maybe they don't. Bottom line is that Leroy remained behind to care for the puppies, while the rest of the folks set off for a week of fun on their cruise.

This is not the first time Leroy had extended what he called a "Senior Chief Discount" to someone. He had given Senior Chief Discounts to sailors and soldiers for such things as rent, car repairs, formula for the baby, and so on. He had given this discount to men and women who busted their ass for Leroy and who counted on him for their daily care and feeding. Leroy was loyal to those who were loyal to him and was giving to those who were giving to him. Juxtapose this with the fact Leroy could not give one stinking dime to the bum with the sign, "need money" when the sign should read, "need job." The Lord helps those who help themselves and Leroy thought that was a philosophy worth embracing.

For years after retirement, when coming across such people, Leroy would stop and offer the bum with the "need money" sign a job. He'd go up to them and say "Hey buddy. I am building this deck and I just need someone to help me. All you need to do is hold the other end of a board, fetch up materials, and if you are really willing, I will show you how to use my tools. At the end of the project, you might actually be able to build a deck for someone else and I will come help you. I have some old tools that still work, and I will give them to you. What do you say? You need money, I need help. It is a win-win for both of us, so come on. But I am not going to beg you to help me out just so I can give you money!" Leroy would continue to beg for help as the bum who needed money would edge further away. Leroy quickly figured out that the "Need Money" signs he keeps seeing, are pretty universally connected to a turd! If there is one out there who is really in need of money then God, please reveal them to Leroy and me and we shall rush to their aid. For the rest of those blights on societys, please keep your signs and your pleas for help out of our range, because Leroy really does not want to accidentally run you over with his car while he is zooming by. If you want a job, say so on your sign. Otherwise get out of the way!

Now, it's noteworthy to say that Cindy's cruise was the first time Leroy had offered money to someone without making them earn it. This included his own children. One might wonder if Leroy was trying to buy Cindy's acceptance and love. To answer this, we have to realize that Leroy's father bought Leroy's love with cars, pistols, rifles, fishing gear, motorcycles and more. Leroy was an only child and this was the only way his father knew how to show Leroy his love. Leroy, following in his dad's footsteps, was much the same way when it came to showing his love for another. One only need recall all the amenities Leroy has paid for and built for Lenora in an effort to demonstrate his love.

Shortly after the cruise, Cindy said as she hugged Leroy, "My dad is gone. Will you be my dad here on earth?" I am paraphrasing. I was backing away when Leroy was hugging Cindy, but wow, what a statement, right? Cindy's father had passed away a short time before the plans had been made for the cruise. Cindy had moved into her father's house after her brother selflessly gave up his rights to half of the house and put the house in Cindy's name alone. Cindy now owned the house free and clear. She shared that she was having trouble paying the taxes and therefore was selling some of her dad's stuff on electronic web sites. She boasted about her successes as she sold one item after another, including her deceased father's motorcycle.

Hearing this, Leroy sprang into action and brought over some new tires from his garage, some new water pumps for aquariums, hydroponics, or whatever, and a lot of tchotchke type stuff for Cindy to sell. Later, Leroy did learn that one of the aquarium pumps had been used. He had simply forgotten that, and later heard that Cindy had likely spent hours cleaning it, instead of just throwing it away. Leroy took the blame, knowing that a 12-year-old would more than likely try and clean a $25.00 pump for two hours instead of tossing it out. Cindy was offered money for the tires Leroy gave her and she turned it down. Again, a 12-year-old would try and get a new price for tires that were new and had never been used, but even so, the tires were 14 years old. A fella offered her $75.00 and she turned him down. Why would she not say "sold"? Because she has the mind and the reasoning of a 12-year-old. Still, it's difficult for Leroy to completely comprehend when things like that seem so obvious to him.

Leroy really was touched by Cindy giving him the honor of surrogate father on earth. Leroy thought, "I have a great relationship with my oldest daughter. I asked her for help selling my old sports car and she gave me some good advice, but using web sites to list the car was something Leroy was not familiar with. Not a problem, he figured. Surely his new daughter Cindy would lend a hand in the same manner his oldest daughter in Seattle had helped as best she could, even from that distance. Cindy had boasted about selling her dad's motorcycle and however you look at it, motorcycle or sports car, each is a motor vehicle with a title and registration and insurance and an engine designed to propel you to your destinations.

So, Leroy reached out to his new daughter Cindy saying, "Hey Cindy! Will you sell my old sports car? Insurance and taxes are coming up on your house and I know you still are not working, so I will give you 50% of whatever you can sell it for." Leroy is thinking that in many ways he's doing Cindy a favor. If the car sells for $3K, then she will have $1.5K towards her upcoming expenses. Leroy asked me if I knew how this technique of selling off junk was going to last year after year and net Cindy enough to continue to pay the insurance and taxes on the house, which we know is in the thousands. We both agreed: This won't work much longer!

In response to Leroy's request for help in selling his sports car, Cindy did not hesitate to tell her new surrogate dad the answer to his proposal. Her response was, "NO. I do not need the stress."

Leroy stifled a snort and his internal negative reaction, and without saying, Leroy thought to himself, "Yeah well, it was awful stressful earning that money for your cruise too. The real possibility of imminent death, dodging bullets, the unrelenting treacherous heat, the constant fear, and anxiety; all of those were pretty stressful. But I recognize that selling my car, like you sold your dad's motorcycle, is way more stressful what with the fact that no bullets are trying to hit you, your home is air conditioned, and by the way - NEVER ask me for anything ever again, even after I am dead!" Leroy opted to keep these words to himself but the pledge those words made, "Don't come near me until after I am dead" were carried out none the less.

Leroy waited a bit in hopes Cindy might realize what she had just said. Leroy felt confident that even a 12-year-old would recognize when she had made her dad mad and figure out what it was that he was mad about and fix it. Leroy waited, longing for her to show some glimmer of empathy, any empathy. He had shown her empathy. Cindy said many times, "Oh how I wish I could afford to pay for this cruise with my family. Oh, how I wish my brother could find time to hang my Christmas lights. Sure am glad my rent got paid back in the day and I did not even have to shovel snow because I wore stilettos." But instead, there was nothing. Not even a simple "Hey Leroy. I am suffering from anxiety (aren't we all) so I can't sell your car, but what I can do is teach you how to use a couple of web sites so you can sell it yourself, and I will get ahold of my brother, Dillon and get info from him because my brother did a lot of the wheeling and dealing for me and I am sure he will help. I will ask him today, OK?" If Cindy had compromised even 1% as outlined above, Leroy would have understood and would not have felt slighted at all. I hope we can all agree the alternative Leroy was looking for has very little stress to it. What little stress there is, is called sacrifice to show your surrogate father that you really do see him as a surrogate father instead of merely some guy who's screwing your mom Lenora and nothing more. Actions speak louder than words.

As mentioned earlier in this story, Lenora also had a son named Dillon. Dillon was younger than Cindy. Dillon had consistently worked for as long as Leroy had lived in New York. Dillon was married with a few kids. To refresh the details from earlier in the story, he lives a stone's throw from Leroy and Lenora. The first thing one notices about Dillon is that he is a pretty good carpenter. He worked for a construction and property management firm called "Build a Bear Construction" off Winton Road in Pittsford. Recently he has moved employment to "G.I. Jane Optics For Less."

It didn't take Leroy long to notice that Dillon works painfully sloooow. Still, Leroy hired him for a few things and asked for help with lesser repairs and Dillon had taken care of them all with good results. It was with this positive track record that inspired Leroy to ask Dillon to tear out a portion of the basement which Leroy had already finished, because there was some mold starting to show. Dillon spent several days removing the old material and asked his mom Lenora to come down and watch as he installed weep holes. Water had become trapped behind the basement wall and was keeping the wall damp, causing the mold. Dillon was about to fix the mold with weep holes. With each weep hole Dillon drilled through the cinder block wall, water shot across the room, in effect draining all the water from behind the cinder block wall. This is something Leroy had not even thought of doing and Leroy was impressed with Dillon's savvy. However, it then took nearly all winter for Dillon to finish the walls in question.

During this project, Dillon's father passed suddenly and Leroy said, "Forget the basement, I will finish it from here." Subsequently Leroy finished the 8-month long project in one day. The whole project should have taken 5 days. When Leroy looked at the new wainscot that Dillon had installed, he noted that Dillon had routed between the vertical boards and horizontal boards. This technique screams "beginner". Leroy had painstakingly assembled the wainscot, routing the horizontal and vertical boards in such a way that there was no router between where they came together and met. This technique is the difference between skilled finish carpentry and the work of a beginner. And yet, Dillon put a herringbone floor in his house that Leroy and I both agreed; we don't think we could have done nearly as well as Dillon did it. Leroy has never said anything about it, but when he sees Dillon do such good work for himself, he pauses and reflects a bit.

Dillon is one of these guys that has his whole house ripped apart with projects, instead of completing them one at a time, and as a result, none of these projects ever gets finished. Years have passed and the same unfinished sheetrock, the same missing trim boards, the same transitions are still missing from the floors and nothing is completed. Lenora always tries to defend him saying, "He works five days a week until sometimes 7:00 at night."

Leroy asked sarcastically, "If he works all the time, then how does he have time to tear up his whole house with projects and then never finish any of them?" Leroy continues, "Lenora, you forget; I started and finished one project at a time, to avoid rendering the whole house inoperable." Leroy went on further, "I finished your kitchen expansion in seven days, not in seventeen months like your son has taken, and while you have your kitchen done, Dillon is still not finished. You were complaining for the whole week about the inconvenience, As If! It took me one week. Think what Dillon's wife must deal with having to live with a kitchen that's been torn up for going on two years." Leroy did not hold any ill will toward Dillon over this. It was his life.

Now by chance, Leroy had discovered that Dillon had access to these purple "skittles" for lack of any other way to describe them. Called Grape Guave Drops, they contained caffeine, ginseng, and a whole bunch of other natural stimulants. They were difficult to find, but Dillon had found them near his work and was happy to pick some up for Leroy. It was on one of these weekly visits where purple skittles were exchanged that Leroy decided to take his relationship with Dillon to the next level. Up until that point, the relationship had consisted of the same interest in Grape Guava Drops and their weekly get togethers in Dillon's garage to exchange funds and purple skittles. Leroy and Dillon seemed to have formed a pretty good bond and after his father had passed, Dillon asked his mom Lenora, "Will Leroy leave if you two ever separate? Do you think he will continue to have a relationship with me?"

When Leroy heard about this, there was a couple of things that Leroy was wondering, "Was this going to be the same bullshit as his sister Cindy had said? And why was he asking his mother Lenora instead of asking Leroy?" After all, how did Dillon's mother know what Leroy would do? Leroy decided he would not assume the worst, and just this one time would lower his shield. While standing in Dillon's garage, Leroy said to Dillon, "Hey, I am looking for a fishing charter. Would you like to go fishing with me?"

Dillon did Leroy one better and said, "Look Leroy, my cousin has a boat and he knows how to catch the fish. I will get us hooked up with him." Leroy is blown away at Dillon's amazing offer. Personally, I am amazed as Leroy nears the age of 60 at just how gullible Leroy really is. For example, Leroy had shown Dillon his rotting decks (see short story about Lowes) and Dillon said to Leroy, "Don't worry, I will get you all taken care of on this."

Leroy was thinking, "Wow. What an incredible offer." Three years later when nothing has been accomplished, Leroy was forced to build the decks himself, despite his physical disability. Leroy made this decision to build the replacement deck himself when he fell through the existing deck and was seriously injured. So just exactly what was Dillon going to take care of and when?

The same thing applied to the fishing trip. Leroy should have gone and found his own outfitter and gone fishing by himself. Every few weeks Leroy would excitedly say, "Can't wait for the fishing trip!" and Dillon would rattle off some excuse about why it wasn't happening. After a while, Leroy stopped listening to the excuses. Now, after more than 3 years of this, Leroy recognizes that the promises of a fishing trip were nothing but lies. Leroy likened this to when he used to meet up with another drunk and say, "Hey! Let's go fishing tomorrow." The drunk would always say yes, Leroy would reward his kindness with beer, and you all know what follows. The day of fishing NEVER came.

Leroy has a neighbor who does exactly the same thing when he states, "Leroy, I work at a body shop and I will detail your car for you." In this case, Leroy's neighbor had done some excellent body work for Leroy in the past so it seemed conceivable that he would do what he offered. But no. It's been three years and counting and there has been no detailing. This is after Leroy had paid his neighbor double what his neighbor had asked for in order to do the body work. Leroy paid the extra money as a way of showing his appreciation for the detailing his neighbor had offered. Once again, Leroy paid up front for the generosity that was offered, only to find out he has paid for NOTHING!

Last year, on Leroy's birthday, Leroy invited Dillon and his wife Ink Squirt, (Ink Squirt's name comes from her love of Octopus) over for a night of billiards and music. Leroy said to Dillon, his wife and Lenora who were all present for Leroy's announcement, "It's my 56th birthday and I have been sober for nearly 7 years now. So, with a clear head I declare that we need to do this once a month. I recognize schedules are tight but I am sure we could find the time. What do you all say?" Everyone got on board with enthusiasm and all agreed that a once-a-month billiards tournament would be great.

After reading the story to this point, Leroy's follow-on comments seem a little harsh, but they are what they are. Leroy said, "Okay everyone. Lenora is the administrator of the family, so Lenora, can you arrange the dates and times for our monthly gathering and take care of the invites?" Lenora agreed. Leroy then turned to Dillon and his wife saying, "So once a month, no matter what, we will keep our promise to each other and get together to attend a monthly billiards tournament." Dillon and Ink Squirt confirmed their attendance with enthusiasm. What followed? The entire clan, including Dillon, never showed up again. Not one stinking time! Leroy and I looked at each other and recognized that neither of us were the least bit surprised. It was just another broken promise and another lie told. Lenora always chastised Leroy for using such a harsh word as lie, but Leroy can't think of any other word as effective and spot on as "lie". What other definition is there when someone tells you something that is not true? You are correct. The word liar nails the turd liar on the head. Leroy does not like being lied to. That is a game stopper in any relationship with Leroy. A liar is like a rabid dog. Given the opportunity, they will continue to bite you with zero regard for you in any way.

Some months later, Lenora asked Leroy to go with her to her grandson's birthday party. Leroy would be going over to Dillon's house and Cindy and some other close relatives would all be there. Leroy showed up at Dillon's house to find Dillon's grandson, the birthday boy, hogging the television playing a one player video game. Leroy sat in a corner, keeping to himself, not really feeling all that welcome. Boredom started to set in and Leroy said to Dillon's son, "Hey buddy. Do you want to play a two-player game or watch some TV?"

Dillon's son responds, "No. I am happy playing this."

Leroy says, "Well, I am not happy" but the grandson remains oblivious. Meanwhile, Dillon is knee deep at work even though it's his son's birthday. He is feverishly managing the company that employs him by working on the phone. As a result, Dillon is ignoring his son and everyone else, including Leroy.

During Leroy's many weekly visits to Dillon's to collect his Grape Guava Skittles, he'd asked Dillon about Dillon getting a work phone that could be passed to his capable men like a watch rotation. Then all the problems would go to whomever has the watch phone on evenings and weekends. If Dillon's watch stander gets in over his head, he could always call Dillon for help, of course. Leroy explained to Dillon, "This tool will allow you to have time with your family and you will not be on call and away from your family every single weekend and evening."

Dillon seemed to listen. Leroy later learned from Lenora that he had listened. He had the right to schedule the rotation of on-call phone handlers and Dillon wrote the rotation schedule thus could put himself on any days he wanted, thus he does not get stuck working through his son's birthday party, or any other special occasion. He was senior man so it was also his right to have first pick of duty days. He set up the schedule and was rotating the phone to different reliable folks besides him, and most importantly, as a result of this, Dillon's weekends and evenings had improved along with his quality of life. The same proved true for all of the workers. Great, right? About as great as the promised fishing trip.

But here was his grandson, sitting alone on his birthday, hogging the television while Leroy sat there bored and Dillon was on the phone with work throughout the entire birthday party. But Wait! Didn't Dillon write the phone on-call watch schedule himself? Leroy too had written watch schedules. Do you think Leroy would have put himself on watch the day of his son's birthday? Of course not. Do you think Dillon wrote himself in as an on-call phone operator on his son's birthday? Well of course he did. Can somebody answer me why? As a result, Dillon was walking all over the house, shouting on the phone and putting out many fires. No doubt, most of them were fires he lit himself, at least from what Leroy and I had observed.

At one point, Dillon did take a breath, and told his son to go get the golf clubs he had just gotten. Leroy excitedly said to the boy, "Yes, yes! Get your golf clubs and I will challenge you to a round of gulf."

Dillon's son simply said, "NO."

As Leroy sat there bored and a bit angry, Ink Squirt whispered to her brother Mike that he should ask Leroy if he wanted some fruit salad. Ink Squirt makes a good fruit salad and yes, Leroy does like it. Leroy has known Ink Squirt's brother Mike for nearly 10 years. The two of them have talked about their love of Sci-Fi, their love of tropical fish aquariums, their love of Thailand and much, much more. Leroy makes it a point to use people's names in conversations with them and is pretty good at remembering names, especially if it is someone Leroy gives a shit about like Mike. But when Ink-squirt hands Mike the fruit salad, Leroy clearly hears Mike say, "What's that guy's name again?"

Ink Squirt says quietly, but not quietly enough, "That is Leroy. He is Lenora's husband."

By this time Leroy has had enough and said, "Ink Squirt, I love your fruit salad but my stomach is off and I do not want any, thank you." But along came Mike with the salad anyway, completely oblivious to what Leroy had just said. Sadly, this feeling that Leroy is an invisible ghost is not unique to this situation. But these kinds of situations are precisely what Leroy must all too often endure.

So out of respect for Dillon's wife Ink Squirt, Leroy horsed down the fruit salad then snuck out the front door and walked home. No one even noticed he was gone until it was time to leave and Lenora got looking for her missing passenger, Leroy.

Leroy decided that day that he was done with the lies. He was done with being told that Lenora's kids wanted him for a surrogate father. If it were true, it would be wonderful. We all know it is not. Rest assured; Leroy is positive that neither child would treat their biological dad like this. Leroy understood these kids didn't owe him anything, and this feeling had just become completely mutual. Leroy had puzzled on all of this for nearly 10 years. The only conclusion and course of action going forward for Leroy was to accept that Lenora's kids only see Leroy as some guy. Why they lied about wanting Leroy for a father figure and wanting a relationship, we will never know. Maybe to appease Lenora? Regardless, there had been far too many lies, the hurt was far too deep, and the damage was done. Leroy takes the blame for this pain, knowing that if you do not let someone in your heart, then they can't really hurt you, can they? But when you foolishly let two kids into your heart because they are beating at your heart's door asking to come in saying, "We want you to be our surrogate dad and will do everything for you just as we did for our real dad," As a result, Leroy made a pact in his heart to treat them like his children. Leroy poured out his love to his new kids Dillon and Cindy, paid for cruises and extended himself in so many ways because, as you remember, doing for others and buying things for others, was Leroy's form of love. It was all Leroy knew and was how he takes care of his biological kids as well.

Going forward, Leroy figures that Lenora's kids can do their own thing. Leroy harbors no ill will towards them but knowing what he knows now, he chooses to cut them loose before they hurt him even more. Believe me, Leroy has been hurt quite enough. Never forget that old saying that if you fool me once, screw you, but if you fool me twice, screw me. For Leroy, there will not be a twice. That is Leroy's rule.

If they want to start honoring a few of their promises and perhaps make a fraction of the sacrifice for Leroy that Leroy has made to help them, then maybe there is hope. Sadly, Leroy knows better. These scenarios will just continue if Leroy continues to be a gullible fool. I am confident Leroy ain't no fool.

As much as he might like it, Leroy knows that any future participation with Lenora's ungrateful children is a fantasy. Leroy recognizes that Lenora's children are prideful and will never see their own faults. Leroy might be just as prideful, but given the past years, it is safe to say he won't be all cuddly with Lenora's kids any time soon. Lenora told Leroy that she was mad that she could not bring the kids to the house. Again, Leroy reiterated, "I am not mad at them at all. They know not what they do or fail to do." Leroy prays that someday they do see their faults and correct them. In the meantime, when they come over to the house, Leroy can make himself scarce, no problem. In no way was Leroy keeping Lenora from her kids. The same cannot be said about Leroy and his kids. But that story is for another time.

In conclusion, Leroy earnestly explained to Lenora that he was not mad that Dillon had lied about the fishing trip. Leroy was not mad that he was going to have to struggle to build the deck by himself after Dillon had promised to find him a labor force. Leroy was not mad because he had to learn how to sell his sports car from scratch. What Leroy was mad about was that those two kids had tried to make Leroy believe they wanted him to be a father figure to them and then, once invited into Leroy's heart, openly and harshly rejected Leroy without so much as a second thought. Leroy had opened his heart to them when he had already been quite content with keeping them at arm's length. He had hoped for a great relationship with his step kids and hoped that they would help him and care about him as much as he helped and cared about them. 50/50 not 100/0. Their actions and attitudes have told another much sadder and more pathetic story. As a result, Leroy refuses to lose any more sleep over something that never existed in the first place: a loving, close relationship with his step kids. He whispers a polite farewell saying," Piss off and don't ever come sniffing around me anymore."

The End

His Name was Tyrell Rucker

For those who have read the other adventures of Leroy; you know that Rucker and Leroy go way back to Leroy's Basic Training in San Diego, California, where Chief Rucker was one of his instructors and influenced Leroy to become a fellow Machinist Mate, which led to Leroy being selected as a Combat Engineer by the Army. Leroy finds it interesting how certain things follow him. Like the number 214. 214 was Leroy's Basic Training company number. The number 214 was Leroy's room number in Snipe's Castle. A Snipe is a bird that only comes out at night and never sees the light of day. A Propulsion Engineer on a WWII class ship never sees the light of day either. Hence the Pit Snipe was born, AKA: Leroy. Snipes Castle was the name of his living quarters during his propulsion engineering school. The number 214 was on the door of his room. Chief Rucker remained in San Diego for the year that Leroy was in school. When Leroy graduated, he returned to San Diego and met up with Chief Rucker and the many other engineers that Leroy would be working with or working for. Chief Rucker took Leroy down to the Shaft Alley, where the propulsion shaft penetrates the hull of the ship and drives the prop. Chief Rucker taught Leroy how to operate the "Donut", so named because it inflates around the shaft and stops the ocean from flooding into the ship if the shaft is damaged. Operating the donut is kind of a kamikaze mission because by the time you stop the flood, the Shaft Alley is full of water and you are drowning. Chief Rucker then pointed at the number 214 imprinted on a bronze placard and said, "This is a hull number. You will see these numbers every four feet and the number gets bigger as it goes to the stern of the ship. Your station is station 214."

Chief Rucker came upon Leroy and some of the other young engineers pondering over how to install this massive motor down into a vertical mounted shaft so it fit properly. Rucker took charge, much to Leroy and his chums' delight. Chief Rucker said, "Go get four chain falls, the coupling and tools to connect it, and get as much light down there as you can. You got it?"

A united "Got it Chief" reverberated into the hot overwhelmingly humid engine room.

A chain fall had a gear that was driven by one-and-a-half-inch chain links. One pulls the chain one way and the object goes up. If you pull the chain fall the other way, the object goes down. Chief Rucker ordered the fellas to hook up four of these chain falls in opposite corners of the massive electric motor. He then showed Leroy and the other kids how each chain fall pulls or releases to give the motor shaft precision guidance. He asked again, "Do you got it?" Again, in union the voices shouted out, "We got it Chief."

The next thing Chief Rucker did was beyond impressive. Chief Rucker climbed down into the bilge where the coupling that needed to be attached was. He laid down into the bilge water which was about 3 inches deep and would have freaked Leroy out if he were to be ordered to submerge in the muck. The bilge water was filled with things too disgusting to write about, and Chief Rucker knew it, as he positioned himself in order to guide the motor into the pump that it would drive. Chief Rucker shouted up from the hole in the bilge, "Hey, you kids! Remember what I taught you about the chain fall?"

The young engineers shouted back, 'We got it Chief."

The young Sailors began to lower the huge motor down on top of Chief Rucker. The motor weighed easily 2 tons and would crush Chief Rucker if the young engineer wannabees screwed up. Now that is bravery! The motor twirled and cantilevered and twisted. Chief Rucker kept barking instructions to the youngsters into whose hands he had entrusted his life. As the youngsters worked, Chief Rucker shouted at them. "NO! you all have to work together. This is a team event if there ever was one. Leroy, you jump down here on the ledge and when it gets within reach, push with your feet with all your might. Do you got that?" Leroy stammered, "Yes Chief. I got it."

Little by little, the motor lowered and before long Leroy was able to execute his order, He pushed the motor frame with his legs with all his might.

Chief Rucker growled, "Are you kidding me? Is that all you have Leroy?" Leroy had to admit that it was indeed all he had. As Leroy gave the motor a pathetic kick with his skinny legs, and Chief Rucker was saying, "Is that all you got?" Chief Rucker grabbed the shaft while lying on his back in the muck, then gave the shaft a solid pull, and with that the shaft dropped into the coupling which dropped onto the pump coupling. With the two shafts in place, everything went into the coupling with one fell swoop. Leroy just looked on in awe. Chief Rucker had just done with his two bare hands what the rest of the wet behind the ears engineers all combined, could have never gotten done. He climbed to his feet, and as his coveralls let loose the bilge water that had saturated them, Chief Rucker worked his way onto the deck plates, Deck plates are diamond shaped skid guards welded to a metal plate to make a non-skid surface to walk on. Water from Chief Rucker's clothes continued to leave puddles as he stood there and gave out some final instructions to complete the assembly and operate the pump and motor, insuring everything was fully functional.

Now understand that Chief Rucker was about six-foot tall, solid muscle, and likely pushed 270 pounds. Leroy would work out with Chief Rucker and half his work out involved standing on the various pieces of equipment so as to add Leroy's 170-pound body weight to the already massive weight on the machine. Chief Rucker would then do rep after rep like Leroy might do with, say, 130 pounds on a bench press. Not only was Chief Rucker huge, he was scary mean.

One time Leroy and about 15 other nimrods, jumped Chief Rucker on his birthday. The objective was to apply a "pink belly" on Chief Rucker's abdomen by swatting him repeatedly with a dust pan. All in good fun, right? I am told all this kind of "Hazing / Tradition" is gone now. Instead of just tempering it a little, they threw the baby out with the bath water. On this occasion, Chief Rucker threw his attackers off like rag dolls until he got to Leroy. I had told Leroy that Chief Rucker was a pass on the birthday tradition, but Leroy insisted he was going to organize a birthday "pink belly" party for Chief Rucker. Guess who found out that Leroy had organized the attack? So, while Chief Rucker was just giving most attackers a good toss, he was gunning for Leroy and had just gotten in range. Chief Rucker grabbed Leroy by his head and twisted hard. I was worried he was going to twist Leroy's head off. I later found out that Leroy had that fear as well. So anyway, Chief Rucker was one bad mutha. And strong as an ox on steroids!

It was some months later and it came time for the arduous task of disassembling many key pieces of propulsion equipment for the purpose of inspecting the components. The propulsion operations of a ship are inspected more frequently and with much greater detail than any other facet of the ship, which stands to reason because without a propulsion system, a ship is just a big metal floating box with no weapons capabilities. Who makes the electricity? Chief Rucker and his mighty men. Who makes all the drinking water, bathing water, cleaning water, and more? Chief Rucker and his mighty men. It goes without saying that those who make it so that the ship has propulsion which can be directed and accurately speed controlled, are of critical importance. Chief Rucker and his mighty men are again the ones responsible for this function.

As Chief Rucker directed the disassembly of the pieces of equipment that would be inspected, he had a plan to get the men some much needed sleep prior to having to perform the duties of reassembling this complicated equipment that they were currently disassembling. Chief Rucker took personal care of his men and finally late in the evening, he went to check in with the Commanding Officer and get permission to put his men to bed so they would be fresh for the inspection ritual in the morning. The skipper said no to going to bed and ordered that everyone continue to clean the propulsion room until morning. Chief Rucker had already accounted for how well clean equipment based on WWII technology ran as opposed to how poorly dirty WWII technology equipment worked. He had ordered his men to make the place shine and shine it did. How much shinier must it be? "Chrome don't get you home." We all remember that motorhead saying.

Chief Rucker never told Leroy or the men about any issues that went up the chain of command. Leroy paid attention to Chief Rucker's example of putting complaints up the chain of command and grew to know why it was done that way, when he himself became Chief. With that said, Chief Rucker needed to get his men some sleep. He took Leroy and all the engineers up to the flight deck. On the edges of the deck there was a fence made of heavy cotton straps which were woven corner to corner on the fence. When the wall was upright and there are no aircraft, then it is just a wall, but when it is lowered flat with the flight deck, then the woven strap wall hangs out over the side of the ship, making a great hammock. How does Leroy know it makes a great hammock? Because this is where Chief Rucker bedded the junior engineers down for a sound sleep in the warm San Diego night. Meanwhile, Chief Rucker continued to report into the Commanding Officer every few hours on the alleged progress of the cleaning of the already clean engine room. To this day, Leroy always wanted to know how Chief Rucker knew the Commanding Officer would not come down into the engine room to check the progress for himself. Had that happened, Chief Rucker would have been screwed. When morning came, Chief Rucker called in a favor with the cooks and a warm breakfast awaited the junior engineers. Chief Rucker had gotten everyone adequate rest and put a warm meal into everyone's belly. A lot of other stories remain untold about Tyrell Rucker, but this one paints a pretty good picture of just how honorable his character was and continues to be if he is still on the right side of the sod..

Tyrell Rucker became friends with Leroy as a result of their running into each other far more often than a normal rhythm of events would allow. Over the years, Leroy would bump into Tyrell, and one year at the Navy Exchange in San Diego, California, Leroy spotted Tyrell. Tyrell was not hard to spot. His size alone made him stand out and just the way he carried himself made him seem more than a little intimidating. Leroy shouted at Tyrell through the crowd, "Tyrell! Hey it's Leroy! Look at me! I made Chief Petty Officer, just like you." Of course, Leroy was nothing like Chief Rucker. Leroy was a wet behind the ear's wannabe. After threading their way through the crowd to one another, Leroy asked Tyrell, "So, you are probably getting close to retirement. I hate to say it but you would make a great prison guard."

Tyrell himself was living in the moment and was enjoying his life as it came. Tyrell Rucker had mastered the ability of taking a forward deployed assignment, meaning out of the country for a year, then would deploy back to a shore duty assignment in San Diego, California. Shore Duty is a term that refers to an easy assignment at home, in this case, San Diego. Tyrell Rucker intended to live in San Diego for as long as he could before it fell off into the ocean. This less aggressive approach to checking the boxes in a career such as Tyrell's had condemned any chances for Tyrell's military advancement. Juxtapose that with Leroy who would check every box that came his way, resulting in fast advancement, allowing Leroy to make Senior Chief shortly after this encounter with Chief Rucker. Leroy felt Rucker should focus on his career. On the other side of the coin, Leroy had it on good authority that Tyrell Rucker was still married to his one and only wife, and had a beautiful home in San Diego which he has owned since 1988. So, who is to boast who made the best career choices?

Leroy wrote in <u>Boxer Edition</u> how his last tour in Afghanistan caused him to end up at Balboa Naval Hospital in the heart of San Diego where he underwent back surgery. As he healed enough to be mobile, Leroy moved to Naval Base San Diego. There he continued to heal and decide if he was going to retire or take the only job he was being offered, which would stick him squarely behind a desk. Given those choices, retirement would win out. Leroy's readers know that a desk job would never bode well for Leroy.

So here was Leroy, living on base in a small but adequate apartment by himself, and his room number was 214. Leroy would go to the gym every day. His neurosurgeon had, most importantly, saved Leroy's back and his quality of life, and almost as important, the neurosurgeon had left Leroy off of medical hold so he would be eligible for advancement to Master Chief. The doctor told Leroy, "I am taking you on your honor that you will do your physical therapy on your own." It is for this reason and for Leroy's physical health that Leroy went to the gym religiously every single day.

One afternoon as Leroy was sweating it out on an elliptical machine, he heard a loud and familiar voice in the dialect of inner-city nuances say, "Leroy? Leroy is that you?" Leroy could not quite place the voice at first but the unique tone was so familiar but was not something he heard often. Could it be?

Leroy turns and shouts back, "Rucker, Tyrell Rucker! Is that you?" A loud inner-city voice responds, "Leroy, Leroy is that you?" Rucker came over beside Leroy as he pounded away on the elliptical machine.

Leroy looked at Rucker and said, "Rucker, damn you got some grey hair going on there."

Rucker snaped back, "What are you doing here in San Diego?"

Leroy smiles, "I am here for my spa treatments. I got blown up in Afghanistan about six months ago and I am here on the mend trying to decide if I should retire or what."

Rucker responded, "So I guess you are glad about Don't Ask Don't Tell huh?"

Leroy looked a bit puzzled, "What are you talking about Rucker?" By now, the folks in the gym focused in on these two men talking loudly to each other and discussing somewhat inappropriate content.

Rucker responds to Leroy's question, "Leroy, it's just that you look pretty gay up on that elliptical machine."

Leroy shot back his response as the laughter of the onlookers settle, saying, "Well, one time long ago when I was just a pup in the Navy, this great big black guy I worked for at the time, took me into a storage closet and I have never been the same since."

The onlookers erupted into laughter. Rucker told Leroy to go fornicate with himself. Leroy responded that he already fornicated with himself to images of Rucker. Laughter from the onlookers grew louder and Rucker conceded that Leroy had learned the art of "How to be a Smart Ass" with a skill level at least equal to his own.

When the dust settled from all the ribbing, Leroy and Rucker caught up a bit. Leroy determined that Tyrell Rucker had retired as a Chief in the Navy. Leroy asked his friend Tyrell, "So Tyrell what are you now doing for a living these days? But before you tell me, let me make one guess: "Corrections Officer." Tyrell Rucker just smiled and shook his head up and down, affirming what Leroy already knew. Let's face it: Tyrell Rucker was built for that job. Leroy has never seen him angry; only quietly assertive. Leroy has seen Rucker show genuine kindness, even for a bunch of engineering eggheads like Leroy and the rest of the group. Rucker was selfless, always giving of himself for the greater good.

As Leroy and Tyrell walked out of the gym together, Leroy turned and looked back. Above the entrance doors to the gym, there in bright gold numbers, was the street number of the gym: 214.

The End

Terry and the Chainsaw

Terry was Leroy's 78-year-old brother-in-law. This was the same age as Leroy's father. Lenora would often go to visit her sister Patti and Leroy would visit Patti's Husband Terry. Terry had been in the Air Force and during his tenure he was a dentist. Leroy had lost a tooth and the Navy dentist had given him a dental implant which, for its time, was a new state of the art method of tooth replacement. Leroy still has that tooth to this day. Terry had opened his own dental practice after getting out of the Air Force. Terry was not only patriotic but was proud of his Air Force heritage. He had placed Air Force stickers, placards, and other such Air Force paraphernalia throughout the beautiful farm house he and Patti had purchased and where they had raised the three children they had adopted from Romania.

One day while Lenora visited with her sister Patti, Leroy was visiting with Terry and he asked him, "Hey Terry. Could you use some help trimming your apple orchard?" Leroy was not being saintly by offering to help with the grueling job of trimming Terry's rather sizable apple orchard. Leroy wanted the wood. He had made some building materials out of his grandmother's apple tree when it had to be cut down, taking the cut apple wood and building several pieces of beautiful furniture. Apple wood has dark reds and then streaks of a light cream color in the wood. If it is lathed, one gets a sort of swirl ice cream cone appearance which is beautiful and unique. Leroy also wanted to cook with the apple wood. His specialty was smoking a whole turkey with apple wood chunks. The process is lengthy but the taste and juiciness of the turkey cannot be surpassed. Perfection has already been achieved.

Terry pondered quite a while about Leroy's offer to clean up the apple orchard. It would be an all-day affair and would be very labor intensive. Finally, with some hesitation, Terry suggested a date and time to meet up to do the job and Leroy agreed. He imagined that Terry was thinking, "Why did I agree to do this with this guy I barely even know? It is bad enough I have to listen to his stories every time he comes to visit."

On the other hand, Leroy was thinking, "I get to cut some trees, gather some wood, and spend time with Terry."

The day of the project came. It was a damp day but not bitter cold and not raining. This is considered a perfect fall day in Western New York. As Leroy's inner voice, I am unclear who came up with the idea, but Leroy and Terry decided to use the front loader bucket on Terry's tractor to raise and lower Leroy into the dead tree branches that needed trimming. Leroy's father had taught him this method as a child, so perhaps it was Leroy's idea. Terry fired up his tractor, doddering back and forth as the tractor dug through the muddy soil, and was soon in position. Leroy jumped up in the front load bucket and rapped on the side of the bucket a few times in order to signal Terry to raise him into position. Leroy later found out that Terry was quite nervous about hurting him when he was raising him in the air with the large branches overhead, but Leroy was having a ball. Sometimes he had to duck low in the bucket, sometimes he was diving to one side as the bucket bounced into a large dead branch but he was loving every moment. Leroy was working at a fever pitch cutting every dead branch in sight and at the direction of Terry, Leroy cut a few live branches for various reasons such as a branch was not growing symmetrically, a branch is going to grow into the tree and not be allowed to flourish, or maybe some dry rot is forming and it is better to remove it now as it is a cancer and would spread quickly. Before Terry and Leroy knew it, they had massed a huge pile of dead branches that needed to be dragged off to a slag pile and burned. Leroy also saw a windfall of applewood he could use as mentioned earlier for cooking, burning, and building.

After a brief break to catch their breath, Leroy and Terry went to work tackling the wood piles. Leroy was cutting and then dragging the wood to be hauled away by him or dragging it to the trailer to be hauled off and burned. Leroy wielded a Makita 16-inch chainsaw. It's nothing fancy but it could handle medium sized branches and logs without a problem. Soon the two men found their rhythm. Terry focused more on gathering up the slag size branches which are too small to be effectively used for anything other than making a nice huge bonfire on some future cold and snowy day. Leroy focused on cutting up the usable wood and then loading it in his hippie van to take home.

Terry had owned his Makita 16-inch chainsaw for several years and it was the same exact chainsaw that Leroy had. At one time though, Terry had dropped his chainsaw from the top of one of the apple trees and the handle had gotten partly broken on one side from the fall. It was still usable, but one would not have as secure a grip on the chainsaw. In keeping with his Air Force pride, Terry had put a thick plastic circle on the side of his chain saw. The plastic circle was an Air Force medallion. Since Terry was focused solely on removal of the slag branches, he had set his chainsaw down near the heat of the battle unfolding on Leroy's turf. Meanwhile, Leroy's tempo increased and increased like the reverse scenario of a windup toy. In other words, as more time passed Leroy became more and more wound up. He was in the groove.

Leroy was very happy as he sawed and gathered all the valuable applewood at his disposal. He looked at Terry who seemed to be content himself. Leroy recognized it as the feeling that we all likely feel when we finally find ourself finishing a chore that we have been avoiding due to its labor-intensive nature. I think it is called, "A sense of accomplishment."

In the fervor of all the activity, Leroy had picked up Terry's chainsaw by mistake and tried to start it, but the handle was broken and it was difficult to hold steady while pulling the start cord. Leroy blurted out, "Cheap Chinese crap. I have owned this for all of a month and already the handle is broken for no reason. Leroy began to assess the chainsaw for a better place to hold on while trying to start the defective chain saw. As he tipped the chainsaw on its side, he spotted the little round plastic medallion attached to the chain saw. Leroy threw the chainsaw on the ground and exclaimed, "And not only is it cheap Chinese shit, they put an Air Force medallion on it. Why Air Force? I worked for the Navy, the Army, the Marines, but I never stooped so low as to work for some prima donna Air Force loser, so why the hell did Makita put the wrong military branch on my chainsaw?"

Terry was enjoying Leroy's meltdown about the damage and wrong labeling of his chainsaw. What Terry did not divulge was that it was his chainsaw that Leroy had mistakenly picked up. Instead, Terry picked up Leroy's chainsaw and started to use it on the task at hand. As the chainsaw cutting came to an end and the afternoon settled down, Terry approached Leroy. Leroy was loading up the last of his precious applewood cargo when Terry came over and said, "Looks like you are all loaded up. Here is your chainsaw. Can I have my chainsaw back?"

Leroy looked puzzled at first, but the light bulb quickly illuminated in Leroy's brain and he put together what had happened: Terry was trying to steal his new chainsaw! Just kidding. Leroy looked up to Terry for many reasons. He was a flawless father and husband. Terry has integrity and empathy for his fellow man. Most importantly, Terry gave Leroy apple wood.

The End

His Name Was Rob

While in the service, Leroy worked in Propulsion Engineering for several years then worked in Cryogenics for a few years and then went back to Propulsion Engineering. If you have read many of Leroy's adventures in engineering, you know that Steam Propulsion Engineering is a technology that came to fruition in 1838 on board the SS Archimedes. It should be no surprise that the technology continued to develop and is still used in the design of a nuclear-powered ship to this day. However, when the Navy fleet shrunk by two thirds, almost all of the remaining ships became diesel electric, gas turbine, or nuclear powered, leaving the Navy's need for Machinist Mates also diminished by two thirds or so. When Leroy realized that the Machinist Mate's pool of advancement opportunities had effectively dried up, Leroy decided to make a bold move.

Leroy had longed to take the war on Extremist Muslims to the tip of the spear. He enjoyed shipboard life but life in the desert via the Individual Augmentation Program seemed promising as well, so Leroy called his Detailer. After a great deal of argument, Leroy finally convinced his Detailer to let him join the program by saying, "Let me talk to your supervisor and see what he says when he hears that you don't want to send a willing Senior Chief into this Individual Augmentation Program." This Individual Augmentation Program was designed to gather sailors from certain career fields who had specific skill sets that were desperately needed in the War on Terror. Leroy had the skills the Army needed in Afghanistan where Leroy would be deployed to help build a (FOB) Forward Operating Base. One example of this is that Leroy would be able to give the airport in Mazar Shariff the ability and freedom to return to commercial aviation after many years of oppression under the Taliban.

Before leaving for Afghanistan, one day while playing basketball with the young sailors, Leroy began having trouble breathing. He went to his doctor who had him take a test where the doctor put an aerosol inhalant in Leroy's lungs that acted like an irritant to his lungs. With each breath Leroy took, more and more of that aerosol inhalant was added. Soon Leroy was struggling to breathe. The doctor told Leroy he was disqualified from his assignment to Afghanistan. Leroy was like, "What are you talking about doctor? I came to you for help and you stab me in the back. Look doctor, at least give me another chance to take this test when I do not have the sniffles." The doctor agreed and the following week Leroy returned to the doctor's office. But before going inside, Leroy took his wife's albuterol inhaler that she used for her asthma and puffed about 6 puffs, which is three times the normal recommended dose of two puffs.

After using the inhaler, Leroy then proceeded into the doctor's office where he immediately began to shake from the extreme stimulation of the albuterol but at the same time, Leroy could also feel his lung function return to a youthful level. Leroy entered the Doctor's office and sat in the visitor chair versus the patient chair in an effort to try and hide the shakes and tremors Leroy had from the excessive albuterol. Leroy was not fooling anyone, because the doctor asked, "Why are you shaking so bad Leroy?"

Leroy responded, "Oh doctor, you know? It was a long night last night and I have lots of coffee in me."

The doctor responded somewhat skeptically, "Coffee huh?" The doctor administered the same test as he had administered last week in order to test Leroy's breathing and reaction to contaminants in the air. Although Leroy had failed that test, by using a high dose of his wife's albuterol, Leroy passed this test with flying colors. After the test was complete, the doctor asked Leroy, "Why on earth do you want to go on this assignment so bad anyway?"

Leroy responded, "I want to be at the tip of the spear again and keep myself viable for advancement." Having been medically cleared for duty in Afghanistan, Leroy returned the albuterol to his wife Racheal without her ever knowing it was gone from her medicine cabinet.

Leroy was on his way to his next adventure in no time. He arrived at Fort Jackson and began training for the mission before him. Leroy quickly learned he was the most senior person to attend the training, and therefore he was in charge. One of the many things Leroy loved about the military was that his fellow Chiefs and Senior Chiefs could have let him fail or even set him up for failure, but instead they lifted Leroy up and showed him how to make up platoons and, in this case assign a chief to each of the five platoons. Leroy put most of his focus on training for himself, or training with small teams in evasion tactics, in going door-to-door, as well as other training that would be carried out by the individual augmentees that Leroy was part of. Leroy also loved learning the tactics of driving in a convoy and what to do if he had to fight back. Leroy would laughingly say, "Sending a sailor to this basic infantry facility is like putting a sailor on a carousel to teach him how to ride rodeo." Before long, Leroy and his fellow Individual Augmentees graduated and they all headed to Afghanistan. In preparation for the tour in Afghanistan, Leroy had begun taking doxycycline to stave off malaria, and Leroy would take one pill daily while embedded in Afghanistan.

Leroy spent a day in Bagram waiting to fly out to his next destination. He was quite interested in how life was going to be once embedded in this command of soldiers. The first thing Leroy noted was that the food was quite good and very plentiful as he gorged himself while waiting for his C130 Plane. Suddenly, for no apparent reason, Leroy began to feel dizzy, almost as if his equilibrium was malfunctioning. The next day when Leroy arrived in Kabul, he was assigned a room with the fella who had picked him up at the airport and when Leroy got up in the middle of the night to pee, he found himself feeling completely dizzy again, which was identical to the experience he'd had in Bagram.

In the morning, Leroy went to the triage center and told the female pretending to be a medic what had happened, detailing his symptoms. Without ever considering the possible impact of the new medication, doxycycline, that Leroy had just been prescribed, the medic immediately jumped to the conclusion that Leroy was dehydrated. Leroy had worked in sweltering hot environments his whole adult life and Leroy knew for a fact that he was NOT dehydrated. But the medic insisted that was the problem and told Leroy to be mindful of his need for hydration and sent him on his way. The following night, Leroy woke and had the same dizzy spell. Given that Leroy was assigned the top bunk, this sensation was extremely scary and very dangerous for Leroy. Then on Sunday at Mass, totally embarrassed that due to the dizzy spells he was noticeably swaying like a drunk, Leroy decided that he'd had enough. Leroy went back to the triage center for help and unfortunately the same wannabe doctor medic was there. Leroy said to her, "Ma'am, I want a copy of the paperwork listing the side effects from doxycycline."

The dumb doc responds, "What do you need that for? I told you that you were dehydrated. Your symptoms have nothing to do with that medication."

Leroy was done being nice and said, "Look! I am NOT dehydrated! I would know if that were the case. I am a Senior Chief who has spent his entire career working in sweltering hot environments and I not only know how to recognize dehydration in myself, I know how to recognize it in those who are working for me. Now, give me the printout containing the info on the drug I just started taking. If you prefer not to give it to me, I'll be more than happy go ask your supervisor for it."

The dimwit doc sighed and went and printed out the data sheet on doxycycline for Leroy. Sure enough, right there in bold print were the words, "Discontinue use immediately if dizziness occurs." Leroy told the tweedled dumb doc that it might be a good idea to make all hands aware of this side effect, since all hands are taking it, minus this one anyway. Sure enough, after stopping the drug, within a day the side effects went away. Of course, the main benefit of the drug, protecting Leroy from malaria, also went away. Leroy was fortunate that during his time in Afghanistan, he never suffered from malaria, in spite of not having the drug protecting him.

Leroy would spend nearly a month in Kabul. Not wanting to get stuck behind a desk, each morning when the command was doing their physical fitness training, Leroy would run with the boss, Colonel Sheffield. Leroy would talk to him about hunting elk on Leroy's ranch, life in Montana and so on. A side benefit for Leroy was that these two men seemed to be the only two who understood how to carry out the physical fitness activities for the day. By pairing up, it became a simple matter of utilizing your workout partner's weight to create the desired resistance that would maximize the benefits of the workout. During these times, Leroy would constantly hint to Colonel Sheffield that Leroy believed his talents would be much better served by working up north around Mazar Shariff. Leroy had gotten wind that Afghanistan was building its first railroad system in history which would run from Tajikistan through the border of Afghanistan at Heriton Gate, onward to Mazar Shariff, eventually branching out from there. Leroy wanted to be a part of that and more. Soon Colonel Sheffield ordered Leroy to go up north and take the lead in engineering whatever was needed by the 10th Mountain Brigade, currently embedded there, and eventually to do the same for the 4th Combat Aviation Brigade that was going to be coming soon. Leroy will forever be grateful to Colonel Sheffield as he sent him on an adventure of a life time.

Leroy arrived at Camp Marmal on Christmas Eve. Camp Marmal was built and maintained primarily by the German Army, and to a lesser degree by the nationalities of other NATO countries stationed on Camp Marmal. It was cold, if you can believe it, and the winds were whipping around. The lights were always kept to a bare minimum in order to discourage snipers, and when Leroy arrived at the camp, it was late and there was no one in sight. Leroy was a little nervous as he had no idea where he should go to sleep or even to get warm, but he was hopeful that someone was expecting him. It wasn't long before Leroy heard the sounds of a large engine in the distance and in the darkness of the night, it seemed to be approaching Leroy. The sounds of the winds whipping around would break the silence every few minutes and when the winds subsided, the sounds of the large engine would be notably closer. Soon a beat up old white Toyota pickup truck came clamoring out of the dark. "Hey, are you, Leroy?" Rob asked.

Leroy responded, "Well, if I am not Leroy, we are all in a lot of trouble." Rob just looked at Leroy through the dark trying to understand what the hell Leroy meant when he said trouble. Leroy simply meant that he was in trouble if he wasn't Leroy, and Rob would be in trouble if he lost Leroy. It was a bit of a joke, nothing more than that. Leroy opened the passenger door and the dome light in the cab of the truck lit up the area giving Leroy and Rob a good look at each other for the first time. Leroy threw his 2 green rucksacks in the back of the white Toyota and jumped in. Rob had the cab warm and for the first time all day, Leroy finally felt like he might thaw out from the cold.

Rob said, "I have a nice warm tent and a refrigerator for keeping cool whatever you want to keep cool. I also have a German bed for you."

Leroy asked, "Why is a German bed so choice?"

Rob responded with only a cryptic, "You will see my friend, you will see."

Before long they pulled up near a row of tents. Rob got out, grabbed one of Leroy's heavy green rucksacks while Leroy grabbed the other, and told Leroy to follow him. Rob led Leroy to a tent and as Leroy walked into the tent it was nice and toasty warm. Leroy thought to himself, "What a relief from the cold." Near exhaustion after the long day of travel, Leroy unpacked just a few things and crawled in his bed just as he was. Now he knew why Rob specifically said he had gotten him a German bed. The bed was made of wood and was much more inviting than a metal bed. The mattress was high density foam, and the blanket and pillow were made of nice soft material, insulated with goose down. That bed was so much better than Leroy had used when he was a shipboard sailor. Then there was the food. It turned out that the food in this camp was also much better than what Leroy had eaten when shipboard.

After some restorative rest, Leroy hit the ground running and in no time flat was running security details from Camp Marmal to Heriton Gate. Leroy was focused on his duties but he took time to notice a large aquarium filled with exotic fish sitting right in the middle of the room. Leroy estimated it may have a 600-gallon total capacity. It was an unexpected treasure, made all the more unique because it was located out in the middle of a desert.

Heriton gate is aptly named because it sits right on the border between Afghanistan and Tajikistan. The Amu Darya River defines most of the border between Afghanistan and Tajikistan, and Heriton Gate is located almost on the bank of the Amu Darya River. Leroy was thinking what a juxtaposition this beautiful aquarium with exotic fish made as it sat in the midst of a massive desert where the river provided the only water to be found for miles in any direction.

The Amu Darya River was quite large and supported a good amount of cargo travel that served the area. Amazingly enough, the river also contained a variety of impressive sized edible fish. Leroy enjoyed a nice dinner one afternoon with some of the civilian contractors for this project, and among the delicacies on the menu was a freshly caught fish from the river. It had huge silver scales and the meat was as good as any fresh water fish Leroy had ever had.

With the railroad project underway, Leroy put his focus on his next project, the removal of personnel mines around the air field and support buildings, the expansion of civilian and military aviation run ways and a modernization of the control tower and remaining technical gear. There was a 737 passenger jet that had been abandoned in the middle of the air strip and it needed to be moved, so Leroy and Rob went to investigate. They climbed into the plane through a window that had been broken out some time earlier, and were greeted by a smell that would knock a person into next week. It was absolutely noxious. It evoked a sensory memory that somehow was a combination of the stink of an old musty basement intermingled with the rank smell of sour body odor. To add to the ambiance, this stench had been trapped in this metal tube and left out in the hot desert sun for who knows how long to marinate and ferment, resulting in what may have been a level three biohazard.

Rob said, "Leroy, what if I operate the tow dolly so we can propel this beast? That only means someone has to sit inside the cockpit and steer." Rob shouted, "Not It!"

Leroy groused, "Damn it to hell! Okay FINE! I will man the cockpit." Leroy would end up having to sit in the cockpit for a good hour and a half while he steered in conjunction with Rob's tow car. Imagine the oppressive heat contained in a metal tube with no air conditioning and then combine it with the oppressive smell that would provoke an episode of violent vomiting in any normal person. Eventually they managed to maneuver the dead plane off into the sand, away from any inconvenience it might cause.

Next on the list was the removal of mines. The current set up was that the Aviation Brigade would take out the mines in and around the air strip itself. They had coordinated small square patterns and contracted with local Afghani residents who would test each grid, square by square. Leroy always wondered what would happen if a grid was to prove NOT safe? But in the meantime, Rob and Leroy had to figure out a way to clear the areas around the support buildings. What the two came up with was to take an asphalt roller that is designed to be pushed by two men, and Leroy and Rob would push this roller around each area that needed to be cleared. They were hopeful there would be no land mines to find, but if they did find a land mine, the theory and their fervent hope was that the asphalt roller would absorb enough of the blast shock to give Rob and Leroy a chance at survival.

Many years later Leroy's sister-in-law gave Leroy some hollyhock seeds. Leroy planted a row of them and carefully tended the row of biennial hollyhocks so that they were always flourishing. You are likely asking what hollyhocks have to do with this story. Well, just as Rob and Leroy were making their final pass with their makeshift mine detonator in the form of an asphalt roller, at the end of the last run, Leroy saw a beautiful and extensive row of deep red hollyhocks. Leroy's fear suddenly faded and he felt the presence of his grandmother. His grandmother had grown hollyhocks, of course. Back in her day, no self-respecting gardener would be caught not growing hollyhocks, but here in the middle of a desert torn apart by endless wars, was this unexpected burst of color. Looking back, Leroy was perplexed at how that species of flower was able to grow with no water and subjected to the constant oppression of the sun and its heat. Perhaps it was a miracle. All Leroy knew was that when he saw them, he had experienced an amazingly pleasant feeling that was downright spiritual. As they made their preparations for the final pass, Leroy said to Rob, "We got this!" When the asphalt roller reached its final destination, Leroy just stared at the hollyhocks.

Rob was both flustered and relieved when he came out with, "Can somebody tell me why?" This would become Rob's mantra when things were screwed up which sadly was often the case.

In spite of the many negatives Rob often encountered, Rob had the kind of personality that had people eating out of his hand in a New York minute. It was amazing for Leroy to watch Rob in action, because not only was it almost magical, it was a skill Leroy had never possessed. Rob's hands must taste really good or something. Case in point; Leroy came back from a day on patrol and was pretty tired. When he returned to his tent, Rob was waiting and told Leroy, "Hey buddy. I got us a hard stand right near the gym and the Dining Facility (DFAC). Pack up your stuff and I will help you with your bags. We're moving up in the world!" A hard stand is a metal container box like you may have seen at a ship's loading dock. They are commonly painted grey. Now take that shipping container, put in a window, add a few florescent lights, and most importantly install an air conditioner. Surround the container with a four-foot wall of sand bags around it, line them up in a row with a shower and toilet plumbed in, and by golly, one has a pretty darn nice place to live. Leroy never did learn how Rob managed to commandeer that posh facility, but the fact he wanted to share it with Leroy cemented what became a lifelong friendship between them.

Leadership of the 4th Combat Engineering Brigade would be arriving soon and the 10th Mountain Brigade would finally be allowed to return home for a rest. Once the 4th Combat Aviation Brigade arrived, they would take on the responsibility for completing the runway.

Leroy had quickly finished his chores for Uncle Sam and was looking for new things to do. Rob walked up on Leroy while Leroy had 5 things going on at once in his head. Rob said, "Leroy, did you get the Joint Operation Review Board filled out for the diesel fuel we need?"

Leroy was keeping his mind on the tasks at hand and so he was somewhat dismissive to Rob. Leroy said, "Yes." and started to walk away from Rob.

Rob called Leroy on his shit saying, "Hey! Don't disrespect me like that Leroy!"

Realizing what he had done, Leroy stopped in his tracks and begged Rob's forgiveness saying, "I have five projects on my mind and although I'm in a hurry, that's no excuse to ditch my buddy. I'm really sorry Rob."

One day Rob asked Leroy if he wanted to go with him to get the diesel tanks filled for the generators. Leroy enjoyed spending time with Rob and was happy to go along. Those who have read the writings of Leroy, knows this was the first mention about Leroy having a friend within the military. The kind of true friend one hopes to hang onto for life. Rob was not the kind of friend you knew was just a friend who called on you when he needed something, and then dropped you like a hot potato as soon as that need was satisfied. No.

Rob was a friend for life, sticking with his buddies through the good, the bad and the ugly. Simply put; Rob was the real deal.

So, Rob pulled his truck up to the diesel tank and when he stopped, dust lifted and poured across the compound. Not far behind Rob was the German soldier named Hans. Hans said to Rob, "How much diesel do you need?"

Rob responds, "Well, I think the diesel tank for the generator is half full."

Then Rob scratched his head and said "No. No, on second thought the diesel tank is half empty. No, wait a minute. You know what? I think I had it right the first time. It's half full. I'm sorry, I finally got it. It's half empty."

Leroy could not hold back a laugh anymore and through his laugh Leroy muttered, "Rob, the diesel tank has to be half full or half empty. It can't be both!" Hans, the German soldier could not figure out what the discussion was about, but Hans suspected maybe they were making fun of him. Rob knew Hans quite well but Leroy did not have a clue who Hans was. Then Rob did what he did best and spoke with Hans on his own level. True to form, Rob who could sell sand to the Taliban for their sand boxes, got all the fuel they needed for the generators. This whole debacle would play out again tomorrow and tomorrow and tomorrow, as the need for fuel to run the generators never ended.

Now a real friend would not expose his buddy's shortcomings in the thick of the nest, otherwise known as the Tactical Operation Center. (TOC) Leroy considered Rob a real buddy but fun is fun. Leroy posted signs all over the TOC such as "Is it six eggs or a half dozen eggs Rob? "Is it 50 cents or a half dollar Rob?" A couple of smart-ass signs got posted each day and while Leroy may have been the only player in the game, it kept Leroy amused for a bit.

After Leroy got the post office squared away so the soldiers could receive mail and packages, Leroy tried to find something, anything, to do that would give him a sense of purpose. That lasted until his supervisor Naval Captain Keety called him aside and told him not to do anything with the Brigades and to do nothing for now. Leroy left Captain Keety's office a bit out of sorts. He had expected to be at the tip of the spear, not hanging around babysitting.

A German Colonel by the name of Thorsten had taken Leroy on as his sidekick. Thorsten was making waffles from scratch, complete with all the fixings, and everyone in the TOC was filing into *Thorsten's Waffle House*, just to eat one of Thorsten's delicious waffles. Leroy was moping nearby and Thorsten said, "Leroy, come have a waffle and tell me your woes." Leroy, with little hesitation, asked for a waffle with whipped cream and strawberries.

Thorsten asked again, "What has you down Leroy?" Leroy began to get a little weepy as he told Thorsten that his captain had benched him with no explanation and that he had thought this tour was his chance to be at the tip of the spear on the war on Extremist Muslims. Thorsten said, "Let me talk to Captain Keety and see what we can do."

The next day Captain Keety seemed a little upset with Leroy, but all he said to Leroy was, "Go ahead and prove yourself out there, but make darn sure you have all the Joint Operation Review Boards (JORB) filled out on time." JORB's were used to purchase everything from bunkbeds to ammunition and all matter of needs in between. Put another way: "Boots Beans and Bullets." Since this was a NATO operation, all members were considered part of a Joint Operation.

And with that snafu behind Leroy, he started working for Colonel Thorsten who was a Tank Commander. The first assignment Leroy would be taking on consisted of making two patrols a week to areas in the city that could be easily pilfered or destroyed, a tactic employed by the enemy in order to disrupt the critical flow of essential products. The other assignment they would be taking on was the training of the 209th Brigade Afghan National Army. During these two day a week excursions and training. Rob and Leroy would part ways in the morning and get back together in the evening. The rest of each week, when Leroy was not in the gym or eating, he was helping Rob with his various tasks for the 4th CAB and those supporting US Forces Afghanistan.

There was one day during the training of the Afghan National Army (ANA) that stood out more than most days. Colonel Thorsten had left the day's activities in the capable hands of Sergeant Muller and Leroy while he went off and ran some errands. Sergeant Muller was a German soldier who was likely half Leroy's age. They had become good chums as they worked together over many months, training those Afghan National Army soldiers. As Colonel Thorsten went to run errands, Leroy and Muller had no idea that what Thorsten was actually doing was going to get his boss and some other key people and bring them back to the ANA facility to recognize the efforts of Sergeant Muller and Senior Chief Leroy in an awards ceremony. With the absence of Thorsten, you know for a fact that when the cat's away, the mice turn into rats, and Leroy and Muller had no intention of breaking that rule. First sign that they were screwing off is when Muller said to Leroy, "Hey Leroy! I'm going to turn you into a puppet." Muller started moving his hands most cleverly as to imitate what a marionette would do, and Leroy, happy to cooperate, moved as if being controlled by the strings. The ANA soldiers erupted into laughter as Leroy and Muller perfected their imitation.

Leroy said to Muller, "You know, I'm pretty sick of these guys. They don't listen, they have no military bearing, they have no sense of discipline, so why do we even bother trying?"

Muller piped up saying, "I have an idea. I have a ton of frisbees in the back of the truck, so what do you say we teach them how to play frisbee?"

Leroy did not hesitate, "Oh hell yes, my friend! Let's do it!" In moments, Muller and Leroy were playing frisbee with the soldiers of the 209th ANA. The two instructors were in stitches at the extreme ineptitude demonstrated by their trainees at the game of frisbee but, at least no one was getting hurt, no diesel was being burned up, and no equipment was being damaged. Muller and Leroy actually got the 86 men present to start demonstrating a bit of improvement at the mechanics involved in playing a game of frisbee. Muller and Leroy got so engrossed in their frisbee game that they did not hear the three vehicles containing Thorsten and several other leaders from different countries pulling up to the area where the games of frisbee was going strong.

Suddenly in mid toss, Muller and Leroy became aware that they had company, and stopped the game. They immediately noticed General Ogdad, who was the boss's boss, and the General was heading straight for Leroy and Muller. As soon as the General got close enough, he made eye contact with Muller and Leroy. Now it's important to note that General Ogdad spoke no English but Sergeant Muller spoke both English and German perfectly. Leroy spoke no German other than a few words that would get him a beer or a brat or a bathroom.

Knowing all this, Leroy looked at the General and began to talk. In English. "The ANA is damaging equipment and wasting a ton of diesel, so Sergeant Muller came up with a plan to save fuel and avoid injury while simultaneously getting the trainees to focus on listening and following orders. All this can be safely accomplished by teaching them to play frisbee and in the process, we saved a ton of fuel and avoided any possibility of injury. In fact, there were no injuries and the trainees were actually listening and following orders for a change." Knowing General Ogdad would not have understood a word he said, Leroy turned to Muller with a subtle wink, indicating the story Leroy had just told was Muller's to tell in German if he wanted to.

Muller began to speak in German, telling the story of the Frisbee and the ANA. The General listened and occasionally chuckled and then put his hand on Muller's shoulder with a nod of approval. Every one of the officers and trainers lined up and a picture was taken. A copy of that picture is still on the wall in Leroy's man room.

As the year went on with patrols and training Leroy and Colonel Thorsten became fast friends and regularly keep in touch to this day. It was late one night when Leroy and Thorsten found enough scrap wood to make a small fire. The sky was pitch black, the moon was new, the stars were unbelievable and the night sky reminded Leroy of nights spent in remote parts of Montana, camping under a vast blanket of stars. As they sat by the small fire, Leroy began to tell Thorsten where his grandfather had fought in WWII. Thorsten paused a minute and then said, "My grandfather fought in that area also." The two men took a moment while they internalized the fact that both of their grandfathers had fought against each other in WWII and just a few years later here were their grandsons, united in the common cause of killing Extremist Muslims. What a confusing and cruel world we live in.

Just weeks before Leroy was to go home to America, he was coming back from patrol and the Croatians were disposing of unexploded ordinance by exploding it. Leroy had never had much interaction with the Croatians, other than when he passed in and out of the security gate. The Croatians were in charge of this facet of the base and Leroy was always bringing through truckloads of building supplies for the expansion of the base and the air strip. This day he was coming back from a combat mission. Leroy had received extensive training in the use and maintenance of the MG3 50 caliber mounted machine gun, a weapon whose use goes back to WWII, only now the cyclical rate has been slowed to 200 rounds a minute in order to give the shooter more accuracy. Leroy liked being the gunner when they went on patrol and had won the second highest award for proficiency in this weapon system during a contest. One could not get any closer to the tip of the spear than that.

So back to the Croatians blowing up unexploded ordinance. Leroy could not speak Croatian and none of the Germans with the team could speak Croatian None of the Croatians spoke English so when Leroy needed to get by their checkpoint, Leroy got frustrated and yelled at the Croatians to let him by. Leroy can only assume that the tone of voice he used somehow conveyed to the Croatians the idea that Leroy knew what he was doing, which he did not. The Croatian's false sense of security, created by Leroy's booming voice, caused them to allow Leroy's tank to pass. The instant the tank got through the gate, the Croatians who were next to the road, detonated a huge pile of unexploded ordinance. The verdict is out on whether the blast knocked Leroy to the bottom of the gun turret or if Leroy dove to the bottom, in reaction to the huge explosion, but no matter. In either case, Leroy was badly hurt. He had ruptured a disk in his back, which later would not respond to cortisone shots or any other pain killer. Leroy was a week away from leaving on his own after a year and a half tour which included time spent training and this happened. Finally, Leroy's boss said, "I am sending you home for surgery and there you will stay." Leroy was tied to the Wounded Warrior Program for the duration home. Thank goodness for the Wounded Warrior Program. Leroy was given a smooth and caring transport to Balboa Hospital in California where he did his best to recover and where he subsequently ended up retiring.

A few years went by and Leroy had retired and moved in with Lenora. Rob had come to visit Leroy and Lenora in Western New York, and during this visit, Leroy told Rob he was getting married in Montana and asked Rob if he would be Leroy's Best Man. Rob was very touched by Leroy's request and immediately said he'd be honored. Now Rob had a friend in Montana by the name of Sam Birky and asked Leroy if it would be okay to invite Sam to Leroy's wedding. Of course, Leroy said yes.

Leroy learned that Sam was a Navy SEAL during the Vietnam war, then he was an airborne, and finally became an Army Colonel Chaplain. Sam was an interesting guy and Leroy discovered that Leroy's dad not only knew Sam but had made friends with him over a common love of fishing and hunting. It turned out that each of them had rights to property containing choice fishing and hunting spots, which formed an instant bond between them, allowing them to enjoy both spots together. I think they call that a symbiotic relationship.

Another who would attend Leroy's and Lenora's wedding was Clint Branger. Clint was a founding member of the Professional Bull Riding club. He was a famous bull rider, having been the only one ever to ride Bodacious to a full 8 second count. Clint had been a family friend forever and Leroy took him for granted. Clint had taken lead on a few cattle drives that Leroy had helped with but the extent of their relationship ended there. Clint was a ranch owner and would often lease land for grazing from Leroy's dad. But the moment Leroy introduced Lenora to Clint Branger, Lenora got all starstruck and said back to Clint, "You are THE Clint Branger. You are really THE Clint Branger. Check this out Clint." Lenora pulled out her phone and pulled up a bunch of videos she has saved. What are these videos? The videos are of Clint Branger riding Bodacious to 8 seconds. Leroy simply did not know what to make of that. Lenora had a picture of Leroy covered in green slime she had acquired while cleaning the koi pond, but she had no videos of Leroy accomplishing any miraculous feats of daring. That might not be completely Lenora's fault seeing as most of Leroy's feats were never captured on video for posterity. But nonetheless, to add insult to injury, there's the fact that Clint was more handsome than Leroy. Leroy is still a little befuddled by all that!

At the wedding, Lenora had her best friend M.J. as her Best Lady. Pastor Bob Bilue was the head of the little Christian Church in Luther, Montana. As the ceremony began, Leroy read a lengthy set of vows and it was clear that while the preacher had a lot more to say on marriage, Leroy had already covered them in his marriage vows, so Bill just pronounced them married, Leroy and Lenora said their "I Do's" and the wedding was over. As we remember, the Catholic Church had not yet granted an annulment to Leroy, so even though they couldn't be married in the faith of their choice, Leroy and Lenora took this experience as the next best option and enjoyed every moment of their uniquely special day.

It was not long after Leroy and Lenora had gotten married that Rob's brother, Leroy, and many friends and family began to coach Rob about the drawbacks of being single, and little by little Rob became convinced that female companionship could be advantageous. While Leroy never knew the whole story, Rob met a Russian woman and was certain they would make very good companions. Everyone approved as she was a perfect fit for Rob and Rob is such a kind and loving man, it was obvious that he was a good fit for her as well. Soon the date was set for the wedding and Leroy flew into San Antonio, Texas to be Rob's Best Man. When he got there, Leroy rented a large minivan in anticipation of playing cab driver for any or all of the folks coming to attend the wedding, should they need it. The investment turned out well as Leroy shuttled Sam Birky, Rob, and several of Rob's buddies, to a small town with more bars than gas stations. Leroy had been sober for just a short time at this point and what encouraged him to maintain his sobriety during the weekend was when Sam Birky said, "Leroy, I like you so much better when you are sober. I'm very proud of your choice to quit drinking." Interestingly, Rob had a ton of friends at his wedding, which was no surprise given how darn likable he was. But what did feel like a disappointment to Leroy, was that over the entire weekend's festivities, there were no fights or property damage. Leroy had made sure those things always existed at his parties.

As of today, Rob is still happily married to his Russian Enchantress. He has a black Labrador for a son. He got a degree in Food Service, but Leroy does not think he knows what he wants to do with it. At one time there was talk of serving Brats and Beer from his food truck, but what Leroy hears today from Rob is that those activities are too hard to accomplish.

Leroy gives his buddy a call, but not nearly often enough. Regardless, this is one friendship that will stand the test of time.

THE END

Paul Spencer

His Name Was Bruce

Leroy and Commander Bruce Becker met 20 years ago from the time this is being written. I am certain we all would acknowledge that if a person appears so vividly in one's memory after 20 years, there's a good chance that person really did you wrong and given an opportunity to destroy them, you would be tempted to take it. Thank God this is not the case with Bruce.

Commander Bruce Becker was the Engineering Officer for the USS Sacramento. To fully appreciate Bruce's talent and love for military service, one needs to know that Bruce had enlisted in the Navy just as Leroy had done. Knowing Bruce worked as an underwater welder, Leroy knew that Bruce was among the elite. There is no room for error, no forgiveness when working with the high voltage power required to weld underwater. Second and equally important is that the option for a failure of a weld in the hull of the ship was simply not an option. The military demanded perfection of its workers, but in this case, perfection actually had to be achieved.

Bruce quickly rose to the rank of Chief which is the same rank Leroy held at the time he worked for Commander Becker. After Bruce made Chief, an enlisted rank, he applied for Limited Duty Officer and specifically an Engineering Officer which is a promotion granted through a presidential commission. Bruce quickly rose through the ranks to achieve Commander which is the highest achievable rank within the Limited Duty Officer program that one could achieve. It was a rank that paid quite well and while you wouldn't exactly call Bruce a tightwad, Leroy was convinced Bruce had the first dollar he ever earned.

Bruce was friends with the Assistant Supply Officer and they regularly attended church together. One day out of the blue, Bruce asked Leroy, "What do you think of the Supply Officer?" Leroy did think of the Supply Officer often. The Supply Officer was a woman who was about 30 pounds over her optimum weight and 20 pounds of that was in her breasts. She was not homely but there was something about her that was damn sure scary looking, if that was your thing. Remember the story *Hertric and the Heavyset Woman*? Women of this size were Leroy's thing.

Leroy gave Bruce his answer saying, "I think when she walks down the hallway, it looks like two racoons wrestling in a gunny sack." That was a most accurate description actually.

Now before moving the story forward, Leroy has one more Supply Officer story to tell. One afternoon Leroy was half asleep on the liberty boat which took sailors to shore so they could enjoy the festivities in the grand city of Singapore. There was a new policy that ordered all sailors to pair up when on shore, and therefore, Leroy was supposed to have a buddy with him. Leroy was not happy with this new policy which, to him, took the joy out of enjoying the sights like every other adult American visiting Singapore could do. It wasn't like they were visiting Baghdad. Singapore is among the safest cities in the world. Compare Singapore to American cities. How many shootings in the cities of America? Right. In Singapore, how many shootings? Zero!

With that rant said, Leroy is awakened from his slumber on the liberty boat by none other than Janis the Supply Officer. She is now in civilian clothes with accentuated breasts that would put Dolly Parton to shame. Janis looked Leroy in the eye and said, "What's your name?"

Somewhat confused, Leroy answers, "Ma'am, you know my name. I'm Chief Leroy."

Janis snaps back, "No. I want your real name! Don't worry, I won't bite. We both need a buddy to go out in town is all!" Leroy told Janis his first name which is Leroy and then he explained to Janis that he did not have a partner because he was not going to leave the liberty launch which was like a mini food court and social area. There was plenty of alcohol there.

Janis said, "Not an option Leroy. I want to go out have a nice meal with drinks, get a couple of motel rooms, one for you and one for me, so let's go. I have all your expenses covered." This was text book fraternization but Leroy figured that the worst that would happen is there would be a flood of rumors flying around, but everyone was too afraid of Janis to even think of crossing her. Including Leroy. After a few days of on shore debauchery, Janis and Leroy rolled back to the ship practically hand in hand.

Six months later, the ship arrived in Bremerton, Washington and shortly after their arrival in Bremerton, the Ship's Christmas Party was held. This event was pretty awesome and the entire ship's crew and their families were invited. The menu included Prime Rib, Sea Food galore and whatever else might whet your appetite, including all the free alcohol you can drink. There was dancing and games for the adults and games galore for the kids. Leroy feasted on his prime rib as he surveyed the room, when who does he spot? Janis, dressed in a shiny red and green dress for the Christmas holiday! Leroy does not see any Mr. Janis and for a moment thinks that maybe a repeat of Singapore could be in order. Sadly, for Leroy, Mr. Janis does appear, and Leroy soon learned he was losing another booty call. The worst of it came next when the entire command was looking at Janis's husband and noticeably chuckling. This all came together when Leroy finally got a look at Mr. Janis. Leroy whispered, "What the hell! He has curly blond hair like me, he is skinny just like me, and he looks like he is the same height as I am." Leroy looked down and said, slightly louder than before, "AND he even dresses like me!" Leroy made the hypothesis that her choosing Leroy for a liberty buddy was not a random choice. Not that Leroy was complaining. Leroy shared this story because Commander Becker teased him about it ruthlessly, every chance he had.

Going back to the story, Leroy arrived on the USS Sacramento shortly after Commander Becker had taken charge as the Chief Engineer. Leroy was confused right off wondering, "How come Commander Becker was the Chief Engineer? I'm an Engineering Chief. Why not me?" The best explanation Leroy could come up with was that Bruce was a commissioned Commander and Leroy was an enlisted Chief.

Commander Becker assigned Chief Leroy to the Ship's Refueling System, or RACE for short. Bruce's decision was based on the fact that there was no Chief in charge of RACE division and there were two other Chiefs still on board to handle the propulsion engineering plants. This meant Leroy was going to get a crash course in fuel delivery and receipt which involved millions of gallons of fuel. Plus, if you spill so much as a thimble full you will bring shame onto the Commanding Officer for poisoning the ocean. So why would Leroy not have complete confidence in his wisdom and minutes of experience? Bruce pulled aside the division First Class Petty Officer who was Leroy's Second in command. His name was Nelson and he was a great second in command. Most of Leroy's responsibilities were taken care of without Leroy even knowing about them due to the competence of Petty Officer Nelson. When it came time for Nelson's advancement, a well written Fitness Report was the key, and Leroy was good at making a well written Fitness Report.

Meanwhile back to Bruce's approach to Petty Officer Nelson. Bruce shook hands and pulled Nelson into him whispering, "Chief Leroy is going to come down here to the control room and frantically ask you what stations starboard are designated JP5. When he asks, you tell him stations 5 and 5A. I want you to follow, though not to close behind, and wait until he goes to the bridge to tell me where the stations are at. You got it Petty Officer Nelson?"

Nelson said to Bruce, "But Sir, you already know all these fuel stations better than we do."

Bruce barks back, "Just follow orders! Now when I enter the bridge, I want you to approach Leroy and tell him you gave him the wrong stations and then give him the correct stations, which are 8 and 8A, okay?" Petty Officer Nelson's brain finally lurched into gear. This was not the first time that he had seen Commander Becker play a well-executed practical joke on who he perceived as the most in need of adjustment and education. This was often the new guy.

The day had come when Leroy would be the RACE Chief in charge of delivering 1.2 million gallons to the coalition ship, in perhaps 4 hours, possibly less, given the situation. Things move fast and it was extremely dangerous work. Leroy had set up the proper fueling stations for delivery to a coalition ship and Nelson, of course, was the real kingpin of the operation. Leroy looked up and said to himself, "Speaking of Petty Officer Nelson, why is he rushing towards me waving his hands?" Chief Leroy annoyingly said to Petty Officer Nelson, "What is it, Nelson?"

Nelson deserved a DiCaprio as he feigned stress in his voice, "I gave you the wrong stations. I gave you 5 and 5A and they're the wrong stations! The correct ones are 8 and 8A!" Leroy immediately panicked and began to sprint across the Weather Decks to the Bridge. Weather Decks are what you call any surface that gets wet and are designed to prevent slips and falls. Leroy got to the wing on the Starboard Side of the bridge but could not physically reach Commander Becker. Leroy could swear that Bruce could see him but Bruce was just standing there, shooting the shit with the Commanding Officer. Chief Leroy finally managed to squeeze through the crowd and get within earshot of Commander Becker.

In as low a voice as possible, Chief Leroy said, "Sir, Stations 8 and 8A are the two stations we are supposed to use."

Commander Becker just looked at Chief Leroy and said, "I know."

Leroy left the bridge feeling a bit ashamed. He knew that anything of the magnitude involved in moving a ton of fuel needed to be in writing, with a step-by-step procedure. Step one was to give your boss the correct information.

Chief Leroy went to the Chief Engineer and as was the norm, Bruce invited Leroy in and offered him a seat. Bruce asked Leroy, "What's on your mind?"

Leroy, feeling ashamed, said, "I screwed up today sir! I told you the wrong fueling stations just before we were to begin refueling."

Bruce asked Leroy, "Who gave you the wrong info?"

Leroy smiled, suddenly assuming this may have been some sort of shenanigan and said, "Sir, no one to blame but me. I thought I had the stations memorized but I did not. I am certain my LPO saved my ass."

Bruce calmly asked, "What have you learned from all of this?"

Leroy looked down at the floor and said, "Never guess if I have a question. If I do not know something, then simply say that I don't know and go find out the answer as soon as I am able."

Commander Becker was testing Leroy to see if he would rat out the Leading Petty Officer who had given him the wrong valves to align, but Leroy knew better than to blame his subordinate when it was, he himself who should have given his Leading Petty Officer the proper valves to align the fuel to for the purpose of delivering fuel to the coalition ship.

Commander Becker was happy to mentor Chiefs and Junior Officers. When Commander Becker needed to align his agenda, he was also skilled at manipulating Senior Officers. Leroy had already learned of the unwavering confidence that the Commanding Officer had in Commander Becker. This allowed Commander Becker a great deal of latitude with decisions that might otherwise require continual requests for permission to do one thing or another. Instead, Commander Becker would report to the Commanding Officer that he was doing a repair or activity as opposed to having to ask permission and then wait for permission before being able to carry out the repair or action.

One morning Leroy walked across the bow of the USS Sacramento and noticed the ship was not sitting straight up and down. The ship had a 7-degree list towards the pier and if this percentage got worse it could snap mooring lines and the ship could eventually come to rest at an angle on the pier. This was an extremely dangerous situation. As soon as Leroy got to the Quarter Deck, the watch stander told Leroy to go see Commander Becker in his office ASAP. Leroy still had on his civilian clothes as he always changed into his uniform when he got to his locker in his living quarters, but Leroy felt the sense of urgency in the air, especially the air of a ship about to tip over onto the pier. Leroy knocked at Commander Becker's office door, went in and sat down. Leroy asked, "Sir, what is going on?"

Commander Becker answered in detail. "The new hydraulic operated fuel valves that were installed at the bottom of the fuel tanks appear to be leaking and several full tanks are equalizing fuel level with empty tanks. As this is happening, the fuel distribution is not correct which means we are unable to keep the ship on an even keel.

The solution to this mess was to pump each tank dry without overflowing any other fuel tank. An overflow of even a thimble of fuel into the water of the bay would incur a huge fine, not to mention that the environmentalists, furious that fuel had been dumped in the water, would promptly put an entire carton's worth of egg on the Commanding Officer's face. Commander Becker revealed that he had worked in RACE division, so obviously he did not need the valve numbers he had asked Leroy to retrieve. As a result of Bruce's knowledge of RACE division, he went over which tanks would be pumped out first and then repaired. Once a tank was repaired and no longer had valves leaking, Bruce would order Leroy to fill the repaired fuel tank to the capacity needed to balance the ship straight up and down and get rid of the 7-degree list. One challenge to this fuel transfer was that when they first started emptying out the tanks one by one in order to make repairs to the hydraulic valves, the ship might list beyond 7 degrees. The degree of list was unknown so communications were set up to monitor and control the fuel tanks as well as to monitor and control the list of the ship.

When everything was in place to make the repairs to the first tanks valves, Leroy climbed down a metal ladder which was fastened to the wall inside the fuel tank. The ladder was horribly slippery due to it being covered with fuel most of the time. No one would be making a mad dash out of the fuel tank on this ladder. To make matters even more harrowing, the valves in the fuel tank that Leroy had to repair were on the opposite side of the escape ladder. Leroy was the only one on the ship who had been educated on these valves. In simple terms there were three Allen screws that needed to be adjusted in unison. In other words, Leroy turned 1 Allen screw at a time, each time turning them just a skosh, repeating the pattern until the fuel stopped pouring out of the valve that was showing closed on the monitor in the operating center but was actually open. The real fear factor of this job was the location of the ladder. If Leroy couldn't fix the multiple valves that were pouring fuel into the tank, then the fuel tank would rapidly fill, trapping Leroy in the tank, because a person sinks in fuel, meaning that one cannot swim in fuel.

As Leroy got each valve to shut correctly, he would have the folks in Fuel Control, operate the valve multiple times until the valve had tested fully functional. As the tank Leroy fixed began to refill, the ship started to right itself and the 7-degree list started to improve. Over the next 5 days, Leroy would complete this process until all leaking fuel valves were fully functional and could be successfully operated remotely. The other Chiefs all got to know Chief Leroy really well as he constantly reeked of diesel fuel as a result of his daily task of fixing fuel tank valves. The other Chiefs yelled at Leroy, "Can't you put on a clean uniform? You are stinking up the whole "Goat Locker." The name "Goat Locker" is a historical reference from days long gone. Picture a large sailing ship with the dietary mainstay being goats. The area next to the goats is called the Goat Locker and this is where, historically, Chiefs would live while aboard ship. The Chief would then have quick access to the goats for acquiring goat milk and goat meat for personal use, which is how the Chief's quarters came to be called the Goat Locker. Leroy could not smell himself since he was saturated with the smell of fuel from head to toe, but thank goodness the day finally came when the all the valves were fully working as designed and Leroy was able to put on a clean uniform at last, but the best news was about to come. The propulsion chiefs were leaving for their next command and the RACE chief had just arrived. Another new arrival for RACE division was the Fuels Officer, named Chief Warrant Officer Hendershot. There were a whole lot of chief and not a lot of Indians on this ship! Chief Warrant Officer Hendershot was a Limited Duty Officer and reported to Commander Becker. He won't ever command a ship but Chief Warrant Officers can fly aircraft and can command small craft, like a patrol boat for example. Chief Warrant Officers (CWO) can go from a rank of 1 all the way to 5. Getting to CWO5 is a feat. Leroy only saw one man reach this level. Every branch of the service has a Chief Warrant Officer program except for the Air Force.

CWO2 Hendershot was a decent enough guy but he was a horrible micromanager and ran himself ragged during fueling operations, constantly second guessing all of his people. Leroy was down in the Engine Room as the Propulsion Engineering Chief, so he no longer focused on RACE division.

Here is a quick aside: When Leroy was a young sailor his chief had sent him down into the bottom of the ship called the bilge to take a bilge sample. This means filling up a pint-sized glass container with bilge water. Bilge water is nasty. Bilge water contains, urine, feces, oil, fuel, dirt and debris. In a word, filthy. Leroy climbed down into the rancid water and filled his sample container to the rim. He then marked the bottle with the date and time of collection along with other various data points. He took the bilge sample up to his chief where many of Leroy's peers were hanging out, observing. Leroy's Chief laughed out loud as he said, "We got you Leroy! There's no such thing as a bilge sample."

After many years when Leroy himself was a Chief, Commander Becker told Chief Leroy to go get a bilge sample and bring it to him. Leroy raised his voice stating, "I'm not falling for that one again Sir! I know there is no such thing as a bilge sample!"

Commander Becker calmy explained, "For your information, bilge samples are now a requirement before pumping bilge water over board." Years later, pumping any bilge water into the ocean would become illegal. Commander Becker gave Leroy a final note saying, "Besides all the above, I need you to get me a bilge sample because I told you to do so."

Commander Becker had Leroy's complete respect and Leroy did not hesitate as he hauled butt down to the bilge and drew a sample of filth that looked like a pile of rust all sitting in the bottom of the sample. He rushed the bilge sample back up to Commander Becker who said to Chief Leroy, "Have a seat if you want. Just keep your mouth shut NO MATTER WHAT." Leroy knew what that meant better than most, having worked for Commander Becker for quite some time at this point of the story. Commander Becker took a fuel sample bottle and opened it on his desk. The bottle was only half full. Commander Becker then took the bilge sample and drained about 2/3 of the water into his trash can, so that what was left in the bilge water sample was a great deal of rust and dirt and debris. Commander Becker carefully poured the bilge sample into the fuel sample bottle until the fuel sample was the correct amount as indicated on the sample bottle. Commander Becker asked Chief Leroy, "Hey, can I use your grease pencil?" Commander Becker wrote on the fuel sample bottle, now full of dirt, the data for the sample which included the fuel tank it came from, the date and time of collection, and when the sample gets centrifuged, the % of water and contaminants is also recorded.

Soon the refueling process commenced and Chief Leroy assumed his position as the Restricted Maneuvering Engineering Officer of the Watch. This watch position ran the engine room and additionally any time the ship was going to be maneuvering up next to a collation ship at 35 MPH, or pulling toward or away from the pier or traversing in a Sound where maneuverability was quite tight, the watch position was in charge of that. After everyone involved had delivered close to 2 million gallons of fuel to one USS Aircraft

Carriers, Commander Becker called for Chief Leroy again. When Leroy arrived at Commander Becker's office, per their previous conversation, he sat in the corner and kept his mouth shut. Commander Becker picked up the JDial. (phone) and called Chief Warrant Officer Hendershot and told him to come to the Chief Engineer's office. Then Commander Becker pulled the sabotaged fuel sample out of his desk drawer. Soon Warrant Officer Hendershot appeared at Commander Becker's door. Commander Becker picked up the filthy fuel sample and told Warrant Officer Hendershot, "You are going to take this filthy sample up to the Commanding Officer and show him the contaminated fuel we just gave to one of our air craft carriers." Warrant Hendershot was beside himself, and his micromanagement failure was about to make Warrant Officer Hendershot explode. After all, he did not make mistakes. Warrant Officer Hendershot took the nasty fuel sample and headed to the bridge to show the Commanding Officer what he had just delivered to the Aircraft Carrier.

Chief Leroy said to Commander Becker, "Isn't that a little rough on him sir? And what is the Commanding Officer going to say?"

Commander Becker just chuckled as he said, "You think I didn't brief the skipper first?"

Leroy thought, "Of course he would."

Commander Becker finished this with, "Hendershot is just too uptight. He needs to relax a little, and this ought to take him down a sizable notch." Leroy never did hear the final outcome of that practical joke, but years later, Norm Hendershot would retire to a spread of land with a nice house in Spokane, Washington. He turned out to be a righteous leader and is a friend to Leroy to this day.

A few months went by and Leroy discovered there was a need for a steam pipe hanger. A steam pipe hanger is flexible because as the pipe it holds heats and cools, the pipe moves significantly. The hanger itself has a spring assembly that holds the pipe relatively stable but it is able to move and flex with the movement of the pipe. This pipe hanger needs to be welded onto a solid metal surface so Leroy went to the Chief Welder on board the ship and asked for help getting the pipe hanger welded. Perhaps you've picked up on how great Leroy gets along with and respects certain people. To merit Leroy's respect, people must care about others and help where they can, as opposed to those who are turd anchovies who may have intelligence but have chosen to care for no one but themselves, and if in business, that extends to the customers they are supposed to be taking care of. Leroy possesses a 3rd grade education so intelligence might be better termed common sense. We have seen all intelligent people who lack all degree of common sense, as well as many "stupid" people who have great common sense. It was easy to be a good person. You simply treat others the way you want to be treated. There are many people who have treated Leroy like shit, so he figured that is how they want to be treated and he was more than happy to give that treatment to them full on! He was way better at this than the turd anchovies would ever be.

With all that said, Leroy did not like the Chief Welder one bit. This chief thought his job was not to help out his shipmates with welding and fabrication, but to find excuses not to weld stuff. A perfect example of the Chief Welder's laziness and self-centeredness was demonstrated one day when Leroy went to the Chief Welder and asked him, "Why can't you weld this pipe hanger so I can safely mount the pipe before it ruptures and kills people?"

Chief Welder responded, "There is a fuel tank on the other side of that metal."

Leroy replied, "There's a two-foot barrier between the fuel tank and the metal overhead where I need the pipe hanger welded. Plus, you can see scabs of other welding on the metal surface. Please take a look at it."

Chief Welder, "Leroy, I already told you no. Now piss off."

Given Leroy's quick qualifications for friendship, how likely was it that Chief Welder would be considered a friend to Leroy? Leroy went to Commander Becker and told him of his plight in getting the steam pipe hanger installed. Commander Becker picked up the Jdial and called the Chief Welder, and ordering him to his office. Soon the Chief Welder arrived and Commander Becker asked the Chief Welder, "What is going on with this pipe hanger that Chief Leroy needs welded?"

Chief Welder said, "I told Chief Leroy that there's a fuel tank on the other side and we cannot weld on that surface."

Chief Leroy responded," I put hands on Commander, and the fuel tank is a full 2 feet from the weld point. One can see other welding on the surface and it's most important to get this pipe hanger installed so as to eliminate a dangerous situation. A pipe swaying in the wind, is a time bomb just waiting to rupture and cook all the sailors in the room with steam."

Commander Becker said to the Welder Chief, "Take me down to the location we are questioning."

The Welder Chief said to Chief Leroy, "So take us down there Leroy."

Commander Becker sternly pointed to the Welder Chief and said, "Excuse me there Chief. I told you to show me the location!" Leroy knew exactly what Bruce was up to. This jackass Chief Welder didn't know where to take the boss because he would never go down in the engine room with Leroy and look at it.

The Chief Welder looked embarrassed as his eyes went to the ground in shame. He had no choice but to come clean with the Chief Engineer and say, "I have never been down there to look at it before, so I'm not sure where it's at."

Commander Becker spoke to the turd master Welding Chief, "Very interesting, very interesting. Leroy, is this safe to weld?"

Leroy said, "Yes sir, it is safe to weld."

Commander Becker looked the Chief Welder in the eye and said, "Get down there and weld that pipe hanger today. When you are done, you are to report to me and I will inspect it personally." (Remember Bruce was an underwater welder.) As a result of this, thanks to Commander Becker Leroy had Mr. Welder Dude in his back pocket forever more.

After 2 years of duty, Leroy departed the ship, going onto another ship of the same class and once again triumph as a second time winner of the Land Speed Record. See the story *Two Time Land Speed Winner.*

After a tour of duty on board the USS Camden Leroy would then go to Afghanistan for a year and a half, after training at the Army installation in Fort Jackson. Many a story has been written about those adventures.

Time flew by and before he knew it, Leroy was back at Naval Base Kitsap near his house in Port Orchard, WA. Leroy had made Senior Chief and was now one rank away from reaching the highest rank an enlisted person could achieve. During this tour of duty, Leroy was in charge of base operations for Naval Base Kitsap. One of his primary duties was to sit as a judge for the base traffic court. As Leroy performed the duty of Traffic Court Judge, Leroy quickly ascertained that the command did not really want him adjudicating parking tickets with a guilty verdict. Every time Chief Leroy took a bunch of people's driving privileges away because the people had four or more parking tickets, The Command would tell Leroy to reinstate them. It did not take Leroy long to see what was going on. When a sailor's driving privileges got suspended, they stayed suspended, but when a civilian shipyard person got enough tickets to result in a suspension, and Leroy suspended them, only to have the Command suddenly reverse the suspensions. Most times these people would go out and get more tickets. Leroy would suspend them again, only to have his legal decisions overturned time and time again. Leroy also took care of drug testing, and was in charge of building new parking structures. Naval Base Kitsap was short nearly 2K parking spaces for the people who lived and worked there so Leroy had come up with a parking pass for swing shift, mid shift, and day shift. This helped open up parking to a limited extent except on the rare occasion when all shifts had to come to work at once.

Leroy also attended all the shipyard meetings to address any needs that fell into his swim lane. It seemed that 99% of the attendees at any given meeting were arrogant to the max and looked down on Leroy in such an agonizingly cold and cruel way that Leroy found himself with little to no motivation for taking care of them. Yet this was his mission, and he was expected to execute it with zero support. In fact, there was the opposite of support. There was what felt like sabotage. When they repeatedly let parking violators go free then bitch incessantly about illegal parking taking away all the ship yard parking, Leroy was left with what felt like a case of the pot calling the kettle black. Chief Leroy, who can be vindictive as you well know, decided to tell the sailors they could park in the civilian lots. Then when the civilian drivers were forced to park in the military parking lot, Leroy had his enforcement staff nail as many of these civilian drivers as they possibly could.

Eventually, at the end of the month, the shipyard managers from the Shipyard and Operations Management at Naval Base Kitsap met in a conference room. Leroy had started to make an introduction when the shipyard leader cut Leroy off and said, "We don't have time for all that. We need to know why there are these sailors parked in our lots, forcing us to park in military parking and get ticketed."

Suddenly a voice from the past came from outside the circle of trust. Leroy recognized this voice coming from the back of the shipyard mob. It was none other than his old boss, now retired Bruce Becker, who was speaking. Leroy could not believe that Bruce could be the enemy representing the shipyard. But much to Chief Leroy's surprised ears, Bruce Becker was defending Leroy. Bruce said, "Sounds like if folks park illegally they should have their driving privilege on base revoked. Then there would be no need for any more of these warnings. Secondly, if sailors cease to exist floating around in ships, guess who is going to become obsolete right alongside of them? You are, all of you! So why don't we all get along? Seems like we need each other." Leroy really hoped Bruce would have some influence on this group which was demonstrating a complete lack of integrity and brain function. With zero support from Leroy's own command, he eventually accepted that what his command wanted him to do was to accomplish the impossible. Leroy had proposed building several parking garages, and two were actually built. One was for the civilian shipyard workers and one was for the sailors.

Before too long Leroy had had enough of office politics. Many of Leroy's shipmates had warned him he would not do well behind a desk and that office politics would eat him up. At the time, Leroy figured they were probably right but this was a way he could be present and care for his daughters who were struggling with all things teenager. Leroy felt optimistic that he could intervene in a way that would save his daughters from the demons they were tangled with, but come to find out, Leroy was as ineffective at this endeavor as he was at trying to unite the shipyard and garner some support from the Command.

Finally, Leroy decided it was time to go do what he did best and leave for Afghanistan again. That was not hard to do because even Leroy's Command had no say in Leroy's decision. Once Leroy signed up for the Individual Augmentation Program, he now belonged to the US Army and would report to Fort Jackson for the training pertaining to his assignment. In the interim, Bruce Becker and Leroy began to have lunch together fairly often. Bruce Becker always drank iced tea and at the time Leroy did not think twice about pounding a bunch of beers. Looking back, Leroy suspected Bruce did not drink alcohol, and felt a bit guilty that he drank in front of Bruce. If Leroy and Bruce ever meet again then there will be no odd moments. Leroy has been sober 8 years now. Bruce would also take Leroy to his house, which was what they would now call a hobby farm, complete with ducks and a few head of cattle, a mule, and various other creatures both furred and feathered.

Over the course of a couple months, Leroy waited for his assignment to Afghanistan to come to fruition and during that time Leroy spent most of his afternoons in the base club drinking copious amounts of beer. One afternoon, Leroy decided he would run for President of the Chief Petty Officer Association. There were about 60 Chiefs that made up the command and a surprising amount of them drank with the same fervor and enthusiasm as Leroy. Leroy was subsequently voted in as President of the Chief Petty Officer Association, and took on the accompanying duties like setting up retirement ceremonies, award ceremonies, and plain old get-togethers to eat and drink. These gatherings were Leroy's favorite part of the job. Now Chief Shawn was the Secretary Treasurer of the Chief Petty Officer Association, and regularly advised Leroy and guided him through all the duties of the job of President. Shawn and Leroy sadly lost touch but Shawn was a huge help to Leroy.

One day while Leroy was into his 4th microbrew beer, the duty phone Leroy was to monitor began ringing. Leroy answered the phone, "Senior Chief Leroy here."

The voice on the phone responded, "Is this Leroy?"

Leroy grew suspicious and answered back with, "Yes, this is Leroy."

The phone voice responded, "Oh good, good. Some of my partners and I have been watching you lead the physical fitness program. We think you would be perfect for us."

Curious now, Leroy says, "What's this all about?"

The speaker on the other end of the phone reached out to Leroy and said, "We think you would make the perfect model for our line of Speedos." Leroy had been looking at a billboard on his way to work and the billboard showed a wiry, well-muscled, guy wearing a Speedo.

Leroy thought for a moment and then said, "Heck yeah. Why not? Sure! I'll do it!"

There is a delay, presumably while the caller was holding his hand over the speaker and laughing out loud. Finally, Bruce Becker could not hold it in any more. He gave an enthusiastic guffaw and said, "Leroy, I can't help you with your blossoming underwear career but I would like to buy you lunch, ok?"

Leroy excitedly said, "Heck yeah Bruce! That would be great you dirty rotten donkey's ass."

On a final note, Leroy was absolutely envious at how Commander Becker was able to tell people to go to hell in such a way that the people would not only ask for directions, but look forward to the journey. Leroy cannot recall a single incident where Commander Becker raised his voice or lost his cool or even showed some excitement. It was that calm that made Commander Becker quite intimidating. Commander Becker was always, unquestionably in charge because folks were glad to follow a competent and wise man who they knew would always have their backs.

THE END

Author's Note:

This is one of my favorite stories in this edition. This story has very little embellishment. All went down as written. I still keep in touch with Bruce and look forward to giving him a copy of this book. This story demonstrates that a competent and wise supervisor is not simply a total joy to work for, but they will keep you alive a whole lot longer as well.

His Name Was Dad

It took a great deal of courage for me to write about Leroy's dad. The relationship had been and continues to be complicated between Leroy and his dad. Leroy's dad got angry when Leroy made reference to Leroy being the son of a wealthy rancher from Montana, because apparently, Leroy's dad did not realize the magnitude of wealth he held. When he looked off the porch of the ranch house, on his left he had a magnificent view of great mountains rising to the skies, and as he looked to the right, there was the East Rosebud River, replete with brown and rainbow trout. Leroy's dad did not see his wealth in having two separate winter homes in Arizona, both of which Leroy and his dad had restored together. And if you can believe it, during that whole time, they got along splendidly. The projects flowed like milk and honey to completion.

Leroy had met his wife Lenora via email when he was in Afghanistan and had courted her for 8 months over that media. Among the plethora of proposed agreements that Leroy presented to Lenora, one of these was the agreement that Lenora would move to Montana and Leroy would build a spacious ranch style home on a piece of his dad's ranch. Leroy would show Lenora the location when they went to visit. Leroy had dreamed of building on this site since he was a young man. Leroy had shown his father his dream and his dad said, "Yes, I too have considered this location. It's just hard to get in and out of." To Leroy, this difficulty with access was among the most beneficial reasons to live there.

Leroy returned from Afghanistan with injuries sustained during his tour. After surgery and some rest and recovery, Leroy retired from the military after 23 years and had moved in with Lenora. Leroy was anxious to show Lenora the ranch so when Leroy's father told Leroy he was in Hawaii using his timeshare and that Leroy and Lenora were welcome to use the house in his absence, Leroy took Lenora to Montana, and to the ranch, hoping she would fall in love both with Leroy and the ranch. On one fateful day, Leroy and Lenora decided to use Leroy's old bedroom to try and make baby rabbits. At age 60 for Meg and age 46 for Leroy, it was highly unlikely they would succeed, but they had decided to die trying. Little did they know that they would come all too close to fulfilling that prophecy of almost dying.

Just as Leroy and Lenora finished playing "The Rabbit and the Hare," Leroy and Lenora heard a frantic rapping on the screen door accompanied by muffled shouts that sounded quite urgent. Leroy put his clothes on and attempted, without success, to straighten out his hair. Still moving a bit slowly after the recent rabbit race, Leroy made his way to the door and opened it wide. Leroy recognized the folks at the door as neighbors who lived some distance further up the valley. They were shouting through the screen door before Leroy could even get it open, "There's a fire on the west rim of your ranch Leroy. Where's your dad?"

Leroy looked sheepishly at his neighbors and said, "My dad is in Hawaii and won't be back until tonight. Lenora and I are using my old bedroom while my folks are away. I'll go get some gear and go work on the fire."

Leroy asked Lenora if she wanted to accompany him to the wiener roast, while muttering to himself, "I hope it's not my wiener getting roasted!" Leroy and Lenora arrived on the fire trail, which is simply a trail where the grass gets plowed down to dirt, and is designed to keep a fire from spreading. Just below the fire trail, Leroy and Lenora saw the fire bordering the ranch. At this point the fire was just a grass fire. Lenora sat in the ATV, or Jitney as it is called in Montana, and watched as Leroy hightailed it down the hill with a big flat blade shovel in hand. As soon as Leroy arrived at the fire, he began tamping it out with the shovel. Leroy's efforts were proving effective and before long he had tamped out nearly 1/3 of the fire and was making good progress on the other 2/3. Suddenly, out of nowhere, several helicopters appeared coming over the ridge from the river. They were each carrying a metal bucket of water that they had filled in the deep parts of the East Rosebud River. Each bucket would contain roughly 500 gallons of river water providing the pilot is able to fill it completely.

As the helicopters started to get where Lenora could see them, she began to wave and point at Leroy as if to say, "Watch out for my husband!"

What all of the pilots saw on their end was, "Hey! Look at that crazy woman with the red hair! She wants us to dump water on her husband to protect him from the fire. Or maybe she's just mad at him, or maybe it's something else, but let's help her out." In truth, not being able to hear her, the pilots figured there could be any number of reasons she would want water dumped on Leroy and were more than willing to cooperate.

Moments later, the opening music from Apocalypse Now started to play from the heavens and the helicopters converged over Leroy, dropping nearly 1,500 gallons of river water on top of him. This was no joke! Water is heavy! The water knocked Leroy to the muddy ground and swirled him around like it was about to wash him down some drain. As the helicopter pilots retreated, Leroy raised his hand to the sky to say, "Thank you." Leroy thought that Lenora's urging to the pilots had been heeded, leading to their generous and precise delivery of 1,500 gallons of nearly freezing melt water from the mountains. At least the water was crystal clear, or is until it hits the mud.

Meanwhile the pilots were all thinking, "I wonder what that moron did to his girlfriend to piss her off to the point that she directed us to dump our payload on her boyfriend?"

True to form, Leroy would quickly get his revenge on Lenora for that stunt, even though Lenora was actually trying to tell the pilots that Leroy was down in the fire and not to dump water on him.

Then suddenly and without warning, the wind shifted in the direction of Lenora's gas-powered Jitney. There sat Lenora, smack dab in the path of an angry new push of fire. Seeing that, Leroy dropped everything and began running full speed towards Lenora. The water that had been dumped on Leroy's clothes was now shedding wild droplets in all directions as he ran. Watching Leroy, one couldn't help but make a comparison between Leroy and that of a long-haired dog after emerging from a pond who was shaking its entire body all at once. Can you picture this in slow motion?

Lenora only had eyes for the fire. She made a quick study of the Jitney, started it and then immediately jammed it into gear and pulled away from the path of fire, leaving Leroy in the middle of the growing fire wall. Leroy's shovel for tamping out the grass fire was down the hill where he dropped it as he had charged toward Lenora, and totally useless to Leroy at this time. Fortunately, moments later a Forest Service water truck came up the fire road and Leroy was able to direct them to the fire that Leroy had narrowly escaped.

As evening started to settle into the valley, Leroy felt confident that the fire was well enough contained that he could go back to the ranch house and clean up. He was relieved that the fire was being well tended by the Forest Service fire fighters. Leroy and Lenora returned to the ranch house and not only was Leroy's face black with soot, he was wet and covered in mud from his helicopter shower. Even covered in grime and smelling of smoke, Leroy had a sense of accomplishment.

Later that evening, Leroy's dad returned from his trip to Hawaii, already having heard about the fire. Immediately Leroy's dad began to make all sorts of preparations for fighting and preventing the fire from reaching the ranch house. He rigged a large plastic tank on his 4-wheel drive ATV, and then filled the tank with water. He hooked a pressure washer suction to the tank and voila, you now have one high-pressure water stream ready to fight the fire. He took his weed eater and cut the grass short all around both the house and the 300-gallon propane tank so as not to feed the fire with the long, dry grass. We won't even think about what might happen if the fire reached the propane tank!

No one got much sleep that night, but what little they got would have to be enough. Early the next morning, Leroy and his dad ventured out to the edge of the Forest Service land to a ridge that overlooked the ranch house. They found numerous unattended hot spots and worked feverishly to extinguish these tinder boxes. All their efforts would be for nought when the Forest Service fire fighters ran Leroy and his dad off the ridge, claiming something about territory and who is supposed to fight the fire.

Leroy and his dad retreated to the ranch house and readied as many hoses as they could find in order to fight the fire that would inevitably be upon them, sooner rather than later. Sadly, the Forest Service failed to stay on top of the areas that were still smoldering. Leroy and his dad knew those hot spots could quickly flash and rekindle the fire, so it came as no surprise to Leroy and his dad when they watched a huge plume of black smoke appear on the ridge, right where the unattended hot spots had been smoldering. It had now obviously flashed up again and reignited the fire, restoring it to all its original glory. It was that fire on the ridge which had caused the sudden cloud of black smoke, and now that smoke and fire were making a fast run towards the ranch house. As Leroy and his dad were getting all their firefighting weapons systems into place, the sheriff showed up. He ran into Lenora first. The sheriff said, "Ma'am, you are going to have to evacuate as soon as possible, and if you stay, I'll need your dental records to identify your body should you not make it out alive!"

Lenora was scared, but what worried her the most was not so much the fire, but what her boyfriend Leroy was going to think, or worse, what her potential father-in-law might think of her if she summarily left both of them on their own, so she stayed put. The sheriff then came to Leroy and his father. Knowing what the sheriff was going to say, Leroy was beginning to chuckle on the inside at the notion of someone telling his dad that he needed to leave his ranch. The sheriff began to talk, but before he could get two words out, Leroy's dad cut the sheriff off and sternly advised the sheriff saying, "First off, you are trespassing on my land. Secondly, all our dental records are protected by HIPPA so you won't be getting them, and finally, you are unnecessarily scaring our guest, so it is time for you to leave. Good Bye." The Sheriff was clearly not happy but he knew his welcome was very much worn out and it was indeed time for him to leave.

As the fire closed in, Leroy and his father skillfully fought the fire with all the tools they'd prepared, and when it was all over, the entire surrounding land was nothing but a charred wasteland. But thanks to the efforts of Leroy and his dad and their skillful preparations there remained a lush green oasis, covering the ground in a 360-degree radius around the ranch house. Leroy and his dad had both been trained in the military to fight oil fires as well as other military oriented fires, so they knew what they were doing. They used their combined skills and their years of knowledge gained through experience, to successfully divide and conquer this fire. They did this herculean task with little verbal communication, and had artfully made sure their efforts were complementary and not a product of a certain flaw embraced by a great many folks, otherwise known as stupidity. Leroy was feeling quite satisfied that he and his dad had coordinated their efforts so well and had managed to prevail over the fire without a word of argument or any feelings of disappointment. Victory!

Leroy then looked up towards the ranch house at the beautiful deck made from decorative stone and some plastic milk bottles that were melted down to look like boards, and there was Lenora with a cloth over her nose and mouth, sitting on a chair and appearing clearly distraught. Leroy ran to Lenora, but it was too little, too late. The damage was done. Lenora was already terrified at the power of the fire and having the stupid sheriff asking her for dental records had not helped. The smoke, the flames and the chaos, all coupled with Lenora's own overactive imagination, had been devastating. She had almost driven away with Leroy's and Lenora's camper van, but had changed her mind and stayed when she saw Leroy fighting the fire. However, any further attempts by Leroy to encourage Lenora to embrace his plan of building the ranch style house he'd always dreamt of, to be located on that special parcel of land on the ranch, had just nosedived.

Leroy knew that a fire had come through the ranch some 25 years earlier and everything had either survived that fire or was rebuilt at the time, so Leroy saw this fire as merely a minor inconvenience. To Leroy, this fire was merely a nuisance compared to living in Western New York where even minor things, which in Leroy's mind includes almost everything, were always a huge inconvenience. When something did not have minor problems, it was because it had major problems which would inevitably end up requiring lawyers and courtrooms and other silly venues to finally make a situation right. Leroy knew a move to Montana would fix all the negativity and conflict he continually felt while living in Western New York, but a fire had just wiped out any chance of that happening. There was no way Lenora would ever feel safe in Montana, knowing that a fire could happen at any moment and in a flash, take away everything and maybe even everyone, she loved. Leroy felt bad that he did not recognize Lenora's fears about the fire, and by not knowing, was therefore unable to put her at ease that it was only a grass fire which is easily contained if one is organized.

Before he had ever met Lenora, it was during a visit to his father that Leroy found the undeniable proof that his dad was a true humanitarian and the best friend anyone could have. One afternoon, Leroy and his dad were taking a little ride together, away from the ranch. Leroy tried to find some common ground with his dad but through no fault of either of them, they simply did not have a lot in common. But on that day, Leroy's dad said, "Hey, my friend Tom needs some help with something. It shouldn't take too long if you'd like to come with me."

Leroy did not care what they would be doing. He was just happy to be home in Montana and sharing some time with his dad, but he was quite surprised when he heard his dad say, "My friend." Leroy didn't recall hearing his father call too many people "friend".

After arriving at Tom's place, Leroy's dad went to work on a plumbing problem under his friend's kitchen sink. As Leroy's dad climbed under the sink with his tools at the ready, Leroy could tell that his dad was in a considerable amount of pain. He could see it on his dad's face each time he climbed in and out from underneath the kitchen sink. Leroy wondered who this guy was that his dad was so willing to be there fixing his sink. All Leroy knew about the man was that his dad's friend was named Tom.

As Leroy's dad continued working on his friend's sink, Leroy found a copy of an issue of *Montana Outdoors* magazine. The magazine focuses on hunting and fishing and expresses concerns about the environment as well as promoting an attitude of conservation. Leroy's favorite stories in the magazine are the ones that inspire the reader. Please keep in mind that Leroy's dad had never made any mention of this article or its contents.

At the time, Leroy didn't have all the details, but knew that Tom had difficulty with speaking and being understood. But nevertheless, while Leroy's dad fixed the sink, Tom tried to overcome his inability to speak as he attempted to communicate with his friend, who happened to be Leroy's dad. Leroy found, to his amazement, that his father was able to communicate quite well with his friend Tom. Leroy figured this was no doubt a result of lots of practice while the two men were spending time together.

As Leroy perused the *Montana Outdoors* magazine, he found an article that really caught his eye. Leroy knew that his dad's friend Tom had become a writer and was writing articles for various magazines pertaining to Montana, such as the magazine Leroy was currently reading, but Leroy had no idea Tom had written an article for this very issue. The article in the *Montana Outdoors* magazine that had caught Leroy's eye was titled, "A Man of God Saves Me and Gives Me Back Life."

As Leroy read the article it took only moments to recognize the article was about Leroy's dad and his friend Tom. Tom had been a driller for natural resources such as natural gas, water, oil, and even did some fracking. He was a seasoned driller. One fateful day, Tom was at the top of the drilling rig when a pocket of natural gas erupted and blew Tom off the rigging. When Tom regained consciousness, his life had changed forever, unfortunately for the worst. He had extensive brain damage and although Leroy was never able to understand him when he spoke, Tom wrote beautifully and eloquently. In the article, Tom went on to explain how he fell into total despair after the accident.

I challenge anyone to experience a disaster such as this and not fall into despair, I certainly did.

Tom's article went on to explain how he had found God and how God would save him from despair. Leroy's dad took Tom to church, he spent quality time with Tom. These two men had developed a true bond and a deep and abiding friendship. One day Leroy's dad asked Tom what he could help him with. Leroy's dad thought Tom might need some sort of home repair or something on that line, but what Tom wanted was not going to be that easy. Tom said, "I want to hunt again. I lived for hunting!" Leroy's dad loved hunting just as much as Tom did and knew what Tom meant, so he thought about it and what he might need to make this happen for Tom.

Leroy's dad went to work, calling in favors and pulling help from his trusted machinists, and before you knew it, Leroy's dad had constructed an elaborate contraption in the back of his truck. It was designed to support Tom in such a way as to allow Tom to once again hunt. Leroy's dad secured Tom in the back of his truck, and explained to Tom how this amazing device would allow Tom to move and brace himself as he fired shots, and how it would do what was needed to allow Tom to put an accurate shot down range. Tom's face beamed with joy. It was a complete and total success and Tom soon had many newly mounted animal trophies in his collection.

Tom closed the article out with this: "A great man took me to church and introduced me to God. Then this great man spent, God only knows how much time and money, building me a device that has allowed me to hunt again. If it was not for this great man, I can only imagine the dark place I would be in. Instead, thanks to the efforts of this man, I am able to experience the joy of hunting regularly and I am no longer a man in despair."

After a couple hours of fixing the plumbing and conversing, Leroy's dad said his goodbyes to his friend Tom, and with that, Leroy and his dad made their way back to the ranch house. Leroy said, "Dad, I read the article Tom wrote about you in the *Montana Outdoors* magazine. Have you seen the article?"

Leroy's dad humbly said, "Yes, I read it. Tom asked me to read it."

A bit annoyed, Leroy said "Why on earth would you not tell me that? You have done the most selfless thing a person can do." Leroy's dad didn't answer. He had done it simply because Tom was his friend. Period.

This just goes to show that the man who would find a way to restore his buddy's ability to hunt after his buddy experienced a life changing event that had made hunting impossible, and then to do it without telling even his own son, is truly a saint. The rest of us would have been tooting our own horns from day one, or more likely, many of us would just have done NOTHING! In Leroy's book, the actions of his dad are what leadership by example means.

THE END

Unlikely Friendships

One of Leroy's college professors by the name of Mark Sample taught American History starting with the end of the Civil War and going up to and including the end of World War II. Professor Sample was bar none the most prepared, most inspirational, and most well-spoken professor on campus. Of all the amazing and beneficial educational gems that Mark provided, the most important was a simple principle to explain why people are so often misunderstood. He wrote on the white board, "Woman without her man is nothing." I know, I know. All the feminist folks are gathering their pitchforks. But this is not all Mark wrote on the white board. He also wrote two variations of the above insulting phrase. The first variation was, "Woman without her man, is nothing." Again, the feminists are at the gate with flaming torches. The second variation goes like this: "Woman, without her, man is nothing." The feminists saw that and cheered. If you look closely, you will see the only difference is in the placement of one comma, but that lowly comma completely changes the meaning of the sentence. The fact is that far too often, major conclusions are often wrongly interpreted simply because of the misplacement or omission of the simple comma. As you read this story, keep an eye out for the commas.

Leroy often frequented Subic Bay, Philippines during liberty port visits for much needed rest and relaxation. Leroy's time as a shipboard sailor was coming to an end with the next phase of Leroy's career soon to take him to Afghanistan to work for the Army. Leroy loved shipboard life a lot and it was going to be a bittersweet departure. He would miss the sea but he would get himself back at the tip of the spear by going to Afghanistan. After docking at Subic Bay, it took a few days for Leroy to get off the ship and when he did, he made a beeline straight to the home of Ronella Punang Bayone. It was the day before Christmas, and Leroy was unable to return to the United States for the holiday. Leroy would be here for few weeks to visit with Ronella and then it was back to work.

Years earlier when Leroy had first come to the Philippines, he had met Ronella. Leroy had been in a bar known as the California Club and Ronella kept bothering him about letting her sit down next to him. She spoke English really well and she was kind but persistent. Leroy never knew when to quit drinking and that night at the California Club was no exception. Leroy was drinking Bullfrog, which is basically a death wish in a bucket for those who dare to drink it. Bullfrog is a complete unknown because it contains a variety of different grains of hard alcohol in it, and because there is no assigned formula to follow when creating it, the alcohol content of Bullfrog varies so much you have no way of knowing how much you can drink without dying. On this particular evening, Leroy felt fine sitting on the bar stool but the moment he stood up, he went down, hard. Leroy felt a power puke coming on and he crawled to the open door, getting out of sight of the other customers. There he laid on the corner of the concrete patio wishing concrete did not spin. Leroy gingerly turned his head and witnessed a massive cockroach skittering up the wall near him. The cockroach lost his grip on the wall and fell on his back, and was kicking his legs in a frantic effort to turn himself right side up. Suddenly out of nowhere, hundreds of ants materialized. The ants literally picked up the whole cockroach and effortlessly carried him away.

As Leroy's inner voice, I was scared, wondering when the ants would be coming for Leroy. All I could picture was a drunken sailor, levitated 3 inches off the ground, and carried away by hordes of flesh-eating ants. I knew that Leroy was too dumb, too drunk, and too stupid to recognize the amount of danger he was in.

In the middle of all this, Leroy heard a rustling from the chain-link fence that partially surrounded the stone patio which Leroy had claimed as his temporary sleeping quarters. Leroy said, "Who is there? What do you want?"

A sweet voice said, "Hey, it is me, Ronella. You can't be out here like this. It isn't safe. I'm taking you home with me." Ronella helped Leroy to his feet and braced him as best she could, given that Leroy was a giant compared to this tiny Asian woman. Ronella dragged Leroy to her house and during the trip, there were several occasions when she held Leroy from behind and comforted him as he continued to projectile puke Bullfrog. When they got to

Ronella's, she laid Leroy onto her bed and got him some cold water and a little food to help settle his stomach. The next morning Leroy emerged with a well-deserved splitting headache and the utter certainty that he would never stop throwing up.

In search of some fresh air, Leroy went out into the courtyard which was shared by many small apartment complexes, including the one where Ronella lived. The courtyard was always bustling with young women. That morning Ronella brought Leroy some hot coffee, a bottle of water and some flat crackers that looked like tortilla shells. They normally tasted rather bland but to the hungover sailor, they were delicious. Leroy ate while he stooped down among the 19 ladies who were all resting before their day of work began. In time, having become a frequent visitor, during his many visits, Leroy had discovered that these young women loved to play bingo and he would always join in. They had a toy for a bingo game, but it effectively served to separate Leroy from his money. Leroy had no problem with that, understanding that a few dollars to him was nothing, but a few dollars to these wonderful people could mean the ability to buy groceries and pay their rent, so Leroy always came prepared for a rousing game or two of Courtyard Bingo.

One day, Ronella asked Leroy if he wanted to go with her to get her son. Ronella's son had been living on the family pineapple plantation, but was now going to be living with her. She told Leroy to finish his coffee and meet her out in front of the complex. Soon Ronella and Leroy were sitting across from each other in the back of an old faded green step side pick-up truck. They sat in quiet companionship, enjoying the beautiful tropical landscape. Within a few hours Leroy could see rows of pineapple plants that stretched across the landscape as far as the eye could see. It was impressive. During the time Leroy had spent with Ronella, he had noticed a pretty horrific scar on Ronella's left knee, but he had never asked her about it, but as they rode along, Ronella noticed that Leroy was looking at her knee. She took Leroy's hand and placed it on her left knee and said, "When I was a little girl working here, I got badly burned on my knee." Leroy was sad for the pain she had felt but also was very honored that Ronella wanted to share that with him. In this country, there are no child labor laws and no OSHA to oversee the safety of the workplace. The story Ronella told and seeing the extent of her scar left a lasting impression on Leroy.

The instant the truck came to a stop in the turnabout of the plantation's main house, Ronella leapt out of the truck, and raced inside the house, leaving Leroy, who was feeling a little uncomfortable, sitting alone in the back of the truck, baking under the hot sun, and enjoying the remnants of his morning hangover. Ronella dashed out of the house in what seemed like a flash. Leroy was surprised. Surely, he thought, Ronella would want to visit with her parents, check her son's packed luggage or something. It just seemed to Leroy that she was in and out very quickly.

Leroy discovered that Ronella's son did not speak any English. Later in their relationship, Leroy would teach him to nod and acknowledge Leroy as if he understood him. Sometimes, Leroy would pretend to speak Tagalog, the language of that area of the Philippines, and Ronella's son would pretend to understand, making gestures in the same way they'd been doing suggesting there was some comprehension there. Now keep in mind that the little boy was somewhere between 7 and 8 years old. He was really smart and a delight to spend time with and this game was great fun for both of them.

When the three of them arrived back at Ronella's apartment, out walked Aunty Behn, Ronella's mother's sister. Leroy never did know her real name, he too called her Aunty Behn. Aunty Behn had decided to assume the role of matriarch in this new family and took over the responsibilities of cleaning, cooking and doing laundry for the entire household. She also took care of Ronella's son when Ronella was working. Leroy was astonished by this. He could not believe the degree of loving generosity embodied by Aunty Behn. What she was doing for this new family of hers had created an entire new family dynamic that lifted up everyone. She was a truly selfless person. Good luck finding one of those in America. Leroy imagined they exist, hoped they exist, but in Leroy's experience, people like Aunty Behn are a rare commodity indeed.

After getting home from the plantation, everyone was exhausted from their travels and went to bed for the evening. Later in the night, seeing they both were awake, Ronella took Leroy's face in her hands and said, "The reason I did not stay longer at the house is that my parents are not happy with me living here, but here is where I can make money to provide for my son and myself, do you understand?" Leroy just nodded his head in agreement.

Everyone had finally gotten a few hours of sleep and morning was upon them. Aunty Behn told everyone they were going to go the beach for the day and to get packed up. Ronella's next-door neighbor was dating a Marine and the two of them were coming as well. The Jeepney showed up to take them all to the beach. A Jeepney is generally overly ornate from stem to stern. It has one seat that runs front to back on the left side of the vehicle and one seat front to back on the right side of the vehicle. It carries 20 people safely but Leroy had seen it loaded down with as many as 40 people, some of them hanging precariously off of the vehicle as it tootles down the road, often at breakneck speeds. Taking a Jeepney is commonplace and is like taking a bus here in America. Without the people hanging off the sides.

As the Jeepney bounced through the many potholes, Leroy began to talk to Ronella's son in his fake Tagalog, and right on cue was Ronella's son working as a professional mime giving an understanding nod to Leroy at just the right time and a shake of the head or waving of the hands, all with impeccable timing. Leroy kept talking his gibberish in a somewhat convincing manner and Ronella's son was enjoying their game. The Marine was taking note of all this nonsense, but seemed uninterested. His focus was on his hot girlfriend, not on playing with Leroy and the boy. Go figure.

Upon arriving at the beach, Aunty Behn broke out some delicious picnic food and carefully staged it on the table that their little group had claimed for themselves. The Marine was quite a bit younger than Leroy, but if you read *Leroy Learns Sibling Rivalry*, this was no doubt one of the Marines he learned it with. When the Marine said, "Leroy, you want to come snorkeling with us?" the Marine knew full well what he was doing. He might just as well have said, "Hey Leroy, are you too chicken to go snorkeling with us?"

Leroy did have a bit of a hard time snorkeling. Leroy would never admit it, but he's got a good amount of fear of the water. When he would dive down to the ocean floor, he sometimes got panicked. Here in the present, Leroy's fear of the water continues.

To date, Leroy has no idea what that fear is about or where it stems from. Unfortunately, an entire staff of mental health workers at the VA are also at a loss to explain it. But at this time, Leroy, of course, joined his brother in arms along with the Marine's girlfriend and off they went in a small outboard motor boat replete with all the snorkeling gear, motoring to a reef about 50 yards from shore. All this supplied for a modest fee, of course. Into the water went the Marine, rolling off the side of the boat and into the sea. Next one in was his girlfriend and finally Leroy tentatively got in the water. Leroy circled on the surface of the water and Leroy watched the Marine and his girlfriend as they swam around down on the bottom. The floor of the ocean was roughly 15 feet down and even Leroy could snorkel that distance with little fear. Both the Marine and his girlfriend had pretty impressive lung capacity but keep in mind this whole next episode took place in less than 90 seconds before they had to come up for air.

Down on the ocean floor, the Marine, bent on impressing his girlfriend, started to stir up the sand and was poking a piece of coral or some other nameless stick of marine life into a hole in the rocks. With lighting speed a moray eel had all 500 of its teeth solidly implanted and buried in the Marine's arm. The water instantly turned a pale red from the amount of blood the eel was drawing from the Marine's arm and that water was swirling around. Anyone else think SHARK?? So, what does the Marine do? Something pretty unimaginable. He grabs the moray eel with his opposite hand and tears it off of his arm, and all the while every one of the moray's sharp jagged teeth were dragging through Marine flesh, shredding it into an ugly mess.

Looking back on it, Leroy was surprised the Marine pulled the eel off in the first place. That should not have happened. By doing what he did, the Marine ended up more than doubling the extent of his injury. But at this point, Leroy was worried less about the condition of the Marine, and far more worried about the frequent shark sightings in the area and all the blood in the water. He figured it wouldn't take long for the blood in the water to draw those sharks in. In any case, Leroy was not wasting any time getting out of these shark infested waters and into the boat. When Leroy was back in the boat, watching the waters for the telltale sign of The Fin, he thought he might as well help the Marine and his girlfriend get back into the boat. Once they were both safely aboard, Leroy stripped off his t-shirt and fashioned a bandage so the Marine could apply direct pressure to his wounds. When they were back on shore, Leroy helped the Marine into the Jeepney, everyone's only form of transportation, and told the Jeepney driver, "Get this injured Marine to the base hospital and after you drop him off, don't forget to come back for all of us, Understand?" The driver nodded. Whether he actually understood, we will never know, but he did return.

Once the Jeepney left and the Marine was safely on his way to the hospital, everyone resumed their fun. Ronella decided to show everyone her parlor trick. Using only her teeth, she could open a beer bottle that usually needed a bottle opener. Ronella grabbed the closed beer bottle and effortlessly popped the top off it with her teeth. Leroy, drunk as always, said, "Give me one of those beers. I can do that, no problem." Leroy took his beer bottle, positioned it on his upper teeth and gave it a good firm pull upwards. Instant agony shot through Leroy's mouth and it's truly amazing Leroy did not shatter all his top teeth. The lid of the beer bottle did come off, although in the process, most of the beer ended up spilled all over Ronella, the food, and the other guests at the table. This made the top 10 on the list of embarrassing things Leroy has done. Ronella was not amused in the slightest and did not look at all happy as she went to the water's edge to clean up.

As the sun began to mingle with the surface of the ocean, the Jeepney that had delivered the wounded warrior to the hospital was back to pick everyone up and soon they were back home. Night fell upon the courtyard where Ronella lived, and everyone turned in for sleep. The next day Leroy felt much better. He had taken it easy on the alcohol the night before and was being rewarded with a clear head. Remember the girls with the toy bingo game? Well, that morning they were out in the courtyard in full force. As always, their objective was to con Leroy into playing bingo for money and then relieve him of his money. Now we have all had this experience at least once in our lives, but on this day, while Leroy played bingo in a courtyard full of women, he had that gawd awful feeling, that ominous rumbling deep in his bowels, start to make itself known, if you know what I mean. This is the feeling that says, "Get me to a toilet right now!" A whole bunch of unregulated booze and copious amount of beer was bound to unbound, said with a smile.

So, Leroy hustled himself off to the toilet ASAP, hoping against hope that he'd make it before the big bang. Next to the courtyard, the toilet and shower for the courtyard residents was located in a dilapidated concrete box only slightly bigger than an outhouse. To flush the toilet one took a bucket, scooped up some rain water, and dumped it down the toilet. Works like a charm. The shower was a single half inch pipe and one faucet. If you want cold water, you turn the faucet on. If you want hot water, you go to the City of Manila and check into a Hyatt Regency.

Leroy was prepared for a healthy movement, so having made it in time, he situated himself on the courtyard's outhouse toilet. Leroy was sitting there, just minding his own business, suddenly without any kind of warning a large rat scurried from a crack in the concrete and climbed half way up Leroy's left leg. Startled, Leroy gave it a swift kick which only frightened and agitated the rat, and this totally terrorized rat then ran up onto Leroy's chest. Leroy grabbed the rat as it tried to bite his hand and tossed the rat with all his might at the door of the outhouse. The rather large and apparently very resilient rat careened off the outhouse door and ricocheted square onto Leroy's chest where it instantly clawed his way around Leroy's neck in an attempt to burrow into Leroy's shirt. Convinced the rat was going to bite him, Leroy could take no more. Leroy busted out into the courtyard where more than 20 women had gathered to play bingo and chat with one another. What a sight Leroy made! His pants and Tighty Whiteys are down around his ankles, he has diarrhea coming out of his butt, and the coup de grace of the event is that he has this enormous rat in his left hand. Seeing this spectacle, the entire entourage of women burst out with a laugh worthy of a 1000 Harpies. While Leroy was more embarrassed than angry, he was angry enough about the entire fiasco that he tossed that rat to the concrete floor as hard as he could. As it turned out, this rat was clearly indestructible because it got up and ran under the fence of the compound, never to be seen again. To this day, if Leroy goes into the California Club or any other night club in the Philippines, for that matter, Leroy will be met with many women chanting loudly, "Rat Boy, Rat Boy." The Marines think the chant is because Leroy has a small penis. The girls at the concrete outhouse know better. Soon Leroy would have to leave yet again, but when Leroy was at Subic Bay, Philippines it was always a time of adventure and there was never a dull moment.

Now that we know how Leroy and Ronella met and have heard about some of the adventures they shared, we need to resume the story at the point Leroy is making his way to Ronella's just in time for Christmas Eve. Leroy knew very little about children, but he figured he needed to get Ronella, Ronella's son, and Aunty Behn each a gift. Leroy got Aunty Behn an extra set of sheets so she did not have to wash sheets so often. This was a big deal. You think Aunty Behn can simply throw the sheets into a machine and come back when they're all clean? Think again. Tide still makes a hard bar of laundry soap and using that bar of soap, Aunty Behn scrubbed the clothes clean, inch by inch, on a relatively small wash board. It was extremely labor intensive. But when Leroy visited, she even washed Leroy's clothes. Hell, Leroy could not get his first wife to wash clothes and she had a machine that did all the work. Seeing the amount of effort these people have to expend to accomplish even the most basic chores gives the term "lazy" a whole new meaning.

Leroy bought Ronella a beautiful pink dress that she had been drooling over in the store window. After finding out what Leroy had paid, Ronella chastised Leroy because he had paid way too much for the dress. She actually took Leroy back to the store and made them give Leroy a lot of his money back. Contrast this with Leroy's first wife. There is a story in this book which will tell you all you need to know about Leroy's first wife, *Father Joe was His Name O.*

In hindsight, Leroy realized his gift for Ronella's son was pretty inappropriate. Leroy had found him a toy that was the exact replica of an M16. Yeah, I know. The little fellow was only 7. But hey! Maybe he will grow up and figure out a solution for ending gun violence. If we all have guns then no one will need to be violent, right? Plus, with an M16, you have to be trained on their use, just like training to get a driver's license. We do not let people drive that do not know how to drive do we? Well, okay, sorta, maybe. Too often we do, so bad example! When Ronella's son saw the replica firearm, his face lit up with joy. He ripped open the collector's packaging, (hey, it was his gift to do with whatever he wanted) and pulled out the replica M16. Leroy motioned to Ronella's son to ask if he could see it. The little boy handed it over. Leroy operated the breech of the rifle and the magazine, handed it back to the boy and the boy performed all the aspects of the rifle just as Leroy had showed him, after seeing it done only this one time. Going forward, Leroy trained a lot of adults that couldn't figure this stuff out, even after having it demonstrated to them numerous times. The kid was smart!

At the time of this story, many Philippine men were joining the U.S. Military, and although they were limited on the types of jobs they could hold, it didn't matter to them. Having already gotten a taste of what living in a 3rd world country is like, you can be sure that compared to living under those conditions, a life of military service is paradise. Sadly, that is a thing of the past. No more Philippine nationals can join the U.S. military. Leroy doesn't know what happened to all the Filipinos who had enlisted, but hopes they've found a way to make a good life for themselves and their families.

On this Christmas Eve, Aunty Behn brought out a beautiful cake that she had made. The cake was impressive by Martha Stewart's standards, but given the archaic tools she had to make it with, it was nothing short of amazing. There were no Duncan Hines or Betty Crocker mixes over there, no electric mixers and nothing that resembled a conventional oven either. It was a work of art and a labor of love. Leroy asked Aunty Behn what the beautiful cake was for and Aunty Behn responded, her face beaming with pride, "I made a cake for Jesus' Birthday"

This was Leroy's first taste of Catholicism and he listened carefully as the family talked about what Christmas was really for. The next day was Christmas and Ronella took her son to church. Leroy asked if he could come with them and Ronella happily obliged. Walking into the church, Leroy was a bit stunned. He did not know what to make of this church he was in. It was large and made of stone, which is an extremely expensive building material for the area. There are no rock quarries anywhere near this spot so everything must have had to be hauled from wherever the quarries were. The windows were beautiful stained glass, the doors were solid wood with gold trim, and the amount of pure gold vessels on the altar was overwhelming. Leroy couldn't help but wonder where on earth all the money needed to purchase all these luxuries and to build and maintain this church had come from. Had the greater church come in and built it? Nope. So where had all the money come from? Leroy knew it could only have come from the same poor people who were cleaning their clothes on a rock, shitting in a concrete shit house and taking cold showers in a shithouse they had to share with the rats, and who oftentimes did not know where the rent or their next taste of food was coming from. Leroy thought that any religion that could convince people who were this desperately poor to purchase expensive and imported rocks, stained glass windows, gold plates and gold goblets for someone else to use, must be pretty great. This was among the experiences that eventually led Leroy to the Catholic church.

In church, as in most places in the Philippines, Leroy stood out because he towered over the Philippine people. Filipinos were originally very short, aboriginal people, but when Spain invaded the Philippines, many of the Spanish stayed rather than returning to Spain and these men would then have children with the local women. Over the course of a few generations, they had mixed their heritage with that of the native people to such an extent that finding anyone today who carries a pure strain of original Filipino DNA is very rare. As a result of this mixture of cultures, many Filipino people look Hispanic and to Leroy's eyes, some of the most beautiful women in the world evolved as a result of this cultural blending.

Once the church service was over, Leroy, Ronella and her son started walking down the street towards home. Lenora asked Leroy, "How long are you here for?"

Leroy sadly stated, "I am only going to be here for a week and then I will need to get back to work. I promise I will come visit whenever I can."

Ronella then asked, "Leroy, can you help me with rent? I hate to ask but I spent so much time with you last month I did not work enough to pay the rent."

Leroy whispered under his breath, "And yet we were just in a church that cost an enormous amount of money to build and which is filled with things worth more money than I will see in my life time, much less anything these folks will see in their lifetimes."

Hearing something, Ronella asked, "What did you say Leroy?"

Leroy just shook his head and said, "Nothing Ronella. I said nothing."

After taking Ronella to the landlord's and paying for her rent, they all went home. A few days later Leroy shipped out and a year later he would no longer live on board a ship again. A shovel and a rifle would be his new lot in life and his time with Ronella and her family would fade into a most fond memory.

When you're in the Navy, the recruiters all promise "Join the Navy and See the World!" Leroy took full advantage of this promise. For his Rest and Relaxation (R&R) time, Leroy did not always go to the Philippines. He would go to many countries and many US Territories in his quest to see the world. One country Leroy often frequented was Thailand, mainly because of its location in the world coinciding with where his ship would dock. One evening Leroy came walking out of the Kit-Cat Club. Amazingly it was not too late in the evening and Leroy was not too drunk. Leroy decided he needed a massage. Leroy would get several massages throughout the day and the next day he would be sore all over. It was soreness in a good way, but he was sore nonetheless. Walking back to the motel where he had intended to stay, he walked into the lobby and an attractive older woman approached Leroy and asked, "Do you want a massage?" Leroy could tell this woman was Cambodian and not Thai by the way she spoke.

During the mid-1970's, millions of Cambodians had fled their country because of a mass genocide that killed 3 million people. They emigrated all over the world, many coming to the U.S. At the time all this was happening, Leroy was in the 3rd grade and his small town in Montana was host to a number of Cambodian refugee families. Some of the children from these families were in Leroy's class, and Leroy still remembers an incident involving a group of idiot teachers. The teachers were on strike, and because many of the teachers were not part of the union, classes were still in session. These strikers were parading in front of the school with their signs and their yelling and their bullhorns and their angry gestures, all of which terrified the young Cambodian refugee children to death as it evoked memories of the violence they had recently fled. Luckily Principal Brittan put an end to that stupidity quickly and with a hint of vengeance in his voice, as he ordered the striking teachers off school property. This show of compassionate awareness came from the same Principal Brittan who regularly spanked children who had done something to incur his wrath. This was in the days when corporal punishment in schools was the norm and every principal had a paddle with holes drilled through it to maximize the sting. And the same guy who responded compassionately to the trauma of the refugee children, was the same Principal Brittan who spanked Leroy so hard and so long simply because Leroy refused to cry while being paddled. What Principal Brittan didn't realize was that at home, Leroy had been hard conditioned to take corporal punishment without so much as a sound, so quite frankly, Principal Brittan did not stand a chance.

Anyway, Leroy did indeed want a massage so he told the nice woman in the motel lobby that yes, he would very much like a massage. Leroy was thinking logistics now so he asked the Cambodian woman what her name was. She responded, "My name Photjiman Pulprinon. What your name, cowboy?"

Leroy looked at her briefly and thought, "How does she know I'm a cowboy?" Leroy answered her saying, "My name is Leroy and I am a sailor."

Photjiman said, "Let me pay for your motel because I can get a discount. Give me some money and tell me what kind of room you want. The top floor suite is available and it has air conditioning."

Leroy looked intently at Photjiman to try and determine if he could trust her. Generally, a good judge of character, Leroy decided he could feel the trust as he said to Photjiman, "Here's $500.00 for the week. I want to go to those limestone escarpments as seen in the James Bond movie. I want to see a show at the theatre and then ultimately, I want my massage."

Photjiman recoiled a little from Leroy and asked, "What else this money is for?"

Leroy smiled as he put his hand on Photjiman's right shoulder and said, "Photjiman, I already told you exactly what I want, nothing more, nothing less."

So Photjiman arranged for the room and when they got to the room, she and Leroy laid on top of the covers of the king size bed. The A/C helped but in the excessive heat and humidity that was Thailand, it hardly made the room comfy. Soon it was morning and Photjiman told Leroy to follow her as she led him down to a courtyard attached to the motel where they were staying. Moments after Leroy sat down, Photjiman brought out a cup of espresso coffee and some muffins and bacon. Leroy devoured the food as he said to Photjiman, "You must have an "in" with the cook huh?"

Photjiman's response? "I am the cook. Eat up. Our ride will be here soon."

Leroy responded, "Ride? What ride? Where are we going?" Photjiman explained to Leroy that she was taking him to see the limestone escarpments from the James Bond movie. She added that the trip will include lunch on an island and then some one-on-one time.

Before long the van came to pick up Leroy and his new friend. They drove for a good distance and eventually pulled up to a pier with an ocean ready boat that carried about 25 passengers. Photjiman and Leroy boarded and the boat quickly pulled away and was in open ocean in no time. After about 45 minutes they came to a small island where a feast had been set up on large round tables staged all over an area of the beach, sitting right on the sand. The food included calamari, octopus, and various types of sea urchins and God knows what other sea creatures were involved. It's a mystery how a man growing up on a ranch could ever acquire a taste for this kind of slimy mixture, yet here Leroy was eating, it down like it was caviar. After all, isn't that what caviar started out as?

Lunch was over and after a nice rest, the passengers boarded the boat and took off again. Before long they were at the spires of limestone as seen in the James Bond film, *The Man with the Golden Gun*. Leroy was enchanted. The boat slowly made its way up a narrow path in the ocean between two massive limestone outcroppings and at one spot, the boat captain dropped the anchor so folks could feed bananas to the many spider monkeys. The monkeys would come down to the boat by way of overhanging branches and reach down to the people in the boat who would feed them.

The water was crystal clear, maybe 20 feet deep, and there were lots of colorful fish of many different sizes swimming in the depths. The boat captain asked, "Who wants to feed the fish?"

Photjiman elbowed Leroy and said, "You're big strong sailor. You can feed the fish." Leroy was fearful of sharks and a bit afraid of the water too. They were still in open ocean and there was nothing to keep a shark from coming into the alcove. But Photjiman had a way of being persuasive when it came to Leroy. She merely needed to stroke Leroy's… ego and she would have him eating out of her hand, or in this case, feeding the fish, in no time.

As Leroy's inner voice, I am convinced that Photjiman knew full well what was about to happen. This was not her first trip to these waters.

Leroy took a loaf of bread from the boat captain who told him to just jump in the water and tear off little pieces for the fish to eat. Leroy felt like that sounded nice. Just break off bread pieces for the happy little fish to eat. So, taking his loaf of bread in both hands, Leroy went to the bow of the boat which was about 8 feet above the water, and jumped in. Due to the height that he'd jumped from, Leroy found himself submerged in the water quite a long way down. Instantly upon Leroy's entrance into the water, thousands of fish mobbed Leroy and stripped that loaf of bread out of Leroy's hands so fast that Leroy had to check to see if he still had his fingers. Large fish were bumping into Leroy from every direction in their efforts to get some pieces of bread, and their size, combined with their aggression was enough for Leroy. Leroy has never surfaced from a plunge in the ocean so quickly. As he surfaced, Leroy had a look of terror on his face and when he looked up at his fellow sightseers, they were all watching him and laughing, but no one laughed more than Photjiman. Leroy calmed down a bit as he witnessed all the laughter. Surely, they would not be laughing if he was being eaten by fish. Photjiman had obviously known exactly what would happen to Leroy when he jumped in to feed the fish and yet she persuaded Leroy to do it anyway. Leroy climbed back on the boat, grabbed Photjiman in his arms and jumped in the ocean with her. The two wrestled around in the water until the boat captain said it was time to go on for some beach time.

The boat captain dropped folks off in various places, giving everyone some privacy. Photjiman and Leroy ended up on a sandy area surrounded by old coral reefs and limestone. As they relaxed on the beach, Photjiman said, "Leroy, I notice you looking at the scar across the top of my thumb."

Leroy said, "I'm sorry for staring. It is just that I have never seen a wound like that." Photjiman started to cry. Leroy put his towel around her, as the cool ocean breeze was a little uncomfortable at times. Photjiman wiped her eyes and told Leroy this story. When Cambodia was under attack, she and her father had escaped to a cane field. Soldiers were on their heels and Photjiman's father gave her a flintlock rifle and sent her to hide up in the woods overlooking the field. She did as her father had commanded and hid where she could see her father. The soldiers surrounded her father and shot him to death right in front of his daughter. Photjiman told Leroy that she had pointed the rifle her dad had given her at the soldiers and pulled the trigger, but the rifle misfired and blew off the top of her thumb, which was how she got the horrible scar. Leroy told her that had the rifle actually fired, the soldiers would have hunted her down and killed her. Her father had saved her life without even knowing it.

After that conversation, Photjiman opened up to Leroy. She told Leroy how she and her grandma had fled to Thailand, which was known as Laos at that time. Her stomach was so bloated from starvation that it made her look like she was pregnant. She said that she had found a carcass of a mule all covered with maggots and obviously rancid, but she and her grandma ate the mule because they were literally starving to death, and even rotten, maggot-filled food was better than no food at all. She told Leroy the only reason they'd survived was that they had some gold which allowed them to purchase a few supplies and to use as bribes. Photjiman went on to tell Leroy she had a son, but her husband had divorced her and taken her son. She had no idea what might have happened to her little boy or even if he was alive. So much for women's rights.

Personally, Leroy thinks that the majority of Americans who bitch about their life in America need to hear this story. It is likely safe to say that stories like this call for a cup of "shut the hell up!"

After telling her story, Photjiman dried her eyes, leapt up in a playful fashion and ran into the ocean. Leroy followed her, amazed at how happy and upbeat she was. Given her awful past, it was a miracle that she was so joyful. As she played in the ocean, Photjiman suddenly ran out of the ocean and climbed up a coral wall. She was only wearing flip flops and a bathing suit, so when she slipped on her butt and slid down the wall. If you don't know, coral is very sharp and easily cuts skin. Leroy ran to her and helped her to her feet but she playfully bolted from him and ran back towards the ocean. As she ran away, Leroy could see she had a wound on her lower back and was bleeding. Photjiman reached the salt water and when she fully submerged, the salt water went to work on her wound. She let out a scream and stood up. Leroy yelled to her, "You cut your lower back and the salt water stings when it gets in the wound.", Leroy took her hand and after helping her out of the water, he once again wrapped her in his towel. They made their way to the tour boat and got settled in for the trip back.

That night Leroy put some salve on Photjiman's wound to help with the sting and then gave Photjiman a massage, trying to imitate her skills. During the massage, Photjiman asked Leroy, "How come you never want sex from me?"

Leroy instantly responded, "How come you never want sex from me?"

Photjiman giggled out loud and said to Leroy, "I guess we don't have that kind of relationship, do we?"

Leroy said happily, "It's a darn good thing we're friends because if you were not my friend, I damn sure would not have let you get away with my little fish feeding experience." Tired after a long day of fun in the sun, the two drifted off to sleep until morning.

The next day they went to a large circus. Photjiman took Leroy to the shooting gallery and stroked his ego, "I bet you good shot, huh cowboy?" Leroy just smiled. The fact that Photjiman clairvoyantly knew he was a cowboy from Montana was reason enough for Leroy to show off his shooting skills. In truth, Photjiman had no clue Leroy was a real cowboy. It was just a term she used like some folks use "hot shot". It took Leroy a little while to ascertain just how bent his front site was. Leroy slipped his Gerber out of his pocket and gave the site a little tweak. The worker overseeing the

215

shooting gallery gave Leroy a concerned look, especially when Leroy won Photjiman a rather large stuffed panda bear, but Leroy wasn't greedy and chose not to clean the guy out of prizes. After winning the panda, the two of them were content to go on to other things.

After a lovely evening walking around the circus, Photjiman told Leroy they needed to take their seats at the dinner theatre. She had arranged for them to see a quite entertaining theatre play and as it was a dinner theatre, the courses of delicious foods just kept coming. It was all totally sublime and Leroy never wanted it to end.

Later that night, Leroy had to ship out again so he told Photjiman to use the money he had given her to develop the pictures they had taken during their time together. With that, Leroy gave Photjiman a big bear hug and departed for his ship.

Leroy's departure was bittersweet. The sweet was that Leroy was headed to port visits in New Zealand and Australia, places he'd always wanted to see. After a week out at sea, Leroy received a package from a most unexpected source. Photjiman had sent Leroy a copy of the pictures they had taken. This cost her a great deal more than it would have if she'd simply kept the pictures as Leroy had instructed her to do. With that said, Leroy was moved by her generosity and moved that her thoughts were still of him.

The bitter came another week after leaving Thailand when the Extremist Muslims attacked the twin towers, killing almost 3,000 people. With that, Leroy never did make it to Australia or New Zealand. Instead, Leroy deployed to the coast of Pakistan and for the next year and a half, Leroy would be at war with the Extremist Muslims. Soon after, Leroy would volunteer as an Individual Augmentee for the Army and the Army would make him a Combat Engineer. From that time until retirement Leroy was no longer a shipboard sailor and he never saw Photjiman again. She had often told Leroy that she wanted to move to America and own a nail salon, and to this day, any time Leroy walks by a nail salon, he always looks for her.

THE END

Author's Note:

Did you notice that after spending time with both of these women, while I was with them, I quit drinking or drastically reduced my drinking? I always considered myself a functioning alcoholic and this story is a great example. Why would I want to be drunk when I could spend time with friendly women instead? No headaches. No queasy gut. No wondering why I was in jail. Instead, I experienced an abundance of kindness from two wonderful and unlikely friends. I do pray with all my heart that they are both healthy and happy.

Acorn Pond Maintenance

Leroy and Lenora sat on their front deck that was prematurely rotting. The pressure treated lumber Leroy had bought from Lowes was not properly preserved and as a result, after only 8 years of use, it had rotted to dangerous levels. Even the structural integrity of the deck was in question. It would only be a matter of time before someone would fall through the deck and then Lenora would have a lawsuit on her hands. Lenora was the sole owner of the house and the property so she would be fully responsible for an injury lawsuit which might result from someone falling through the deck and getting hurt. Read the full story in *Lowes Pressure Treated Lumber.*

Leroy and Lenora were not giving the rotting wood malfeasance any thought on this day. Their thoughts were on the warm sun, a beautiful day, and a yard full of opening tulips, daffodils and a plethora of other early spring blooming plants. Since Leroy always cleaned the pond, one might wonder why both Leroy and Lenora were sitting on their lazy butts. Lenora was supposed to be getting her cleaning gear and climbing down four feet into the pond using her two new knees. Lenora had had both of her knees replaced which is why Leroy called them new knees, and which we all know are not nearly as flexible as the original knees. But both Leroy and Lenora were sitting on the deck enjoying the spring warmth. To find the answer to why they were simply sitting there instead of cleaning the pond, we need to go back a few months when Leroy had asked Lenora to put in a claim with the Better Business Bureau (BBB) for the failed pressure treated lumber. Lenora resisted saying, "I know nothing about what caused the rotting wood. I have no understanding of the warranty so you need to do this one Leroy." Leroy was not happy; he had given Lenora all the data she needed and had practically written the submission for Lenora. However, Leroy had learned from the great Kenny Rogers, "You gotta know when to hold 'em, know when to fold 'em, know when to walk away, and know when to run." This was a situation that required option 3: Run.

While Leroy was retreating to the word processor to tackle the BBB submission, he asked Lenora, "So, since I am doing the BBB submission, that means you are going to clean out the koi pond this spring, right?" Leroy was being an ass to Lenora because Leroy knew Lenora could not climb down a four-foot rock wall that was not only sheer but slippery, in order to clean the pump, walls, and floor of the koi pond. Secondly the two filters, weighed nearly 50 pounds each, which was far more weight than Lenora could lift. Leroy assumed Lenora would find some way to barter with Leroy for the koi pond cleaning. The barter might involve food or be sex related as either of those would motivate Leroy. But Lenora had no intentions of cleaning the koi pond, nor was Lenora, in any way, going to tickle Leroy's libido or whet his appetite with promises of some gourmet experience just to get the koi pond cleaned. She certainly was not going to climb down into the pond and clean it herself, so what was left?

That question was answered when a big white Ford truck pulled up to the end of the driveway and parked. On the sides of the pickup truck there was a large decal with an acorn at the top and the words "Pond Maintenance and Repair" written under the acorn logo. Leroy just looked at Lenora and said, "Well fry me on a griddle with butter sauce. You went and hired a pond cleaner?"

The owner of Acorn Pond Maintenance arrived first and introduced himself as Tim. Tim's mail order bride followed along behind Tim, just like a puppy. Leroy considered verifying that she was okay and able to leave on her own free will, but Lenora, of course, was talking up a storm with her in no time. This was despite the woman's complete lack of English and Lenora's complete lack of Spanish. This woman scrubbed every stone, scrubbed between architectural stones, vacuumed out all the fish poop, algae and leaves from the decorative gravel, and finally, she cleaned the pump suction so well that the flow of water was the best Leroy and Lenora had seen in years. Please do not think that Leroy calls this woman a mail order bride because she speaks Spanish. He means to say that due to Tim's ill-mannered treatment of her, she seems like she'd have to be a mail order bride. Lenora would tell Leroy to piss up a rope if Leroy ordered her around, or better said, tried to order her around.

While the mail order bride was working up a sweat doing an amazing job of cleaning the pond, her worthless husband Tim was telling Leroy and Lenora about all the seminars around the country he had attended, about how he knew every aspect of koi pond maintenance and that he was known as The Pond King. Mail order bride's efforts were wasted on Tim because her husband Tim was completely clueless and his cluelessness was what eventually caused the pond to turn into a green goopy mess. Worst was that Tim failed to match the pond chemistry from the old water to the new water, mainly the 20 pounds of dissolved salt that was removed and never replaced. Koi thrive in brackish water. Koi die without brackish water, something a pond king would know right? This 1st day noob move resulted in the tragic death of all but 4 of the original 87 fish. Some Lenora had named and were large valued at $5K. (look up Koi value for yourself.) Leroy was not one to engage in name calling so here is what Leroy had to say to back up his claim that Tim is as much a pond king as Leroy is a famous neurosurgeon. NOT!

First Tim tells Leroy, "Looks like you have built a pretty good pond here."

Leroy's response was, "I am a retired Combat Engineer in the military. Although I never put fish and plants in the drinking water tanks, they were a whole lot bigger than this koi pond. Multiply that with the fact that I picked the brains of every nursery pond guy I could find and bought all my supplies from the folks at Sara's Nursery because they were by far the most helpful of all the folks I've talked to. So, I think you mean VERY good, not PRETTY good, right?"

Tim just ignored Leroy but a moment went by and Leroy approached Tim as he was taking the filter medium out for cleaning. Leroy said, "Hey Tim, I have all the parts for my ultra violet filter laying on the work bench when you get to that part of the job."

Tim's response was to say, "We don't believe in a UV filter. What you need is plants and an aerator."

Leroy's blood pressure spiked but this was Lenora's show, and he knew it's best that he leaves it alone, but Leroy can't help himself as he blurts out to Lenora but definitely within earshot of Tim, "Pond King! How about Pond Jester! I was looking forward to one thing and that was that I would not have to assemble that UV Filter!"

Leroy had been told by every pond expert he'd spoken with that the UV Filter was the key to a healthy koi pond. The filter works like any ultraviolet light works. It kills algae and parasites in the water, and delivers a crystal-clear pond. For Tim to claim he did not believe in them was the first blaring proof of Tim's Intelligence quotient of 1.

Next thing Tim does that proves stupid is as stupid does is to convince Lenora to put these Bio Balls in the filter. They are supposed to replace the lava rock that Leroy had put in the filters nearly 10 years ago. Bio Balls are small grey plastic doggie balls. After 3 weeks Leroy pulled out the Bio Balls and showed them to Lenora. Leroy asked Lenora how good biologics were supposed to adhere and grow on plastic. Leroy then showed Lenora one of the pieces of lava rock like the ones Tim had thrown away. Lenora could immediately see why Bio Balls are stupid and lava rocks will stand the test of time. Leroy enjoyed the privilege of paying for more lava rock so much. Thanks Tim.

Then as Leroy continued to remove the filter, he found further proof that Tim was the King of Stupid Pond maintenance guys. Tim had put the fine filter in first and then the coarse filter in second. Now think about it. Here is how these filters work: water is pumped through a hose from the bottom of the pond, and the flow of water goes to a bucket with a hole in the bottom of it. The water flows through the hole, then flows through a bed of lava rocks, and then it should flow through the coarse filter first, filtering out leaves, large sized pond debris and that sort of detritus. Whatever is small enough to get through the coarse filter then gets caught by the fine filter which catches things like the occasional grain of sand. Can you just imagine when shit for brains Tim reversed them? All the debris both large and small clogged the fine filter leaving the dirty water to run straight back into the pond. Ergo, the amount of dirt removed by Tim's contraptions? Zero.

But wait! There's more! It doesn't stop yet. Soon Tim is trying to tell Lenora that an aerator will fix all her problems. Lenora grabs Leroy and tells him that Tim wants to put an aerator in the pond.

Leroy came over to Tim and said, "Lenora tells me you want to put an aerator in the pond. Isn't that just going to keep things swirling around so the pond will never settle out and clear up?"

Somehow Tim still managed to convince Lenora that they needed an aerator. As all this was going on, Leroy was finding it harder and harder to even be around Tim. He was supposed to clean the pond which his lovely wife had already done 100%. All Tim did was to make a huge beginner's mistake on the filters and throw away Leroy's lava rock. And don't go anywhere! There is much more! There's even worse proof of a complete lack of grey matter still to come.

Since Time had gotten on Leroy's last nerve, Leroy told Tim, "Go ahead and install your aerator but use the outlet by the pond because one, it sounds like a boat motor zooming through the water and I don't want to have to hear it, and two, because the outlet under my covered deck is MY outlet that I use for my summer plug in devices."

Once Leroy had given Tim his marching orders, Leroy went out front and asked Lenora how much she had paid this idiot. Lenora said, "$2,000.00 but that was also supposed to cover any problems Tim found with the koi pond. Hearing that, Leroy was just plain pissed. This asshole Tim had ripped off his wife for $2,000.00 when the most his pathetic service was worth was nothing! And of course, later over 80 fish, some valued in the thousands of dollars would be dead. How much would you pay the "pond king" for that?

Leroy returned to his koi pond and once again, Tim's stupidity and just plain disrespect knew no limit. Tim had plugged the aerator into the one place Leroy had specifically told Tim not to use. He had specifically told Tim, "Don't plug that piece of shit in this spot and do not put the aerator within reach of my hearing. Leroy looked at Tim and said, "I know I told you not to plug it in there or put it there, so what do you do? You completely disregard my instructions and frankly, I want to know why." Tim was one of these guys who really was stupid. If he suffered from some sort of intellectual disability, Leroy would be sympathetic, but Tim just suffered from being Tim. He was a liar and an idiot, which is sadly pretty run of the mill these days.

Leroy asked Tim again why he had ignored his orders concerning the outlet he used and the location of the aerator. Tim sheepishly admitted that he had moved the aerator because it would not reach from the back outlet. Later Leroy learned just what a lying turd bird Tim was but at the time, Leroy sarcastically said, "Hey, thanks Tim. This roaring boat engine next to my deck really adds to the ambiance, oh, and thanks for covering up my clematis with your fake rock. They should grow really well in the dark that way. My complete thanks go out to you for taking my outlet away so now I can't use my fan. You literally took away my cool. That was the best $2,000.00 ever spent, says no one!".

Tim and his mail order bride drove off never to be heard from again, hopefully. About three weeks went by and the koi pond kept getting greener and greener. Leroy thought to himself, "Didn't Tim say UV Filters don't work and aerators do when it comes to making the pond clear?" The sorry truth is that Tim is someone who is completely uneducated in anything other than how to get his mail order bride through the State Department. As far as being knowledgeable about pond maintenance, the koi have more knowledge than Tim. In fact, Leroy was surprised Tim had the mental acuity to string words into a sentence, especially a sentence where Tim tells the truth.

About three weeks after the pond was cleaned so well by Tim's Mail Order Bride, the koi pond was looking and smelling horrible and fish were dying to the tune of several a day. Before long, all the koi, except for the largest, had died. A total of 80 fish, lovingly raised for years were now gone, but why had this happened besides the fact that due to the bubbling caldron of green in the pond, the fish couldn't even swim in their little 4,500-gallon pond due to the aerator which was rated for a ¼ acre pond, not a 4,500 glorified aquarium. Leroy knew that Lenora had even named some of the fish, and these were now among the casualties because, as it turned out, the water was missing the critical minerals that are essential to koi life. Leroy was surprised Lenora did not ask him for help in finding the solution for the problem that was killing their koi, and after another week went by, Leroy couldn't stand it anymore. He ripped apart the pond filters that had been put in backwards, and then yanked the aerator out of the pond and threw it across the yard.

It was while ripping out the aerator that Leroy learned what an ass faced liar Tim was. The cord for his aerator was wrapped around the pump so many times it could easily have gone half way around the yard and reached the area Leroy had ordered Tim to put it. I use the word "order" because I can assure you there was no, "please" built into Leroy's vernacular so yes, he ordered Tim to put the aerator in a specific place. Leroy was now wishing he could place the aerator in a specific place but that would require Tim to be present and to bend over. Maybe later.

While Leroy was loosely wrapping the power cord around the aerator, he noticed a metal plate on the side stating that the capacity of this aerator was designed for a pond that had a size of between ¼ to ¾ acre. No wonder Leroy and Lenora's little 4,500-gallon pond was converted to a big boiling pot of split pea soup! What moron would put an extremely oversized aerator that was meant to work in a small lake, into Leroy's and Lenora's little pond? It was ludicrous!

Leroy tackled the UV filter and after a couple tries, he got it working. Keep in mind that the whole reason Leroy looked forward to Tim's service is that of all the jobs associated with cleaning the koi pond, Leroy hated the job of assembling the UV Filter the most, and any logical person would expect someone billing himself as The Pond King to know how to assemble a UV Filter. Every one of these conferences Tim claims to have attended, ALL preach the value of the UV filter. They've been around for nearly 20 years and are a must for keeping any pond with fish in it clear. Tim obviously does not have a clue. If he did, the pond would have cleared up in spite of the Bio Balls and with the filters installed backwards, in combination with an aerator rated for a Tilapia farm. No, no, no. Under Tim's leadership, almost all of Lenora and Leroy's fish were dead, and as a bonus, they got to listen to a motor cycle engine run continually while they sat on their covered deck.

It was while Leroy was ripping out the aerator and playing "Catch the Asphalt" with it four or five times when a thought jumped into Leroy's head. "That shit stain on life Tim did not replace the brackish water critical to the survival of koi!" Do you still think Tim is the King of Pond Maintenance? Neither do I! After Leroy introduced 20 gallons of salt into their 4,500-gallon pond, not a single fish has died since. Leroy and Lenora both beat themselves up for not thinking about the salt, but isn't that why folks hire someone for $2,000.00 though? They're supposed to know to do this automatically. It's a no brainer. I am absolutely certain that if it happened to Leroy and Lenora it has happened to other victims of

The Pond King. When you get your car washed, they do not drain out all the oil in your car and send you on your way do they? I am certain that would result in a lawsuit and that is why you should know for certain that this situation is also grounds for a law suit. Leroy and Lenora's dead fish were worth $8,500.00 at a minimum! If you think that the price of koi is high look up cost of koi on the internet. That $8,500 is actually very low. Add in the years of caring for these koi and the value skyrockets.

After a week and a half later, having put the pond filters in correctly, recleaning the pump suction which was full of algae, reinstalling the lava rocks and finally, after a couple of tries getting the UV filter working, all the effort paid off and the pond turned crystal clear and has remained crystal clear to this day.

Leroy went to the bank where Lenora and he had separate bank accounts. He was withdrawing funds for himself when he asked the teller if he could deposit $2,000 into Lenora's checking account. The wonderful bank teller happily accommodated Leroy and he put funds in Lenora's account to cover the cost of the koi pond cleaning. Not surprisingly, Lenora did not even notice the deposit was made. Almost a year later, Leroy told Lenora that he felt guilty that he had not cleaned the koi pond and had deposited the $2K to cover Lenora's investment.

Leroy knew that the mail order bride from Acorn Pond Maintenance had done a much better job cleaning the koi pond than he ever had and going forward, it was Leroy's plan to pay no more than $800.00 for a koi pond cleaning ONLY! There is no doubt that with an artificial pond, artificial means are required to keep it clean. Tim's operational methods are as follows: take a koi pond, turn the homeowner's outdoor space into a monster truck rally, kill all their fish, and make their pond a beautiful, tumultuous green bubbling mess in the process. If that is beautiful to you, go for it. If not, then keep your distance from Tim. He is poison to koi in the worst way. Tim is about to find out he will be paying Leroy for all Lenora's fish that he so artfully managed to kill.

On a final note, Tim told Leroy and Lenora their koi pond was full of algae because they had no plants. Leroy knew that was also a lie. Yes, plants in one's pond are wonderful. In large amounts they may keep down some algae by using the fish poop as food.

However, if one has an environment with two huge waterfalls and a 5,000 gallon per hour pump providing constant circulation through their koi pond, then plants aren't much use as aerators. They do provide some cover for the fish and if one is lucky, perhaps some flowers will arise from those plants in the koi pond. The reason Tim was lying again is that the koi pond had been crystal clear for 6 years with little to no plants. It had only been in the last 2 years that Leroy had failed to get the koi pond clear. Leroy had a hunch that cleaning the koi pond would remove the poop and other debris that has a lot of nutrition for algae growth, and it stood to reason that by eliminating all the debris in conjunction with the proper use of all the conditioning products Leroy had learned to apply, the koi pond would turn crystal clear.

Once it was clear again, Leroy bought a beautiful red water lily so Lenora would be happy that the koi pond had plants. It blossomed multiple times last summer and every day the flowers brought a smile to Leroy's and Lenora's faces. Leroy and Lenora are considering replacing all their lost koi but the blow of Tim killing all their pets is just too much to bear for now. Payback will be served 10-fold, of this I can assure you. All too often Leroy hears folks say, "Leroy you have to let it go. Leroy you can't make a difference. Leroy you cannot win."

Leroy's response to all those comments is, "So if a man murders all your fish, something I will never be able to reverse, am I supposed to do nothing? What if Tim murdered my kids or my wife? Where do I draw the line?" Well, for Leroy, when you live with integrity, both in what you expect from yourself and what you expect from others, then there is NO LINE to draw!

THE END

Author's Note:

This is a true story. In my next book *Speedo Edition,* I will bring you all up to speed on what follows from here. The take away from this story is the audacity of some people. How do people of this caliber stay in business? My assumption is that they manage it because folks who give Leroy the advice to let it go are the same folks who would let Tim kill their fish, ruin their pond, and do absolutely nothing about it. I have news for you: All it takes for evil to exist is for good people to do nothing! Doing nothing is the worst thing you can do. What if before Leroy and Lenora hired the man, three or four folks had reported the unethical business practices of Tim and Acorn Pond Maintenance, as Leroy fully intends to do? If all those disgruntled folks who had hired Tim with disastrous results had reported the wrongdoing before Leroy and Lenora had the misfortune to hire him, by the time Tim got to Lenora and Leroy, maybe he would have at least been afraid of killing their fish or afraid to do a half-assed job. Or maybe after he got taken to court a few times, he would remember to put the correct amount of salt in people's ponds, or would install a UV Filter correctly, or would get rid of Bio Balls, or would stop using aerators rated for Lake Ontario. Then he might actually avoid killing all his customers' fish. I am quite certain Tim does not have an advertisement on his web page reading: "We will gladly kill all your fish for you and kick you in the nuts while we are at it." Tim did tell us that we may lose a few fish due to stress. I totally accept that as true! But Tim needs to say you will lose all your fish and will have to start all over the years of dedication given to these expensive, and beautiful fish that are now dead. Maybe this is why I had a bumper crop of roses with all those dead fish to bury around the roots. No matter. It's still not a fair trade.

LeafGuard: The Great Mistake

Have you ever had real and true buyer's remorse? The kind where you realize all too soon but all too late that you have been completely suckered by a well-crafted shake-down that has robbed you of a considerable amount of your hard-earned money while leaving you little recourse to obtain any sort of redress from the scum sucking thieves? Well, this is exactly how Leroy felt after buying LeafGuard. Who has not seen the thousands of advertisements for this LeafGuard product, despite the fact that in many climates with temperatures that go below freezing, it is completely defective? Not to spoil the story, but the major design defect with these gutters is that in the winter, when there are six inches or more of snow on the roof, the roof snow starts to slowly melt as it is warmed by the sun. The melted snow then gets to the LeafGuard gutter opening, which as we have all seen on the commercials, consists of a long narrow slit on the top/front edge of the gutter. And as soon as the water reaches this drain opening in the gutter, it promptly freezes and all remaining roof melt slowly leaks onto the walkways below. The massive amount of water delivered on the walkways, then freezes into an impassable ice-skating rink coating all of the home's walkways.

But I am getting ahead of myself. Let's start the story with Leroy, sitting in Western New York, home of blizzards, Nor'easters, Alberta clippers, and lake effect snow, watching the television as it showed a LeafGuard commercial demonstrating an amazing looking product. After being taken in by this demonstration, he would later come to find it was all false advertising, but Leroy did not know, as the commercial aired, about the ridiculous lies and withholding of the truth, particularly as it pertains to the LeafGuard system in cold climates. If it's too good to be true, IT IS! So as Leroy and Lenora were sitting watching Jeopardy and the LeafGuard commercial came on, Leroy became enamored with the whole idea and called the number on the screen even before the commercial ended. A good phone center person scheduled an appointment with Leroy and LeafGuard.

A few days went by, and then Ashley showed up from LeafGuard to sell Leroy his new gutters. Truthfully, Leroy did not really know why he was buying these gutters. First of all, to clean the gutters currently installed on the house, which were working exactly as they should and without any hitches, Leroy simply got up on the roof using the railing on the back pool deck, which happened to make a perfect step onto the roof. As a result, Leroy did not even need a ladder, and simply carried a plastic bucket to hold the debris. Secondly, Leroy speculated when he could no longer safely get onto the roof, he could hire a handyman for $500.00 a year to do the job for him. With that expense compared to the cost of the LeafGuard System, Leroy calculated that he could hire a handyman to clean his gutters for the next 23 years.

As Leroy's inner voice, I can promise you that Leroy will not be living anywhere even close to Western New York in 23 years, so one has to wonder why was Leroy spending $12K for gutters. Even if the gutters worked, which we now know they don't, they still would not be worth much more than $6K. Why was hindsight always 20/20? Cuz it's hindsight, not foresight.

After Ashley made her intros to Leroy, she and Leroy walked all around the house to inspect the old gutters, the condition of the facia boards, and such. Ashley took Leroy over to his little stone fire pit which was arguably too close to the covered deck, but which had functioned without incident for 10 years, with the only down side being that it left a noticeable amount of soot on the old gutter and on the surrounding posts and overhang. It never bothered Leroy or Lenora and they didn't usually even notice it. But as Leroy reached Ashley she said, "Leroy, do you see all this mold around here?"

Leroy looked at Ashley and this blunder immediately put Leroy's stupid watch on full alert. Leroy answered Ashley's question about the mold, "Ashley let me show you something." He wiped his hand over the soot on the surfaces and then showed Ashley as he said, "Do you see any bluish hue on my hand?"

Ashley looked and responded, "No I don't."

Leroy asked, "And what does that mean?"

Ashley started to squirm a bit as she said, "I don't know what that means,"

Leroy pointed to the fire pit nestled too close to the gutter over head and said, "Could it be soot from a dangerously placed fire pit and NOT mold at all?"

Having no response to that, Ashley and Leroy then went to the front deck and began negotiations. Ashley told Leroy, "The LeafGuard gutter had 30% more capacity than your current gutters and the downspouts were called Big Mouth, which means they can handle a lot more flow than your existing gutters." Ashley then got out the wool to pull over Leroy's eyes and committed her first shenanigan. She told Leroy he would need 2 additional downspouts to ensure the warranty was intact. Lest we forget, Leroy was a former Combat Engineer, so the logic according to Ashley that says the gutters take 30% more water combined with the lure that the existing downspouts would be replaced with the Big Mouth downspouts, allegedly allowing a ton more water to flow, made a lot of sense to Leroy. This was in spite of the fact that Leroy's old gutters had worked flawlessly for 35 years as long as they were not clogged with leaves, which did occur every couple of years. As negotiations began in earnest, Leroy accepted the purchase of the two additional downspouts because Ashley said he needed to have them for the warranty to be valid. More lies from Ashley. Now that Leroy was on the hook, it was time to reel him in. Ashley pretended to fiddle with her papers a bit and then told Leroy, as if stating the cost of a donut, "Leroy, good news! We can get your gutters done as early as next week. They will only cost you $17,000.00."

Leroy just laughed in Ashley's face as he told her, "Well okay then. Thank you for your time." Screw the notion of buyer's remorse. Instead, let's build a time machine and let Leroy use it to go back in time to this precise moment. Wouldn't everyone want to use such a machine occasionally? Leroy sure would!

As Leroy made his way back into the house, Ashley said, "Hey Leroy, do you have any military experience?"

Leroy laughingly stated, "Ashley, you know I retired from the military as a Combat Engineer. I'm certain I boasted about that at least three times."

Ashley then said, "Well, we can give you a military discount which will bring the price down to $14,500.00"

Leroy stood back up again, unaware that Ashley was playing Leroy like a fiddle. No. Stop. Ashley is playing Leroy like a one-man band replete with colorful balloons and a dancing bear. Ashley then said, "Leroy, hold on. Are you or your wife aged 65 or older?"

As Leroy's inner voice, I have never seen him be snookered like such a big fool as he was this time. It is as if in the dictionary under "fool" there was a picture of Leroy: the poster child for the word!

Leroy stupidly responded, "Ashley, I know what you're doing with this little game. You are going to see how much I will pay for this product. Leroy sat back down and continued, "In answer to your question Ashley, you know I am retired from the military, just like you know my wife Lenora is 70 years old. You know all of this because I told you several times while we inspected the gutters. Ashley, please stop with the games. What is the bare minimum you can sell this to me for? You have one more shot at this negotiation." That's far more shots than anyone else dealing with Leroy generally got, but Leroy really wanted those LeafGuard gutters.

Ashley responded with, "Leroy, the very best that I can do is $11,500.00."

Leroy smiled and said, "Interesting. That's almost half the price that you originally asked. May I ask, does anyone ever pay your initial offer? Never Mind, don't answer. Sadly, they must or you wouldn't use such underhanded techniques that I can only assume is meant to test the depth of customers' pockets."

So, the contract was finalized, the next week came and before long the installers had the new gutters installed, but in the process of installing the gutters, they forgot to install one of the two additional downspouts, in accordance with what Leroy paid for. They left one of the additional downspouts off which will help in showing one of LeafGuard's many blatantly underhanded moves. Seeing the error, Leroy contacted the store manager for Buffalo LeafGuard, a man by the name of Joe Geodardi, and told him he wanted the downspout installed per his purchase order and to make sure the warranty would be valid. Joe told Leroy, "Ashley told you wrong. You do not need that downspout. I will refund you the $750.00."

Leroy took the $750.00 for the one extra downspout that didn't get installed and as soon as he received his refund from LeafGuard for one of the extra spouts that was sold under false pretenses, applied to get his money back for the second one as well, because the other extra downspout is an exact mirror image of the downspout that Joe told Leroy he did not need. Leroy agreed with Joe that neither of the two new downspouts were needed and selling him those two downspouts was clearly one of many scams LeafGuard has pulled and will pull as we push forward through the story.

As he dealt with the extra downspouts, Leroy found out there is no warranty except a "No Clog Guarantee" which has to do only with leaves. So, Ashley lied when she told Leroy he needed the downspouts for the warranty. What warranty? There is no warranty! Ashley had spun her lies and managed to dupe Leroy out of the cost of two unnecessary downspouts, and now Ashley had to go for the jugular and finish Leroy off.

The final hassle with Ashley came as Lenora came out and told Ashley she wanted the cream-colored gutters. Leroy had not given it much thought so thankfully Lenora had. Ashley had picked out the generic white gutters, which were the cheapest gutters available. Lenora had Ashley adjust the color of the metal gutters in quick order.

As Leroy's inner voice, I just look at this whole mess and I am astonished Leroy fell for all this. I guess when you want that shiny baseball card you will go to a lot of extremes to get it and these LeafGuard gutters were the equivalent of those shiny baseball cards to Leroy. I can assure you there is absolutely no other way that Leroy would be so dumb.

Leroy cannot blame Ashley for what comes next. I am certain that in search of the highest commission possible, she had picked up all these unethical habits from her mentor, Joe Geodardi. Teaching a young impressionable woman how to be a money-grubbing gutter whore, which is a horrible crime in and of itself, instead of teaching her how to conduct business with honor and to have pride in the product she's selling. Instead, Joe Geodardi and other LeafGuard scum have just mentored her into a lying turd dressed in sheep's clothing. Joe Geodardi has a PhD in the practice of how to be a money-grubbing gutter whore and takes great delight in passing on his knowledge of deceit, unethical business practices, inability to string words coherently and even more trouble stringing words together without lies.

In pursuit of his quest for justice, Leroy demanded that the extra downspout, which by LeafGuard's own admission is not needed, be removed and the cost of the downspout reimbursed. Leroy would soon learn his answer to that demand. There is no answer. He first reached out to Joe Geodardi, the Buffalo store manager to get this problem taken care of in a timely fashion, but as of the writing of this story, the request has been in for two years and the ONLY response has been for LeafGuard to ignore any and all communications from Leroy. Finally, after Leroy put his lawyer to work on the problem, there has been a few signs of activity. Stay tune for <u>Speedo Edition</u> for the conclusion to this part of the story.

Once all the hassle of the purchase and installation was behind Leroy and Lenora, they enjoyed their yard, deck and pool throughout the summer. Soon fall arrived and Leroy said to Lenora, "Hey! I don't have to clean up the leaves anymore! Yay for me!" Lenora rolled her eyes at Leroy. Lenora knew it was Leroy's money and he was welcome to buy those gutters for Lenora's home if he wanted, but it sure seemed like an awful lot to spend to replace something that seemed to be working just fine. Leroy felt the gutters were pretty pricey as well, but if they worked as promised, then it was all good with Leroy and he would not have buyer's remorse.

In the summer they sort of worked except they have a varmint guard, and like most things LeafGuard, it is screwed up. Varmints such as moles, mice, rats and other small pests will go into the spout unimpeded and then get caught partway down the downspout at the varmint guard. If the varmint starts from the bottom, he won't nest straight up and down, but will nest on the flat part of the down spout where there is no varmint guard, impeding the flow of water through the downspouts.

What happened to Leroy and Lenora is that the downspout varmint guard got clogged up, the rainwater goes down the downspout until it reaches the clog and then the water shoots out into Leroy and Lenora's koi pond. Koi are extremely sensitive to their environment so when the runoff water from the roof went down the LeafGuard downspout and shot out of the varmint guard into the koi pond, Leroy and Lenora panicked, wondering what toxins were in that water and if it was going to kill their koi. LeafGuard eventually came and fixed the one downspout by the koi pond but all the downspouts responded the same way within a few months. Given that Leroy and Lenora have no intention of keeping the LeafGuard gutters and will replace them as soon as possible with the old-style gutters that Lenora had for over 35 years of trouble-free operation, Leroy and Lenora could give a rat's ass about the varmint traps.

As per Mother Nature's rules, after fall it becomes winter and Western New York has difficult weather and unpredictable weather. One year the snow comes at a rate of a foot or more at a time and the total snowfall amount can be excessive. Other winters, it rains all winter, the snow plows rust in their stalls, and the snow shovel begins to collect cobwebs in the corner of the garage. The first year of Leroy's LeafGuard ownership, it snowed a lot. Remember in the beginning of the story where you learn about the winter phenomenon as it relates to the effectiveness or lack thereof that is a LeafGuard gutter? This is a design defect so severe there is no way people should tolerate it, and if they are tolerating it, then someone ought to tell the cowards to take a stand against the turds, scammers, and folks who would sell their own children for a buck!

Sadly, and without any warning Lenora's son's wife (remember Ink-Squirt?), lost her grandfather to a heart attack, which of course delivered a heavy emotional blow to Ink-Squirt. Lenora was quite close to her children and although Leroy called them "mama's kids" he understood the closeness of Lenora's family and got on board the support train by putting meals together, making constant visits, and doing anything else Lenora asked Leroy to do. In less than a month, Ink-Squirt suffered another horrible blow when her father also died of a sudden heart attack. It doesn't sound very original, but that's how it happened. As a result, Leroy and Lenora were continually shuffling between Lenora's son's house, and Ink-Squirt's mother's house, and then at times, Leroy and Lenora would try to get everyone out of the house for a spell, hoping a change of scenery would help by providing at least a temporary distraction. The entire time that all this sadness and death was happening, it was snowing up a storm and roughly a foot of snow had settled on Leroy's roof. During the day when the sun hit the roof, the snow would begin to melt and trickle into the gutters until the resulting phenomenon described at the beginning of the story began to leave walkways so treacherous, they could not be walked on. Leroy and Lenora were afraid for their safety and the safety of anyone coming to the door. The LeafGuard gutters had become completely blocked with ice and the water just ran right down the front of the LeafGuard gutter and onto all the walkways which were then choked with ice. It was not only dangerous; it was a major lawsuit waiting to happen.

When Leroy finally got his head above water, so to speak, he called Joe Geodardi. There should be no doubt that any empathetic, generally kind person, would understand when Leroy said, "I'm just getting around to getting a refund on my gutters. I did not get photos or videos of the ice-skating rinks aka the sidewalks, or the cause of them which was the LeafGuard gutter system, because we had 2 deaths in the family back-to-back, and believe me, taking care of family trumps dealing with dipshits and defective equipment."

Joe said, "Well, I'll have to come over and see if it is installed correctly."

Leroy snaped back, "You are not welcome on my property anymore. I want the warranty for my gutters honored, the gutters removed and I will be out of your way Joe. You told me the gutters would be properly installed in the first place, and they are, which I can clearly see for myself. The problem is that they are defective and that is something which is never going to be fixed by any sort of different installation."

Now Joe is one of these guys who thinks their shit does not stink. In reality, the smell is repulsive and Dr. Dipshit, aka Joe, is just one of those people who has a smug attitude and the tone to go with it. Joe said, "I need to come out to your house first, and then we can talk about a refund." Joe arrived at the house and one of the installers checked the gutters. As the installer went around to check the gutters, Leroy explained to Joe all the issues that resulted due to the design defect of these gutters. Leroy explained that his wife hated the 4-foot-long torpedoes hanging off the house and that one of her Yorkshire Terriers was injured when about 20 pounds of ice from the LeafGuard gutters fell on him. Leroy further explained to Joe that the gutters freeze over within 30 minutes and then all remaining roof melt pours onto the walkways and freezes, forming a thick slippery surface of solid ice. Leroy knew Joe knew all of this already. It was in no way unique to Leroy. What kind of dirt bag would do this? Joe that is who.

Joe proves his kinship to all those who possess that wonderful quality of moronic stupidity when he suggests to Leroy, "Why can't you break the icicles off every day? And why can't you take a roof rake and rake your roof? And why can't you put salt on your pressure treated wood decks?"

Leroy looked at Brainless Joe and said, "First, I never had to do any of those things with my old gutters. Secondly, if you possess the ability to read then go online and research the effect of salt on pressure treated lumber. If you still think you're brilliant for coming up with those solutions, then sadly I won't be surprised. Finally, rake my roof? Seriously? Trying to do that in a foot of icy snow would be crazy. It would be a whole hell of a lot easier to just clean the leaves. I'll pass on trying any of your suggestions. I just want my money back! Bottom line is, I bought LeafGuard to relieve work not create a shit ton more work you replication of pond scum."

Joe told Leroy that he will need one month to get an answer back to him. (Unbelievable delay tactic that a 6 YO would not fall for.) Leroy just laughed, "You have 2 days Joe! This is 2021 not 1821. Pick up a phone, send an email, and it will take you no more than a day. Are we clear?"

Joe waited through all his complete line of bullshit products, to tell Leroy, "There is no money back guarantee. There is only a No Clog Guarantee which states that if leaves do clog the gutter, LeafGuard will come out and clean the gutter, but only if there is no flow coming from the downspout, and believe me, it's gonna get horribly clogged before that measure is met."

Leroy has thought many times about calling LeafGuard about this No Clog Guarantee. because their measure of a clogged gutter is limited to having no water coming out the downspout. On every occasion where Leroy's gutters were completely iced over there was no flow coming out of the down spouts, so perhaps Leroy will test this soon.

Later that summer while Leroy and Lenora gathered the evidence, they needed to put LeafGuard in their place, Leroy's phone rang and it was Joe on the other end. Leroy was cordial to Joe and Joe offered to pay for the installation of heat tape on the gutters to avoid the mess from last winter. Leroy was a little speechless, wondering why all of a sudden, the change of heart? OH, RIGHT! Hell, no worries that their usual snake in the grass behavior is trying to slither up Leroy's ass. This time Leroy is onto them. Leroy asks Joe, "How many bids do you need me to get?"

Joe says to Leroy, "I want you to get three bids."

Leroy responded excitedly, "I appreciate this. If this fixes the problem, I promise I will consider the matter closed. Now, all I need is the Manufacturer's Installation Manual for the Heat Tape for the LeafGuard system." (pay attention here. Leroy finally gets the upper hand.)

Joe responds to the demand for the Manufacturer's Installation Instruction for heat tape saying, "Leroy I don't have anything like that, but not to worry. If the heat tape installers need help, they can call me."

Leroy basically told Joe to find a flaming cauldron of shit to jump in because the ridiculous, half-assed plan that Joe just uttered was just one more inanity in a long line of stupid things that came out of Joe's mouth. Leroy raised his voice asking, "How do you know this will work when you don't even have instructions to make it work? And are you going to pay for the increase in my electric bill to cover the cost of running the heat tape during winters that have been known to go below zero and stay there for weeks?" Joe Geodardi had saturated Leroy's brain with the heavy syrup of complete stupidity, and Leroy could take no more. He decided it was time to go to the District Manager, Tim Spring. It only took about 5 minutes for Leroy to recognize that Tim was just as stupid as Joe. In fact, Tim was Stupid Joe on steroids, and not in any positive way.

Leroy told Tim that when getting the estimates from the three electricians, all three had asked Leroy, "How do we install heat tape on this menagerie? And even if it can be installed, to be honest with you, we don't really believe it will work." Tim lied again, just like Joe had, and claimed there was no Manufacturer's Instruction for the installation of heat tape. Leroy asked for that in writing and Tim refused, asking why Leroy needed it in writing. Disgusted, Leroy said, "Because I can trust your fat ass about as far as I can throw your fat ass."

Tim then uttered the Mount Everest of stupid and said to Leroy, "You don't need a manufacturer's installation manual. The gutters are your gutters Leroy, and you can do whatever you want with them."

Leroy did not miss a beat and said, "Well, Hell, Tim. Why didn't you say that in the first place? I just need that in writing and then I can take my Sawzall, and cut the tops of the gutters off so they'll go back to the way they were for 35 years. Then when the gutters fill with leaves, I can call in my "No Clog Guarantee.""

Tim started back peddling, "Leroy, now don't be silly. You know that won't work."

Leroy responded, "First of all, you waste of planetary oxygen, call me silly and I will teach you just how silly I can be. You are the one who is completely silly, to think I will believe these gutters are mine to drill and saw on with no instructions and no written guarantee that what I'm doing is perfectly acceptable. Wow Tim. Does your mother have any living children?"

Leroy's lawyers are now working on this little project. LeafGuard never did buy the heat tape, but Leroy did get statements from the heat tape installers who agreed that LeafGuard gutters were an absolute joke if you get snow. Leroy's lawyers have a mediation set up for a time in the near future when they will sit down with LeafGuard's representatives in an attempt to resolve this, but Leroy has his suspicions as far as where that particular strategy is headed. Either way stay tuned to Leroy's Shorts: Speedo Edition.

THE END

Lowes Home Destruction Store

Leroy worked hard in the military and Leroy's goals were to take the next tough duty assignment and keep himself viable for advancement to the next rank. When it came to money, Leroy sent his paychecks home to his first wife Racheal with the belief that Racheal would use the money wisely, sparingly, and for good purpose. Instead, Leroy would come home to credit card debt upwards of $25,000.00. Leroy had purchased a house in a gated community near a semiprofessional golf course where membership was included in the home owner's dues. The children had their own bathrooms and bedrooms and the house was to be the nicest house Leroy would ever live in. Every deployment of Leroy's, Racheal would max out the credit card to $25,000.00, and every time Leroy would refinance the house in order to pay off the credit card debt. After several of these catastrophes, Leroy owed more on the house than its current valuation. Leroy had been pushed to the end of his rope when Racheal had tried to kill herself with gastric bypass surgery. This was a surgery she'd gone ahead with despite the fact that Leroy had sternly warned her and her doctor to wait until Leroy got back from his latest tour to Afghanistan before doing any surgery. Leroy had explained he would not return from Afghanistan to take care of Racheal, but his oldest daughter would take care of her sisters, no matter what happened to Racheal. As a result, Racheal would be completely on her own.

Secondly and most importantly, Leroy said to Racheal, "You've had a couple of years to get this done, while I have been stuck stateside as Senior Chief in Charge of Base Operations. Now I'm leaving for Afghanistan after nearly 6 months of training, on an assignment that will give me the rank of Master Chief and I am taking it. If you selfishly choose to interfere with my goal, then I will consider your decision to be a betrayal of our marriage and thus, grounds for divorce." Because Leroy's marriage to Racheal had completely run its course by this time, Leroy knew he would not be totally disappointed if Racheal defied him and went ahead with the bypass surgery, thus forcing a divorce and setting Leroy free!

Suffice it to say that Racheal unequivocally told Leroy to piss off about her not getting the surgery. Leroy thought Racheal may get cold feet and not want the surgery but when Racheal said, "I am getting the surgery," that was the final nail in the coffin of their marriage.

Leroy may have well told Racheal, "Go ahead. I dare you to get the surgery!" In his mind, Racheal stuck out his tongue at Leroy and went, "Nan-a- nan-a- nu- nu." A kiss of death to the relationship that was now over for good.

Everyone knew not to say "No" to Racheal. She would cut off her own nose to spite her face, and sure enough, about 4 months into Leroy's last deployment to Afghanistan, a Sergeant Major approached Leroy and most unsuccessfully tried to convince Leroy to return home to look after his wife Racheal. Leroy had an epiphany as he realized he was finally free of Racheal and had zero guilt about it. Guilt had mastered Leroy's life for the last time.

Just before he was due to come back to the states, Leroy was injured, and this injury ended Leroy's career. He could continue behind a desk but that was as far from the tip of the spear as one could get, and Leroy found a great deal of desk work to be politically oriented, not mission oriented. I will bet most of you feel the same way in your job environment. When Leroy's injuries had mended well enough that he was mobile, Leroy contacted several divorce lawyers, all who were absolutely clueless when it came to their profession as divorce lawyers.

By the time the divorce was final, Leroy owed his divorce lawyer $30,000.00. This amount bought Leroy the contractual obligation to give Racheal half of Leroy's pension for the rest of Racheal's life. Racheal had done a number of destructive things to Leroy's career but had not done a single good thing. So, half Leroy's pension? For what? Leroy's lawyer originally promised Leroy he would keep his entire pension. This was the first lie spoken by the lawyer. Racheal got all the cars, all the household goods, basically everything, including stuff Racheal was supposed to give back to Leroy like woodworking materials, military paraphernalia, and many other hobby tools that Leroy had. None of it got returned. Leroy felt certain all those keepsakes got thrown away as yet another example of the depth of the completely unwarranted seething hatred and desire for revenge that Racheal felt towards Leroy. Why she felt this way is beyond Leroy's ability to understand. Racheal was the one who drew first blood by refusing to wait until Leroy was home again and going ahead with the gastric bypass surgery in the first place. In any case, this so-called settlement reminded Leroy of the old saying, "She got the gold mine, I got the shaft."

The one thing the lawyer got Leroy was his house. No victory there! The house was completely upside down financially, and in the end, Leroy decided not go back to the house. He just left it for the bank to foreclose on. So, there was Leroy owing $30,000.00 to his lawyer and Leroy did not have a pot to piss in. Leroy's dad had bought Leroy a van and driven it up to Seattle, knowing Leroy no longer had a vehicle after the fiasco of the divorce. When Leroy's dad heard about the lawyer's ineptitude, he walked straight up to the lawyer and asked him, "Do you really think you earned $30,000.00 today? Don't answer because you and I both know you did not! If you had done your job, my son might be able to afford to pay you, but you can see he has no money to pay your fee, either now or in his near future, due to your incompetence. Here is how this is playing out; I am writing you a check for $6,000.00. I suggest you take it and mark my son's account Paid In Full, because it's all you're getting from this family. Do I make myself clear?"

Leroy knew his dad was serious. In addition, Leroy's dad had a hell of a lawyer on retainer for his business interests and Leroy was certain that his dad would have introduced his lawyer to Leroy's clown of a lawyer, if the need was to rise. Leroy's bozo lawyer was at least smart enough to know when he had been outmatched. Bozo was like a player in a T-ball league while most other lawyers were playing in the Majors. Bozo the clown lawyer took Leroy's dad's $6,000.00 check and that's the last anyone has ever heard from him except when he makes an occasional appearance at Chuck E Cheese or Mickey D's where he pursues his true calling as Bozo the clown.

Leroy's dad then negotiated with the Credit Union that held Leroy's maxed out credit cards which was the same Credit Union that held the mortgage on the upside-down house that Leroy had been given by the divorce judge. Leroy's dad then got the credit cards reduced down to a fraction of the original amounts, and then paid them off for his son Leroy. Leroy's dad mitigated all potential damage resulting in foreclosure and Leroy's dad explained to the bank that the house was now property of the Credit Union. The Credit Union had grossly over extended the amount of money they allowed Leroy to borrow against the value of the house, which was now dwarfed by what Leroy owed on it. For folks who bought houses in the mid 2000's, you may remember stories of this happening over and over. Some got through it but not Leroy.

Leroy's dad gave Leroy a 2011 Chevy Express hippie van as a gift for his retirement from military service. Leroy expressed his thanks to his dad. Leroy's dad always scoffed when Leroy referred to him as wealthy. But wealth is measured in smarts as well as monetary goods. Leroy's dad had a fountain of knowledge on finances and as a result, Leroy got more sound advice and counsel from his dad than he did from his ring a ding-ding lawyer. Furthermore, Leroy's dad had given him money. What had the lawyer provided other than legally undoing Leroy's marriage? Trust me, nobody knows.

After expressing his appreciation towards his dad, Leroy asked if he could paint some large flowers on his new van along with a couple of peace and love symbols. Leroy does not object to the peace and love movement at all, but the truth is, by suggesting the paint job, he was really trying to get his dad's goat, which was not much of a challenge. Leroy's dad immediately boiled into a fury as he said, "You can put flowers and all that liberal crap on my van over my dead body." Leroy backed down quickly before he lost the van. With a pat on his back from his dad, Leroy got in his van and over a 30-day period made his way across the country.

Leroy longed for the day when he could explore the country in his hippie van nonstop for 2 or 3 years straight, but this little mini adventure of 30 days was enjoyable enough and provided Leroy with a nice taste of what solo travel over an extended period of time was all about. It was a dream that Leroy savored, in anticipation of the "someday" when he could do this for a couple of years. Over the 30 days he was traveling, Leroy did some successful fishing, he camped out up in the woods and in beautiful meadows. He stopped and ate delicious food at many local diners and eateries. Prime Rib was a favorite of Leroy's, so anytime there was signage boasting of the best Prime Rib in whatever state or county the restaurant was in,

Leroy would stop to test the boast of "Best" to see if it was legitimate or not. Leroy knew full well that the use of superlatives are always subjective, but nevertheless, Leroy felt obligated to add in his personal perspective which is unusual for Leroy, right? Right?

During the trip, Leroy walked along lovely waterfalls, took in a number museums and points of interest, and lived in his van for the full month it took him to travel from Washington State to the little village where Lenora lived, located in Upstate New York. During his trip Leroy had lots of time to reflect on his future. Leroy had thought and pondered about his future that was coming at him hard and fast and knew he needed to once again find a way to become financially secure. Leroy came up with a dozen or so ways he could get some cash flow started. He would start on them when he got settled.

When Leroy arrived at Lenora's house on September 1, 2011, the two kids at heart, fell into each other's arms and began to snuggle down together for at least two days. Months earlier, Leroy and Lenora had sat together in Lenora's garage. The weather was bone chilling as the two lovers looked out the window in the back door of the garage. Leroy had two propane space heaters blasting into the garage but the heat was all escaping up into the uninsulated ceiling and then going to the outside. As Leroy and Lenora held each other for warmth, Leroy began to tell Lenora all the things he was going to build her. "Lenora," he said, "I am going to start by putting a wood shop in the garage and fixing the flaking floor. This will include insulating everything so the space heaters will heat up the space nice and warm and will do it quickly. Second, I'm going to finish the basement and put a second bathroom in down there. Next, I am going to build you a kitchen that will more than double its current size and will put down a hard bamboo floor." Years later, Lenora and Leroy began to breed Yorkshire Terriers, and the hard bamboo floors turned out to be a great decision. The four-legged kids are hard on flooring.

Within a few years of living in Western NY, Leroy looked at his life. His injuries from Afghanistan had healed and Leroy's permanent disability was not as serious as it could have been. In short, Leroy loved building. He had done so in the military in one capacity or another creating many things using a great variety of materials.

When Leroy had finished all the plumbing, electrical and construction projects on the remodel for Lenora's house, he felt a real sense of pride in his accomplishments. All these remodeling projects were not only completed but were done with flawless craftmanship. Another feeling of pride occurred for Leroy when despite Leroy's undeserving ex-wife Racheal ravaging his financial standing. Leroy had brought into existence, several of his money-making ventures and was making a TON more money than Leroy would have made if Racheal was still leeching off him.

A year after the afore mentioned projects were complete, Leroy managed to scrape together enough money to build the deck systems of Lenora's dreams. It was not only a work of art, but also very labor intensive. Leroy's dad had a saying, "I earned the $35,000.00 to buy the lumber, concrete and other building materials so I could build my deck; at $3.00 an hour." That sure put things into perspective, Leroy worked hard to manage his money in order to pay for the 850 square feet of decking he had built. Leroy used Sono tubes, which are just a cardboard tube that Leroy used to put the 4X4 posts in the ground. The Sono tube and 4X4 combination that made up the support for the decks was then filled with two fifty-pound bags of concrete. Do you know how much a 50-pound bag of concrete weighs? Leroy knew because he lifted 110 bags by hand from a pallet sitting on the driveway over to the various post locations throughout the deck system. The Sono Tubes keep the wood out of the dirt and away from any accelerated rotting. Leroy used 2X6's in various lengths for the joists and the top boards of the decks.

There were four deck heights involved in the whole deck system. The deck that went to the swimming pool had a half circle that took a bite out of the deck, which then perfectly matched the circumference of the pool for the length of the deck. With a skill rarely found, Leroy created the end by bending it so that the end 2X6 joist that faced the round swimming pool, was bent, vs having the top deck boards just cut with a jigsaw. Everyone knows those top boards will snap off as soon as someone heavy set, dares to stand on the edge. You may remember that when Leroy first came to visit Lenora, he had gone swimming with Lenora and had stepped on a 2X6 that had been cut with a jigsaw. It broke and Leroy panicked as he said loudly, "Holy shit! What if I had broken my ankle just before returning to Afghanistan?" In contrast, Leroy's curved deck was built with solid craftmanship and structural integrity. Leroy would not create a hazardous deck, designed to break ankles and maim swimmers. As a wood sculptor, Leroy used his skills to carve leaping dolphins across the front of the board facing the swimming pool. Leroy also made a hobbit door which was partially round and has a heavy frame. The hobbit door was built on the side of the deck that overlooked the koi pond. Along the entire side of the deck where the Hobbit Door was located, Leroy carved flowers, vines, butterflies, leaves and other various artistic designs. The lowest deck next to the koi pond had a full permanent cover over it. Leroy and Lenora often sat on the deck in the shade under the permanent cover, and enjoyed watching the soothing swimming of the koi.

Coupled with the labor, and Leroy's and Lenora's continual use of the decks, you can deduce that going from no money and no prospects, to slowly building up a little nest egg and having some money, made Leroy what some might call a real miser so parting with $35,000.00 to buy materials was a huge deal to Leroy. Leroy had skillfully built all 4 deck systems, totaling more than 850 square feet, and both Leroy and Lenora enjoyed their new decks immensely. The pool deck was large and accommodating and the ornate railings replete with carvings and cut outs of hearts, humming birds, and flowers were custom and beautiful. Lenora and Leroy would sit in the shade of the covered deck, with a hurricane fan providing a gentle breeze, watch their koi swim about and listen to the lovely music of the waterfalls cascading over the stones. Leroy and Lenora would sit on the deck between the house and the pool deck, where they would watch thier four-legged kids frolic in the yard. When Leroy was cooking in his outdoor kitchen, he would sit and watch the grill from this deck. The last of the four decks was in the front of the house. Lenora had bought a huge metal chiminea that was so heavy that Leroy and the delivery man had to take it apart just to be able to lift it and then reassemble it. The nice delivery guy was awesome to do all that grunt work for nothing other than Leroy's profuse thanks.

For the next 6 years the decks were great. There was the annual chore of pressure washing the decks and staining them with a recommended sealant but Leroy had gotten proficient enough to complete all the washing and staining in a day and a half. Lenora worked for days each spring making up 53 flower pots. Some were too heavy for Leroy to lift while others were much smaller and easier to move. When Lenora would get a few pots completed, Leroy would hump them into place where Leroy and Lenora were able to enjoy them all summer. Every year a great deal of summer joy was captured from these decks.

The spring of the 7th year, Leroy noted several surface boards were rotten. Leroy thought. "This must just be a fluke." Leroy purchased approximately $300.00 worth of Pressure Treated 2X6's and replaced all the rotten boards in the decks. Leroy and Lenora enjoyed another summer of gardening, swimming, and lazily watching the world go by from the beautiful decks that Leroy had crafted. Come the spring of the 8th year after Leroy had originally built the decks for Lenora, Leroy saw that the koi pond deck was halfway rotten. If one stepped on the boards they would fall right through. The boards were rotted beyond recognition. The pool deck was sagging due to the severity of the joist rot and in rough enough shape to make holding the weight of a small adult questionable. The deck between the house and the pool deck was rotten throughout. The screws in the top boards all were sticking out of the wood, because there was no wood left on the joists for the screws to adhere to. The rot was so bad that while checking out all of the deck surfaces for safety, Leroy fell right through. I guess that part of the deck was not safe, said with a smile.

After falling through the deck, as Leroy picked himself out of the mud under the deck, he suddenly noticed he had large amounts of blood squirting from his neck with enough force to make it across the deck. Leroy was instantly worried that he had punctured his jugular vein. Leroy rushed in the house; blood continued to squirt all over the kitchen floor. Leroy called for Lenora, "Hey you! Get in the kitchen! I stabbed myself in my 'getting screwed 'neck." Lenora sauntered into the kitchen from wherever she had been. Leroy had kept pressure on his neck with his hand which had provided some measure of help, but really, how much pressure could he put on his neck? At least the blood was not squirting out anymore.

Lenora told Leroy to take his hand down so she could tend to his wounds. Many of you know from other stories of Lenora, that she worked in Oncology and Hospice care where she picked up a vast store of knowledge regarding wound care. Leroy was sure Lenora had seen worse than an old man stabbed in the neck by his own deck boards, but when Leroy removed his hand from his own neck at Lenora's command, the blood immediately resumed squirting and now it was squirting all over Lenora's kitchen, not on an outside wall that could be washed down with the garden hose. Lenora hollered at Leroy, "Cover your neck! Cover your neck now Leroy! You're getting blood all over my kitchen!" Leroy followed Lenora's orders and the squirting blood stopped. Shortly after stopping the flow of blood, Lenora had several bandages of different sizes gathered on the kitchen counter and patched Leroy all back up. Leroy figured he was good to go, but Leroy would soon find out he was not good to go. More on that later in the story. So here was Leroy, head in hands, somewhat in shock from his accident, as he realized that he needed to replace the deck systems after only 8 years, which meant spending another $35,000.00 in materials - or more due to inflation – and necessitating the performance of an arduous amount of physical labor by this 100% disabled soldier that was Leroy. One might ask why Leroy does not use his disability money to hire someone? (Keep reading…)

Rewind with me for just a spell. When Leroy had initially gone in to purchase all the materials to build Lenora her deck systems, Leroy had met a real nice man by the name of Simian. Simian worked the Pro Desk counter for Contractors at Lowes Home Improvement Store and dealt with the large purchases associated with building 850 sq. ft. of decking. Simian showed Leroy the warranty which read, "Top Choice Pressure Treated lumber with a Limited Lifetime Warranty." The limited refers to acts of God such as a plane dropping from the sky and hitting the deck square on. In those types of cases, the damage will not be covered by the lumber manufacturer. That made sense to Leroy as long as the Lifetime Warranty guaranteed the wood would never get cancerous rot from fungus that eats the wood completely. If you go for a walk in a forest and you will see that these funguses have purpose. Without them the forest floor would be piled with downed trees and logs. Because of this fungus; the trees are rotted back into the earth quickly. Relatively speaking. Maybe over a couple hundred years. Leroy did not get a copy of the Warranty, but there was one laminated copy on the Pro Desk to look at. Had Leroy known what he knows now he would have demanded a hard copy of the warranty but his balls were not clairvoyant nor even made of crystal you know.

After falling through the rotted deck, Leroy went back to Lowes only to discover that Lowes does not honor the warranty that Leroy saw printed out. Leroy also discovered that the company that might honor the warranty is the chemical treatment company that sells the copper oxide which is supposed to be the new environmentally friendly treatment to prevent lumber from rotting. Leroy had taken down the two old decks Lenora's ex-husband had built 35 years ago. The decks were still solid and were only a little rough from weather. Compare that to pressure treated lumber that is a mere 8 years old and has no structural integrity! Leroy wondered about that, thinking, "Can somebody tell me why we would go backwards and allow such a huge swing and a miss? Harmful to the environment? How environmentally harmful is the practice of taking twice as many trees to build a deck because the wood rots every 8 years. Leroy knew that any subsequent purchases of the new and unimproved pressure treated lumber would not last any longer. That was all the more reason Leroy would insist on having a warranty in place, complete with a hard copy signed by the manager of whatever store ends up selling it to Leroy. No wiggle room, no tricky verbiage.

In search of some help with the lumber warranty, Leroy went to Lowes Home Improvement on Greece Road and sought out David from management, who very plainly told Leroy that it sounded like it was a Leroy problem. So, Outa Luck So Sorry Chuck. Leroy looked at him and said, "Another asshole in a position to provide customer service, but instead you serve up a taste of your empty brain cavity replete with the "Tru-Self" machine you are wearing."

Clueless, David asked Leroy, "What are you talking about, "Tru-Self?" I am not wearing any machine."

Leroy further explained to David, "This machine you are wearing projects an accurate holographic image of a person's true self, such as the Lowes house manager, which would be you David, let me see YOUR image, here it comes; a self-centered turd muncher?" Yep, the machine works every time.

As Leroy's inner voice, otherwise known as his conscience, I must admit I am pretty small, but what there is of me constantly strives to convince Leroy to wait to piss people off until AFTER he has gotten what he needs from them. I think the stubborn old coot finds his way a challenge, rather like a matador waving his red cape at the bull in order to get him angry before he goes up and milks him. I have questioned Leroy's tactics, because, after all, a ranch boy from Montana should know that the milk coming out of that bull may not be what he expects. Though it may soothe the bull. Maybe Leroy should have milked David. At this point of utter frustration anything is on the table. So, after Leroy got David real spun up with his accurate insults, Leroy asked David for a copy of the warranty on the wood he had bought 8 years ago. Top Choice, and Moron Walking, AKA David, sends Leroy the warranty for "Ecolite" which is the pressure treated lumber Lowes currently carries and does Leroy absolutely no good.

The first action Leroy took on after this debacle was to go after Lowes for the cost of the wood. As you heard earlier that is not how it works with Lowes. Instead of Lowes telling Leroy how it did work, they just continued to do NOTHING for Leroy. Lowes told Leroy he would need all the plastic end pieces from the boards. Leroy did not know that because he had no copy of the warranty to read along with the installation instructions. Keeping plastic tabs is something Leroy never did in all his 23-year military career using pressure treated lumber to build. Yes, Leroy built plenty of structures out of pressure treated lumber. Leroy said to David, "I do not have the plastic tabs. I had no clue that I needed to gather them because I only got a brief look at a copy of the warranty. Nobody gave me one so there was no way I could follow the directions within. Now what do I do?"

David's complete lack of empathy for anyone including David's own mother, was purely disgusting. Leroy imagined that David's mom let David live in her basement which he had adorned with his

"Hanna Montana" posters, jammies and matching bed spread. The basement he claimed as a bedroom had way too many autographed pictures of "Hanna Montana" who is a girl that children idolize until they are around 13. Leroy is not saying David was emotionally stunted and had the maturity of a tween. No. David himself thought he was hot shit. Leroy agreed with that as long as you remove the word "hot." Every couple of days David's mother would ask David to bring up his dirty socks and poo-poo undies to the laundry room. David's mom was clearly in pain as she'd just had a recent knee replacement surgery, and she was hoping her son David would be a good little boy and bring his clothes to the laundry room. Instead, David yelled up the stairs, "Ma, I am going out to meet with my friends at the video arcade. Don't forget, my clothes are down in my bedroom and I'm almost out of clean clothes so make sure you get them done today." As Leroy's inner voice, do you want to chicken choke David as much as Leroy does, figuratively speaking of course? Of course.

So, Leroy bypassed David and found the district manager for the Lowes Home Improvement stores in the area. The district manager, Tom, was only slightly better than David but at least he did possess some intelligence and a tiny bit of empathy. Tom is a gold mine of concern compared to most, but the bar is set pretty low. Leroy explained to Tom that shortly after he retired from the Service, one of the Lowes cashiers told Leroy that he needed to get a My Lowes card in order to keep getting his military discount. Leroy took up the flyer for the My Lowes card, which Leroy still has. The flyer read," With your My Lowes card you will not need receipts for returns. ALL purchases will be tracked by your card. Leroy thought, "What on earth am I wanking about?" The My Lowes card would show Leroy had purchased the wood and when he purchased it. Unfortunately, the My Lowes card does NOT save a record of purchases forever as advertised on TV and in the flyer. It saves them for 5 stinking years. When did the deck rot? That's right. At 8 years old and now it is no longer structurally safe to walk on. Out of desperation, Leroy asked one last question of Tom, "If I buy future pressure treated lumber and I follow all the installation instructions then will you help me get my money back should the need occur?"

Tom answered "Hell No!" and went on to explain that the manufacturer of the treated lumber is who covers the warranty on the wood. In some weird twist the warranty is covered by the makers of the chemicals that gets injected into the wood. Imagine with this parallel scenario for a moment: You purchase a royal blue GR86 from the Toyota dealership in Greece and a few years later you start to experience issues with the car. You take the car to the dealership and the Service Manager says, "Sorry Leroy but the only way you are going to get service on your car, which is still under warranty, is to drive it to the manufacturer in South Korea." Seriously, that is exactly what the pressure treated lumber business wants us to expect. Frankly it's on par with most catastrophes that occur to Leroy as he attempts to retrieve goods and services.

The trip to the New York border was lovely for Leroy. However, never intending to stay in WNY when he entered the state, he was immediately chewed up, shit out, and then shit on over and over again! Yes, that is a lot of shit, for sure and it just keeps coming with almost every transaction. It's like being swallowed up by a giant beast with no way to get out of the beast's belly. "God, I love New York," Leroy thought. "NOT!"

The next phone call Leroy would make was to his lawyer. Leroy tried lawyering up on this debacle, but this is why these assholes win! They know most of us don't have lawyers so the threats aren't taken seriously by the offenders. Well Leroy did have a lawyer and he was not afraid to use him. Leroy asked Lenora to have the lawyers find ground contact pressure treated lumber with a lifetime warranty, which would provide a very clear path to getting one's funds back. After all, wood that lasts the life of a human is something Leroy will believe when he sees it. Or maybe when he sees pigs fly out his butt which is far more likely to happen. Leroy gives the new wood 8 years before Leroy figures he will be replacing it again. If the industry standards that are set for pressure treated wood remain ecologically "sound" then building with pressure treated wood is an exercise in futility. Hopefully, if this fight with Lowes proves successful, Leroy won't end up paying $70,000.00 total on these decks and he can claim victory. If not, then Leroy's lawyer better make sure the warranty going forward on new pressure treated wood is iron clad. Otherwise, Leroy will have to take care of the lawyers and the wood salesman and…. It really gets exhausting to be Leroy, can't you tell?

Remember where Lenora bandaged Leroy and we said this is not the end of this story? Well, here is what happened a few weeks later. Leroy was licking his proverbial wounds head in hands, as he rubbed his cheeks with both hands, he felt a huge ball of pus under his right ear. You guessed it. It was right where Leroy had stabbed himself with the deck board when he fell through the rotten deck. Leroy immediately called his old primary care doctor at the VA. Doctor Gerwig who Leroy to go to the emergency room. Now Doctor Gerwig knew better than anyone that Leroy suffered from panic attacks, debilitating anxiety and other mental health demons and that going into an emergency room full of drama and trauma and people needing way more critical procedures than an infected neck, meant that Leroy would get to enjoy this lovely soothing environment where Buddhists come to meditate for a really, really, really long time. Leroy's response was pretty typical for Leroy, "Give the head set to someone with a brain Dr. Gerwig." Leroy educated Dr. Gerwig again on the years of history that Dr Gerwig and Leroy had. Leroy was unable to believe his doctor had given him such stupid advice. Sending Leroy to the emergency room was absolutely the height of stupidity. Leroy pressed Dr Gerwig to at least look at the infection. Doctor Gerwig agreed to look at it and examined Leroy's neck and indeed found the pus ball.

Dr Gerwig sent Leroy for a scan to see if there was foreign matter in the wound. Leroy did not believe he needed some stinking machine to look for foreign matter in his neck because the only reason his neck had a pus ball was because there WAS foreign matter in Leroy's neck. Nevertheless, Leroy went for the scan and when the results of the scan came back, Doctor Gerwig called Leroy and said, "Leroy you're all good. There is no foreign matter in your neck."

The pus pocket continued to get worse so Leroy went to Urgent Care where the on-call doctor gave Leroy a half dozen shots, 2 bottles of pills, but no other care. Leroy said, "Doctor, just take the tip of your scalpel and lance that pus pocket. Then flush it like crazy with saline solution. I will just bet it will heal. I saw a lot of this on the battlefield all the time. A person can get an infection from the tiniest of foreign object and wham! A pus ball forms and that is exactly what I have." The doctor at Urgent Care, told Leroy she was not allowed to lance the pus pocket and told Leroy he needed to go to his primary care doctor, who is the same doctor who had already refused to treat Leroy claiming he did not have the staff. (THEN GET THE STAFF!) Can you believe it?

To say again, did you hear this? How many times have we seen Leroy go after a problem, only to be sent full circle? No exaggeration in that statement whatsoever! Leroy ends up full circle with the lumber from Lowes and now has gone full circle in his quest for medical care. Leroy received nothing from either weasel. Can somebody tell me why?

Leroy was having lunch with his friend Bill who is literally old enough to be Leroy's father. Leroy and Bill met at church and was featured in the story *Leroy down the Parkway*. Bill has been one of those friends to Leroy that no matter what Leroy needs, Bill would put real effort into helping him. Bill went beyond kindness as he cared for a number of folks, Leroy among them. After listening to Leroy's tale of woe regarding his neck, Bill said to Leroy, "Hey, I have a young Greek primary care doctor who is taking new patients." Leroy had been unable to leave the VA completely because he just did not know where else to go. Thanks to Leroy's friend Bill, Leroy had an appointment with a non-VA Primary Care Physician who would take on Leroy as a patient and who would also take Leroy's medical insurance. The problem of course is that it would be another three weeks to get in to see the new doctor.

Meanwhile, Lenora said, "Leroy just let me lance that pus pocket and flush it." Leroy was all for the home procedure except he knew just how painful it was going to be. Had one of the of otherwise useless doctors done it, they would surely numb it up, or so one would hope anyway, but maybe they no longer know how to do that either. Sober for many years, Leroy could not even get drunk to help with the pain. What kind of bullshit is that? But the need to get the pus ball taken care of allowed Leroy to push back his fear and he said to Lenora, "Okay. You can do it, but be careful." The thing about Lenora is; she gets it done! She took her scalpel and literally carved out a hole in the pus pocket. The room immediately smelled of decay and there was at least a half cup of goo that flowed out of Leroy's neck. Lenora doesn't let moss grow on the river rocks. She immediately shoved a beaker straw into the hole she had made with her buck knife and started to squirt the salt solution into the hole in Leroy's neck. Leroy couldn't decide what hurt worse; having a chunk of skin cut out of his neck or having salt sprayed into his raw flesh. After what seemed like one very long time, Lenora said she was done and she showed Leroy a dirty, bloody, gooey, pus-filled napkin that held seven pieces of pressure treated lumber, that had been festering in Leroy's neck. Yep, seven pieces of pressure treated lumber, the ones that the VA doctor said did not exist. Guess they must have re-formed somehow, was that it?

Leroy said to Lenora, "Save that big piece there, the one the size of a tree trunk. I am going to build a bird house out of that wood for Dr. Gerwig."

Lenora responded to Leroy, "Let it go Leroy. You don't have time for bird houses now." Soon after Lenora had performed triage on Leroy's neck, the neck started to heal and the wad of pus under the skin of Leroy's neck diminished almost completely. There was still some inflammation around the blunt trauma wound inflicted by the deck, but Leroy was not worried he will drop dead of sepsis any time soon. Leroy eventually met Bill's doctor; Dr. Kathsolis and it was love at first sight. Leroy asked what Dr. K would do for his neck and Dr. K told Leroy he would send him upstairs to a surgeon to get the neck infection lanced immediately. Leroy asked why the VA had not found the foreign matter. Dr K went on his computer where he was able to tap into all medical data. Dr K turned to Leroy and said with kind of a disturbed look in his eyes, "The VA used the wrong test. They were never going to find that wood in your neck I am afraid."

When Leroy retired in 2011 the treatment offered by the VA sucked so bad veterans were getting anxiety and stress, not from their residual Shell Shock but solely because of the lack of any organization combined with a complete lack of empathy from the VA which was and is supposed to be a place that would serve as a lifeline for veterans, not as a noose. Want to help a Veteran? In Leroy's dreams, someone could start by firing all the employees and burning down the entire VA. For the 2 of you workers who were competent and caring, just take one for the team. For the other millions, good riddance.

In the next book in this series, Speedo Edition, I may try to write about the VA experience if I can find the courage among the many flashbacks, trauma, and images of poisoned wood in my neck, none of which was caused by my 23 years as a military combatant but sourly caused by the VA itself. Perhaps I will write about the first time they tried to kill me. Poisoning me with wood fungi was the second time they tried that stunt. And still, even in this endeavor, the VA is still a failure, just this one time, Thank God!

There is a final chapter to this story involving **Jeff from Cactus Contracting** located in Spencerport. Leroy had no clue why Jeff called himself a Contractor. He was a landscape person. Looking at his landscape artistry, it kind of looks like the landscaping created by the skillful and wanton digging done by Leroy's talented and enthusiastic Yorkshire Terriers. The decks on Jeff's web site for Cactus Construction are equally pathetic. For someone who brags about his deck building prowess, there are only a few pictures of shipping pallet style square wooden boxes that must be meant to hold wood for your fireplace? Be your own judge. What Leroy wants to warn everyone about is this: After reading *Angi* one would know that Leroy would never call Angi again. In fact, it had been over a year since Leroy last called Angi and the huge volume of spam calls had finally stopped when Jeff called Leroy around 7:30 at night. Jeff must have been desperate for work because he usually quits for the day around 5:00 PM. Jeff spoke, "Leroy, I am calling you from Angi. I see you are requesting a deck, is that true?" Keep in mind Leroy's most well-deserved hatred of Angi is due primarily to the number of times Leroy was forced to give all the information on the details of the construction of the deck: not once, not twice, but three times. Three times!

Leroy responded to Jeff, "Oh, I see you use Angi. I normally do not work with contractors who use Angi because any contractor that would purposefully use Angi would purposefully screw over their customers by subjecting them to the absolute stupidity that is Angi."

Jeff got a little uncomfortable as certainly, Leroy figured he was one little tweeker of a powder puff, scared of his own shadow and it turns out, scared of Leroy as well, as we will soon find out.

Leroy then said with sarcasm in his voice, "So. Here's the deal. I explained my deck three time to three different phone reps, spending a total of 1.5 hours of my time repeating myself, and now I will have to explain it to you as well, coming to a grand total of 2 hours. Oh, and I got to enjoy hundreds of spam phone calls from Angi and I NEVER found a single service provider who was able to meet my needs coming from those hours with Angi, in spite of the fact that the services I was looking for were all based on some pretty vanilla needs." Leroy continued, "Look. Today is January 4th and if you want to build my deck, I will agree to that and I will need a warranty for both labor and materials, of course."

Jeff came back with a one-year warranty. Two guesses as to what Leroy came back with. Leroy explained to Jeff that pressure treated wood has a warranty, usually, a Limited Lifetime warranty. Jeff, a self-proclaimed expert on decks, knew nothing about the warranty process for pressure treated wood. How many poor saps had this shit for brains built a deck for, only to have it dissolve in 8 years just as Leroy's deck had done? Leroy's deck rotted but the difference was that Leroy did not own a deck building business. Said with a smile. Leroy would posit that Jeff didn't own one either. Jeff needs to build a quality deck first. After nearly four months of discussions, Leroy had educated Jeff on how the pressure treating process worked, having already taught Jeff about the warranty process for pressure treated lumber.

It was now early March and the window for hiring a quality contractor for a spring project was closed. Any quality contractor would be booked solid by late February and a quality contractor already knows a 1-year warranty on a $35,000.00 expense is 100% on the stupid chart providing 100% is the most stupid one can be. Put another way, Jeff is 100% stupid. And now, in early March, for the very first time, Jeff asked for pictures of the decks. Do keep in mind Jeff works out of the Village of Spencerport which is only about 15 miles from where Leroy and Lenora live. Lenora sent Jeff 30 pictures of the decks and that evening Jeff called Leroy. The first words out of Jeff's mouth were that the deck was entirely too complicated for him to build. Can you believe this 6-foot pile of fresh horse shit? All this came about months after Jeff bragged to

Leroy about his skills and it turns out he couldn't even make a 2X6 contour for around the pool. He said, "I don't know how to build those doors or do those carvings."

Leroy responded, "I already told you over the phone a long time ago that I would do all the carvings and if you needed me to, I would make the curved 2X6 for the pool edge of the pool deck. What I need is workers to install the decking because after getting blown up in Afghanistan, my back is taxed by heavy lifting." Jeff again agreed to take on the job. If you count how many times Leroy had begged Jeff to build his deck, BEGGED! It comes to three so far. At this point, Leroy knew there was absolutely no other contractor who would take on building the deck this late in the spring. They are already solidly booked. At least Leroy had Jeff and he could keep Jeff on track.

On the 5th of March Jeff called Leroy and asked if he could come by the house to look at the decks. He said he would be by at 10:30 the next day. At 10:30 the next day Jeff called Leroy and told Leroy that he had changed his mind about building the deck as it was just too complicated and therefore, he was pulling out of the project.

Leroy reminded Jeff about their first conversation and how Leroy had made an exception for Jeff who was one of those people stupid enough to subject their customers to Angi. Leroy reminded Jeff that he had told Jeff he'd made an Angi exception for the last time by hiring Jeff. On the fourth of January Jeff and Leroy had made a verbal contract, followed up by numerous text messages, detailing the specifics of their agreement. These texts remain preserved on Leroy's cell phone, and totally contradict a liar named Jeff who would have folks believe that he and Leroy hardly know each other. Leroy went on to explain to Jeff, "Jeff you have no idea who you have just wronged and that while the retribution won't happen today, it will happen! There are many tools in my toolbox that are going to allow me to make your life miserable, Jeff." Then Leroy decided to further intimidate the shit weasel and asked Jeff, "Hey Jeff, it will be easy enough to find you as you well know, but how about you give me your address and I'll come over and discuss this with you in person?"

Jeff said, "I don't think that is a good idea."

Leroy responded, "Well Jeff, I know YOU are not a good idea that is why I am on my way to your house right now, I know you are there." Leroy knew the turd was home by the background noises on the phone. Then Leroy said to Jeff, "Are you recording my call?"

Jeff said, "You bet I am and I have you making threats to me."

Leroy laughed and said, "Thanks Jeff for admitting to a felony. First off, in the state of New York you cannot record me without my permission. Secondly, you sorry excuse for a sub human, you will never record me making threats because I don't make threats. Do you think I threatened the Extremist Muslim before I emptied 20 rounds of NATO 556 caliber into their head?" There will be no warning for all turds, and that means Jeff AKA: King of the Turds and lover of Angi especially because he can't get ANY word-of-mouth work. Now I know why. You have to satisfy your customer for that advertising tool to work."

Jeff hung up so he could change his shit filled drawers. Leroy waited for the next guests on the docket and sure enough, soon the police were at Leroy's door. Leroy pulled his military identification card out of his wallet with his driver's license. The policeman asked Leroy what happened between him and Jeff. Leroy tried to temper his anger towards Jeff but hey, there's no law against being angry, is there? Leroy answered the policeman, "I absolutely told that little weasel that he did not know who he had messed with and that there would be repercussions." Leroy was way too smart to SAY he was going to do harm to Jeff. What Leroy did say to the police is that he was going to write to the Better Business Bureau, Consumer Reports, Attorney General and a couple of Chamber of Commerce folks about Jeff's shoddy business practices. Leroy told police that he had told Jeff that he will soon discover what Leroy meant when he said, "You have no idea who you just screwed over!" The police officer said that Jeff claimed that Leroy had threatened to beat Jeff up. On the other hand, when the police saw how skinny Leroy was and what a big jug head Jeff was, the police could clearly determine what a stinking liar Jeff was and still is. Leroy knows the real reason for turd chaser Jeff to leave Leroy in a lurch is that Jeff was getting his feelings hurt when Leroy had to teach him his profession as an alleged carpenter, because Jeff's only real profession would seem to be Professional Bitch Boy!

In closing, this story has not yet ended. Lenora is working with the lawyers on the lumber. Leroy has decided he is going to use a junk company to remove all the rotting wood and then start from scratch and build all the decks all by his own damn self, just like he did 8 years ago. Leroy had better NEVER hear the words unemployment, can't find work, or any other defeatist nonsense. Leroy has money to pay someone to build his deck and yet he is building it himself, 100% disabled and all. THANK YOU, AMERICA! Not. More to follow on this story in Leroy's Shorts Speedo Edition.

THE END

Author's Note:

I don't want to offend my readers, because after all, only readers of discerning taste read books called Leroy's Shorts Tighty Whitey Edition. I was once on welfare before I went into the military. I was between jobs and the apartment Joe Welfare put me into was significantly nicer than what I had lived in when I had a job. Strike one. Why was I living in an apartment that was so much nicer while on welfare than I could afford when I was working. I am not saying I should have lived in squalor while on welfare, but some place clean and small would have encouraged me to want to get a job and move up. Instead, I never wanted to leave. Secondly, because of food stamps, I had so much free food I literally could not eat it all. Now if I was a drug addict, I would have sold the food or even the food stamps themselves for drugs. Happily, I am not a drug addict so instead, I gave the food to my hard-working grandparents. They did not especially need the food, but since I'd made a habit of stopping by their place on a daily basis to eat, and ate heartily, eating them out of house and home, I was trying to give back to them. Strike two, mismanaged money! Finally, welfare gave me a check for $700.00 each month. I was not a drug addict but as you all know I was and am an alcoholic. So, what did I buy with most of the $700.00? You already know the answer. A big strike 3 and you're out. Out of excuses for such crazy talk as a high unemployment rate.

Author's Editorial:

For my part now, I HAVE WORK!!!! and I WILL PAY YOU!! and I WILL TEACH YOU!! Are my mantra. What I won't do is simply give you money. That is the whole damn problem with welfare and unemployment. Never talk to me about unemployment, welfare, food cupboards or other handouts. Starvation is a hell of a motivator; trust me I know. As a man of faith, I would always help my fellow man/woman, but the government and its ill-advised programs that are supposedly designed to combat poverty, is a broken system and as a result, it hurts people and keeps them down. That is the moral of my author's editorial on the lack of a work force in this country. There is absolutely no reason for it.

Starry Night Publishing

Everyone has a story...

Don't spend your life trying to get published! Don't tolerate rejection! Don't do all the work and allow the publishing companies to reap the rewards!

Millions of independent authors like you are making money, publishing their stories now. Our technological know-how will take the headaches out of getting published. Let Starry Night Publishing take care of the hard parts, so you can focus on writing. You simply send us your Word Document, and we do the rest. It really is that simple!

The big companies want to publish only "celebrity authors," not the average book-writer. It is almost impossible for first-time authors to get published today. This has led many authors to go the self-publishing route. Until recently, this was considered "vanity-publishing." You spent large sums of your money to get twenty copies of your book, to give to relatives at Christmas just so you could see your name on the cover. However, the self-publishing industry allows authors to get published in a timely fashion, retain the rights to your work, keeping up to ninety percent of your royalties instead of the traditional five percent.

We have opened the gates, allowing you inside the world of publishing. While others charge you as much as fifteen-thousand dollars for a publishing package, we charge less than five-hundred dollars to cover copyright, ISBN, and distribution costs. Do you really want to spend all your time formatting, converting, designing a cover, and then promoting your book because no one else will?

Our editors are professionals, able to create a top-notch book that you will be proud of. Becoming a published author is supposed to be fun, not a hassle.

At Starry Night Publishing, you submit your work, we create a professional-looking cover, a table of contents, compile your text and images into the appropriate format, convert your files for eReaders, take care of copyright information, assign an ISBN, allow you to keep one-hundred-percent of your rights, distribute your story worldwide on Amazon, Barnes and Noble and many other retailers, and write you a check for your royalties. There are no other hidden fees involved! You do not pay extra for a cover or to keep your book in print. We promise! Everything is included! You even get a free copy of your book and unlimited half-price copies.

In twelve short years, we have published more than six thousand books, compared to the major publishing houses, which only add an average of six new titles per year. We will publish your fiction or non-fiction books about anything and look forward to reading your stories and sharing them with the world.

We do all subject matter, fiction, or nonfiction, scholarly works, cookbooks, self-help, etc. Our company might not be huge in size, but we currently have more than 6,500 clients, maintain an A+ rating with the Better Business Bureau, of which we are an accredited member, and have won the "Best of Rochester" Business Award four years in a row, making us a member of the Rochester Business Hall of Fame.

We sincerely hope that you will join the growing Starry Night Publishing family, become a published author, and gain the world-wide exposure that you deserve. You deserve to succeed. Success comes to those who make opportunities happen, not those who wait for opportunities to happen. You just have to try. Thanks for joining us on our journey.

www.starrynightpublishing.com

www.facebook.com/starrynightpublishing/

Made in the USA
Monee, IL
15 June 2023

35737246R00148